Britain's Coast at War

This book is dedicated to my Great Uncle Ernest Griffin and all who served on Britain's coastal defences during the Second World War

Britain's Coast at War

Invasion Threat, Coastal Forces, Bombardment and Training for D-Day

Neil R Storey

Pen & Sword
MILITARY

First published in Great Britain in 2021 by
Pen & Sword Military
An imprint of
Pen & Sword Books Ltd
Yorkshire – Philadelphia

ISBN 978 1 39900 122 9

Printed and bound in the UK by CPI Group (UK) Ltd,
Croydon, CR0 4YY.

FSC
www.fsc.org
MIX
Paper from
responsible sources
FSC® C013604

Pen & Sword Books Limited incorporates the imprints of Atlas,
Archaeology, Aviation, Discovery, Family History, Fiction, History,
Maritime, Military, Military Classics, Politics, Select, Transport,
True Crime, Air World, Frontline Publishing, Leo Cooper, Remember
When, Seaforth Publishing, The Praetorian Press, Wharncliffe
Local History, Wharncliffe Transport, Wharncliffe True Crime
and White Owl.

For a complete list of Pen & Sword titles please contact

PEN & SWORD BOOKS LIMITED
47 Church Street, Barnsley, South Yorkshire, S70 2AS, England
E-mail: enquiries@pen-and-sword.co.uk
Website: www.pen-and-sword.co.uk

Or

PEN AND SWORD BOOKS
1950 Lawrence Rd, Havertown, PA 19083, USA
E-mail: Uspen-and-sword@casematepublishers.com
Website: www.penandswordbooks.com

Contents

Sentry of 2/5th Battalion, West Yorkshire Regiment keeps an eye on the visitors allowed to use the beach at the fisherman's gap on Sheringham beach, July 1941.

Introduction

Their brasses shone in the bright winter sunshine and the streets echoed with the sound of studs in the leather soles of ammunition boots crunching along, as men from Regular Army battalions of the British Army marched from the railway station to the docks at Dover. To look at the troops it could almost have been 1914 with their stiff peaked caps, service dress uniforms, puttees and 1908 Pattern equipment; even many of the rifles they carried bore dates from the First World War, but this was January 1935 and British troops were leaving Dover bound for the Saar Basin.

The Saar was an industrial area with numerous coal mines bordered by Alsace-Lorraine on one side and Germany on the other. It had been governed

Soldiers of 1st Battalion, Essex Regiment and 1st Battalion, East Lancashire Regiment marching to the dock at Dover to embark bound for the Saar Basin, January 1935.

by Britain and France under the auspices of the League of Nations since the Treaty of Versailles had been signed in 1919; now it was up to the people of the Saar to decide by plebiscite whether France or Germany should govern them. In the interests of peacekeeping during the voting, British regular army battalions along with those from Italy, Sweden and the Netherlands were sent to the Saar. When the votes were counted however, it came as a surprise to many observers when the region voted overwhelmingly to reunite with Germany, a country that was by that time governed by the Nazi Party under the leadership of Adolf Hitler. The Saar was the first and often forgotten annexation of a number of regions in Europe that would be achieved by Hitler before 1939 when he began to obtain control and occupation of countries by far less diplomatic means.

The British Army battalions that had been sent to the Saar left them to it soon after the vote had been declared and returned via France where they had a brief tour of the battlefields of the First World War. It would be far from the first and most certainly not the last time task forces and expeditionary forces of the British Army were to leave these shores. It was, however, a rare occasion when all who left would return unscathed by active service.

This is a book about places I hope we all have the pleasure of knowing and loving around the great British coast. Many of us have known them all our lives for it is a coastline so diverse, offering beautiful places where we can find quiet, solitude, wild nature and wide-open skies. It is also where we had fun growing up, playing on the sands, rock-pooling and going crabbing over piers and quaysides, enjoying a trip to a funfair, playing the slot machines, laughing at summer shows, eating treats like sticky sweets, rock, candy floss and ice cream and then enjoying it all over again with our children and grandchildren. For those of us born after 1945 we have been fortunate to always know and enjoy our coastline in peace and freedom. Indeed, for so long now it is easy for us to forget and take such things for granted, but during the Second World War Britain's coastline became its front line defence against Nazi invasion.

When I was growing up in the 1970s I recall seeing rusty joints from scaffolding on the beaches we visited in East Anglia and Kent. At the time I wondered what on earth they were for and asked the family members I was with about them. Fortunately, my grandad and a number of great uncles had all served on coastal defences at some point during the war. They were able to explain the rusty objects were the joints from what they knew as Admiralty scaffolding that was erected on the beach, often with mines attached, to foil enemy vessels if they attempted to make a landing. This would often lead to other stories about their time crewing guns on coastal batteries, being out on lonely patrols along the cliffs at night and keeping a watch on the horizon

A Royal Navy Chief Petty Officer instructing Sergeant Gunners on the Oerlikon 20mm cannon near a Port Signal Station in Northern Command, June 1942. Note the Admiralty scaffolding behind them.

across the sea just in case Hitler chose to send his invasion barges over under the cover of darkness.

The stories were told to me with a twinkle in their eyes, but those who told them and thousands of others like them had kept that vigil when the threat of invasion was very real. Anti-invasion patrols were carried out on land, in the air and at sea, but for those on land it was not just the threat of invasion that was a cause for concern, there were also acute shortages of weaponry and equipment. Local Defence Volunteers and even some army units in May and June 1940 were being armed with nothing more offensive than pick-axe handles to defend their stretch of coastline if the Germans had decided to land there. However, there were thousands of miles of barbed wire, thousands of mines being laid and more being made in quick time. So many pillboxes, defences and gun emplacements were being built it caused a national shortage of concrete.

Despite the majority of the coastal anti-invasion defences being removed over the years after the end of the Second World War numerous pillboxes and structures associated with artillery and rocket batteries were still around. I remember them well, I played in some of them, but now many of those I knew have tumbled onto the beaches and are now lost forever; some became unstable, their entrances have been bricked up or they have been demolished and removed.

That said, there are still reminders of Britain's coastal front line that linger on; most obvious are the remaining pillboxes and casemates that housed coastal gun batteries. When you look at some historic structures along the coast look out for large, oblong embrasures cut out of the ancient stonework. This might just have been for a machine gun, there are often concrete spigot mortar bases to be found if you know what you are looking for and thousands of concrete anti-tank blocks that have now been repurposed as sea defences. Just consider all the wartime sites you know around the coast, the objects you have seen on the beach and heard about too. The last beaches to be certified as clear of mines were handed back for public use in the 1970s, but there are still mines being uncovered and ammunition lost and discarded during wartime training exercises is found on occasion to this day.

Sometimes it just takes heavy rains and high tides for a beach to have a scour and reveal the anti-invasion defences that have been buried unseen under the sands for decades, like those revealed on Blyth beach in Northumberland in

London evacuees Maureen and Maurice Foley at Bideford harbour, North Devon 1941.

2019 that were so numerous it was compared to looking like something from the set of *Saving Private Ryan*. Rather like the agricultural fields where the Battle of the Somme was fought, where farmers still have an 'iron harvest' of weapons and ammunition from the battles of the First World War, we will continue to rediscover our wartime defences and artefacts on the beaches of our coast for many years to come. It certainly gives an idea of the scale of our coastal defences that even after clearances and the passage of time so much of it is still around today.

In the late 1990s it was my great pleasure to be involved with both field work and research for the Defence of Britain project which set out to record the 20th century militarised landscape of the United Kingdom with a view to its preservation. There are also some superb books on pillboxes and fixed defences as well as books charting the story of specific counties and places during the Second World War, but what I feel has been sadly neglected is the wider story of what happened around our coastline and the impact of war on the people who lived and worked in the resorts, towns and communities during the war years.

This book does not pretend to be encyclopaedic; instead by selecting key events, first-hand accounts and reports accompanied by evocative photographs it will reveal the dramatic, moving and often previously untold stories of Britain's coast during the Second World War.

Neil R. Storey
2021

The 'Scottish fisher lassies' pose for the camera at Great Yarmouth in the early 1930s.

Chapter 1

The Last Summer

Though things may not look bright
They all turn out alright
If I keep painting the clouds with sunshine

Lyrics of a popular song performed by
Jack Hylton and his Orchestra 1939

The British coast in the 1930s shared a common story of two halves, one of fishermen and allied industries and the other of the holiday trade which had become a valuable lifeline for the economy of coastal communities since the late nineteenth century. In rural areas untouched by the holiday trade fishing communities with families working small boats catching crabs, lobsters in pots and netting what fish they could in waters just off the coast worked in much the same routine as they had for centuries before. Many fishermen also developed valuable sidelines of shellfish such as cockles, mussels, whelks and shrimps too, all of which they boiled up themselves to supply to local fishmongers and often sold direct to local people and holidaymakers from their own yard or garden.

The railways also provided a valuable link to towns and cities and 'crab trains' became a regular feature on the east coast lines carrying crate loads of crabs and lobsters down to London. Times, however, were hard especially in the more rural fishing communities away from railways and the tourist trade. Fisherfolk were fading away as younger generations of many fishing families were not carrying on the family business, migrating instead to busier towns and resorts to work on boats there or giving up the coastal life and the sea altogether to find more lucrative work in construction, municipal works, factories and industries in towns and cities.

Improvements in deep sea fishing vessels, notably the steam-powered drifters and light machine-made cotton nets, during the late nineteenth century enabled unprecedented catching power. These developments, combined with access to international markets thanks to larger, faster, efficient merchant shipping and railways, brought about a massive expansion in the

The Fishing Fleet at Fraserburgh, Aberdeenshire, Scotland in the 1930s.

herring industry. By the early twentieth century as many as 30,000 vessels were involved in herring fishing off the east coast alone. The zenith of the herring industry had been in the years immediately before the First World War. During the 1907 herring boom, 2,500,000 barrels of fish (250,000 tons) were cured and exported, the main markets at the time being North Germany, Eastern Europe and Russia.

The fish caught off the east coast were seasonal but when one fish became scarce another filled its place and kept the trade going. In May and June there were mackerel, with occasional hauls of 'midsummer herrings' from mid-June to mid-July. With the autumn came the shoals of herring, known affectionately as 'silver darlings', and as they left sprats made good catches in November and December.

Above all, the herring season was the boom time on the coast. Fishing boats and associated industry workers followed the shoals of millions of herring down the coast of Britain. Herring were caught off the north coast of Scotland and Shetland in the early summer and then, as they migrated south, they made rich pickings all along the east coast through summer and autumn as they made their way to their spawning grounds in the Dover Straits and off Brittany. With the fleet came a veritable army of merchants, curers and general hands, not forgetting the Scottish fisher girls who would come down by the train load because they were considered unlucky on fishing vessels and were not allowed to travel down aboard the fleet.

2

Mate and Third Hand mending nets on board the Grimsby trawler SS Righto while on the North Sea, 1945.

Crushed ice being fed into the ice room so the fish that had been caught were kept fresh aboard SS Righto at Grimsby docks, Lincolnshire 1945.

The bows of the trawlers line up along the quayside in front of Lowestoft fish market in the 1930s.

The drifters would put to sea in the afternoon, quite a sight as the smoking funnels of around 100 drifters steamed out from the harbour 'crossing the bar' from the calm waters to the stirring waves of the North Sea. Their departure and return the following morning would always draw a crowd of onlookers, it was, in its day, a remarkable spectacle and very much an established feature of coastal life. In every port, haven and harbour where the herring fleet docked there were fish quays and docks created for the fish to be landed and covered markets where they were auctioned. As the boats docked side by side the morning air would fill with a smoky smog from the funnels of the boats and the size of the fleets were said to be measured by the distance you could walk along the decks of the moored boats; in Norfolk for example, it was said you could walk from Great Yarmouth to Gorleston along their bows. The smell of those busy docks, a heady blend of drifter smoke, wet fish, sea water and damp wood would be affectionately recalled by anyone who experienced it.

Once the herring were sold the fish were sorted and packed into crates on the quayside and loaded onto horse-drawn carts and lorries that waited to transport the fish to the gutting and curing yards that spread over large areas near the docks. The industry provided welcome employment for local people on the fishing boats, and thousands more on the curing yards, curing works, in the smoke houses and in allied trades of seamen's clothing manufacture, boat building, coopering, basket, wooden box and net making. The work was particularly welcomed by agricultural labourers. Low on work out of harvest time, hordes of strong labouring men would walk to the fishing ports to find work. The gutting yards became famous for the Scottish fisher girls or lassies employed in them. These women came from fishing villages from all along the coast of Scotland and were called 'girls' or 'lassies' no matter what their age. Most of them had begun gutting and packing the silver darlings from about the age of 15, learning by eye, then doing it themselves.

The 'fisher lassies' travelled throughout the fishing season from Stornoway to Lerwick, to Peterhead, and then followed the fleet down the coast. In a busy season there would be thousands of women employed in the yards. They wore tarpaulin aprons, drab headscarves, rubber wellies for work and, when on a day of rest, swathed themselves in brightly coloured shawls, linked arms and knitted as they walked and talked along the quayside – all for a good reason, knitting to keep their fingers nimble and linking arms in case they became so engrossed in their chatting one of them might stumble over the edge into the water if they had not been arm in arm with their friend. Just like many fishermen, most of these girls could not swim.

The lassies worked in teams of three, two of them gutting the fish with a deft flick of their sharp knives and the third grading and packing them into baskets. They were a popular sight to be seen by visitors to the yards and the speed with which they worked was truly remarkable, their hands were a blur yet they carried on animated conversations with their neighbours. Their labours appeared effortless and easy to the onlooker (until they tried it for themselves). One girl was timed and recorded as gutting fifty-seven fish in one minute!

Once the baskets were full the team of three would share the carrying of the baskets to the barrels. There one girl would remain to salt and pack while the other two returned to gutting. The filled barrels were lidded by the cooper and stacked for about ten days after which time the barrel bung was removed and the brine poured out. The barrels would then be topped up with more cured fish then packed off for export. There were also smoke houses where as many as 24,000 herring could be smoked to create the famous 'bloaters'. By the 1930s it had become a novelty to send a box of Great Yarmouth bloaters to friends and family when visiting the town. As many as 5,000 boxes of bloaters were being handled every day by the Post Office.

However, the First World War saw the loss of the major foreign markets and in the years after the war the industry never really recovered and had dwindled to half the size it had been in 1913. In the late 1930s there were great hopes for something of a renaissance and a national campaign to popularise the herring to the home market as a staple article of diet was begun in 1939 with Herring and Kipper Weeks being held in a number of fishing ports around the country.

In August 1939, after a two-year absence, the Scottish herring fleet returned to the coastal waters off North Northumberland and were observed as they lay off the coast to stretch from Embleton Bay to Boulmer, a distance of 4 miles by land. Joined by local fishing boats, they would take their beats between 6pm and 7pm and then, as the sun set and darkness descended, the sea was decorated by the long ribbon of bobbing lights of the fishing boats. In the early morning they would set off with their catches to the markets at North Shields. Catches were large, demand was high, prices realised from 42s to 66s per cran and hopes were raised for a restoration of the good old days of the herring industry.

* * *

The other side of Britain's coastal economy was the holiday trade and by the 1930s the British coast had become established as *the* destination for day trippers and holidaymakers for generations. Days off were precious, times

British holidays were often advertised as for 'health, fitness and fun' in the 1930s.

had been hard and as the country tried to pull itself out of the recession many folks would save all year for a few days away. Things were looking up after the Holiday Pay Act was passed in 1938 which meant workers would now receive pay during their days of annual leave.

It was very unusual for the majority of British people, regardless of class, to take foreign holidays; the prices alone were prohibitive for many and as a society many people found the concept so alien they simply did not consider foreign travel as an option. If the average British holidaymaker did cross more than a mile of water to reach their destination it would usually be by ferry or steamer to the Isle of Wight, the Isle of Man, Ireland or Jersey in the more distant Channel Islands.

For most people location was key to their choice of holiday destination. At a time when most families did not own a car travel to the coast would have relied on what was then the most remarkable, proudest and reliable railway network in the world. The other factors were tradition and habit because by the 1930s generations of families had made a particular resort their chosen destination, the attitude of the time being very much: 'If it was good enough for dad and grandad it's good enough for me.'

The annual holidays of many people in industrial areas were held at the same time, for example in the potteries of Stoke-on-Trent it was 'Potters Holiday' in late June and early July, in the industrial north it was 'Wakes Week' or 'Factory Fortnight' when mills would shut for maintenance of machinery and boilers were thoroughly cleaned and overhauled, usually during July or August. Works would organise holidays for their staff which would enable employees to make a contribution from their wages each week to save for the holiday. Better rates would be obtained for group bookings and you would have the chance to holiday with the friends and colleagues you already knew.

There were also 'holiday fellowships' of various hues, some faith based, others based around social groups often either for men or women only. Some of the largest fellowships had their own holiday homes for their groups, hotels were available but were often too expensive for the average holidaymaker so most people would stay in a 'private hotel' or guest house which would provide a bed for the night and breakfast. Guest houses were an intrinsic part of coastal resorts, each with its own name, such as 'Bide-a-Wee' (Scottish for stay a while), 'Rise and Shine', or named after other well-known seaside places like 'Cliftonville' or 'Sandown'. Others were named after national figures, heroes and royal estates and just about every permutation featuring sea, 'Sea View', Sea Crest', 'Sea Spray', 'Sea Croft' 'Sea Breeze', 'Sea Grove' and 'Sea Marge' to name but a few.

For those who decided to break with family tradition and try other places there were no online travel reviews then and, with only limited information from adverts in newspapers or guide books, holiday makers had little idea of what they were letting themselves in for when they booked a place to stay. There might be a picture of the exterior of the establishment, facilities such as hot and cold running water would be mentioned, but all you could really expect from the guest house would be the provision of a bed for the night and breakfast. A communal bathroom with a flush toilet and a bath with hot water would be a real treat. How modern or clean the rooms were would only be discovered on arrival, so when folk found a good guesthouse they tended to return to the same one again and again rather than take pot-luck each year.

Guests would also be subject to house rules, notably the curfew of a set time for return because the doors would be locked and bolted at midnight and woe betide anyone who returned late and had to wake the landlady to be let in. The landladies that ran these establishments varied too, some were warm and welcoming, others made guests feel more like an inconvenience, and some were absolute harridans who treated their guests with contempt. The seaside comedians who ended up staying at the poorer establishments over the years (usually because they were cheap or the only ones with available rooms) certainly got their own back by drawing on such experiences and seaside landlady jokes became a staple of their stage routines.

All of that said, a holiday provided the experience of getting away, having a few golden days off from what were often hard-working lives. Great efforts and investments were made by seaside councils, entrepreneurs and impresarios to make these resorts as appealing as possible for everyone. Advertisements would extol the clean golden sands, lido, open air swimming pools, amusement parks, beautifully maintained tennis courts, bowling greens and miniature golf courses, boating ponds, ornamental gardens, parks and green spaces. Many had bandstands where bands would play throughout the summer and pavilions and winter gardens for shade or shelter where teas would be served to the accompaniment of light music.

There would be ice creams and lollies, fish and chips eaten out of newspapers, novelty rock emporiums, souvenir shops and entertainments on the beach, piers with theatres and shows. In the seaside towns there would be more theatres, dance halls, ice rinks, cinemas and ballrooms for the evenings or if the weather proved inclement and then all could walk home by the light of the seaside illuminations.

It was a gentle world, one where the entertainment was innocent compared to post war and modern tastes. Perhaps the rosy tint of nostalgia for those times was magnified in the minds of those who lived through the Second

The Spa Bandstand at Scarborough in the 1930s.

World War, but they were times looked back upon with immense affection by anyone who experienced them. Bradford born author and broadcaster J.B. Priestley drew specifically on this special part of British life in his contrasts of home at peace and hell of war in his famous *Postscripts* BBC radio broadcast of June 1940. Priestley was unlike many of the voices heard on the BBC at the time. Listeners were used to hearing the clipped English accents and received pronunciation of announcers and news broadcasters like Alvar Lidell and John Snagg, whereas Priestley spoke with a rich voice marked with a regional accent which, when combined with his eloquence, meant he did not speak to the nation, he spoke for the nation and would be dubbed 'the voice of Britain'.

He spoke with such affection of the 'ridiculous holiday world' of 'pierrots and piers, sandcastles, ham-and-egg teas, palmists, automatic machines and crowded, sweating promenades' which he contrasted with the paddle steamers from this world of fun that went with other 'little ships' into the inferno of Dunkirk to help rescue soldiers from the beaches. Some of these ships, of course, did not return. Priestley's broadcast proved to be one of the most poignant and memorable radio orations during the war. He stuck such a chord it resonated into the British psyche and did much to crystallise the 'Miracle of Dunkirk' in the minds of British people after the Dunkirk evacuation.

So, let's take a whistle stop tour of that more innocent world catching the highlights at some of the most popular British coastal holiday resorts in

The paddle steamer **Gracie Fields** *mentioned by J.B. Priestley in his famous* **Postscripts** *broadcast as one of the vessels that sadly did not return from its Dunkirk evacuation mission in May 1940.*

1939. Beginning our tour in Scotland the famous 'Glasgow Fair Fortnight' saw shipyards and factories closed for a week at the end of July allowing a rare period of time off from work. Other areas in Scotland had similar 'trade holidays' during the summer months and although there were some seaside resorts around their coast, the Scots knew only too well their local weather really could not be relied upon. Traditionally many took steamer trips 'doon that watter' of the river Clyde to the Ayrshire coast, but with the improved railway links and cheap fares Blackpool had become the resort of choice for the Scots, hence the Caledonian themed names of hundreds of the guest houses in the town.

Further down the north east coast in Northumberland the Geordies loved Whitley Bay and its Spanish City amusements. For Yorkshire and their stretch of the east coast it would have been Scarborough or Bridlington where the newspaper coverage of the annual regatta in 1939 raised an eyebrow at the increasing numbers of women becoming active members of the Yorkshire Yacht Club. The Midlands had Cleethorpes, branded as a health resort in

London North Eastern Railway advertisements that claimed the destination was 'Lincolnshire's health gift to Britain – Your health comes first so Cleethorpes must always come first.' There was also Skegness with its iconic advertising image of a jolly fisherman skipping along the shore and the motto 'so bracing'.

It was near Skegness that Billy Butlin, having been inspired by the early Warner's holiday camps, built his first camp at Ingoldmells in 1936. By 1939 Butlin had camps at Skegness and Clacton and with more in development he rapidly became quite a phenomenon. Butlin's publicity offered 'holidays with play', a play on words with the new holiday with pay scheme he had helped to lobby for. He offered a week's holiday for a week's pay. In 1939 a week's wage would have been between £2 and £3 and a stay at Butlin's would have cost 45 shillings (he undercut Warners by 5 shillings). For this you would receive exactly what was offered on his advertisements: '*separate chalets, four good meals a day prepared by expert chefs under ideal conditions served at separate tables, all amenities and entertainments free*'. Despite being aimed at a mass audience, his 1939 advertising assured potential guests these were 'The most luxurious holiday camps in Europe.'

Holidaymakers from all over the country steamed in by the train load to 'Meet the sun in East Anglia' at Great Yarmouth and Lowestoft. At the latter popular radio comediennes Elsie and Doris Waters, known to all as 'Gert and Daisy', were packing in audiences at Sparrow's Nest Theatre and Jack Musikant and his Musikaneers were playing in the park every afternoon at

Multi-view postcard showing some of the delights of Skegness in the 1930s.

Southend Pier, Essex during the 1930s.

3pm. Local people, however, were often drawn to their own smaller and more sedate resorts and seaside towns like Hunstanton, Sheringham and Cromer. Piers being structures with a high wood content were prone to fires and tragically it would be Hunstanton that would suffer a blaze in June 1939 when its pavilion theatre caught fire. Miss Doris Bassford of Leicester and Miss Winifred Taylor of Wembley were trapped at the end of the pier and only escaped with their lives by jumping into the water below. Thankfully the tide was in and the water was deep enough to break their fall.

Further down on the Essex coast the resorts of Clacton and Southend hold many happy memories for

Harry Gold's Margate Entertainers 1939.

12

Londoners. Southend had a yachting week in June, county cricket weeks, an open bowling tournament, carnival week and illuminations planned for autumn.

On the 'sunny south coast' of Kent Harry Gold's concert parties entertained visitors for many years on the sands at Margate and Ramsgate. Ramsgate's 'Merrie England' funfair proudly announced new attractions such as an Electric Brooklands Racing Track, Moon Rocket, Mademoiselle d'Alba 'The Australian Television Wonder Girl', along with all the old favourites of dodg'em cars, ghost train, big wheel, slot machines and side-shows. There was Scott Gordon's Ramsgate Revels at Granville Pavilion and Billy Merrin and his Commanders played at the East Cliff Bandstand.

Shipping companies around the south coast offered day trips across the Channel to Boulogne, Ostend, Calais and Dunkirk on steamers. J.B. Priestley reminisced:

We've known them and laughed at them, these fussy little steamers, all of our lives. We have called them 'the shilling sicks'. We have watched them load and unload their crowds of holiday passengers – the gents full of high spirits and bottled beer, the ladies eating pork pies, the children sticky with peppermint rock. Sometimes they only went as far as the next seaside resort. But the boldest of them might manage a Channel crossing to let everybody have a glimpse of Boulogne. They were usually paddle steamers, making a great deal more fuss with all their churning than they made speed; and they were not proud for they let you see their works going round. They liked to call themselves 'Queens' and 'Belles'; and even if they were new, there was always something old-fashioned, a Dickens touch, a mid-Victorian air about them.[1]

There were also reports in local newspapers of renewed attempts to revive the question of a Channel Tunnel, but as the clouds of war gathered there were pros and cons for such a venture. The French were very keen, Marcel Boucher, Deputy of the Vosges Department commented:

Just as in 1914, Great Britain and France suddenly realised in September last, in face of common peril, how sadly lacking was the Channel tunnel. Between two nations whose every existence faces the same risks a rapid and safe communicating link is of capital importance and of utmost urgency.[2]

He went on to quote Marshal Foch who had claimed if a Channel tunnel had existed in 1914 the World War might have been avoided.

Day trippers and holidaymakers from London and the Home Counties made for the Sussex coast to stay at such destinations as Hastings and St Leonards and Eastbourne. In the summer of 1939 Eastbourne Royal

Hippodrome was billing 'Here Come the Band' headlined by Bertini and his Radio Boys 'bringing all the gaiety of Blackpool to your door'. Supporting Bertini was Harry White described in the advertising for the show as 'a boy discovered by Bertini singing in the streets of Manchester'. There was also Tommy Walker, 'Lancashire's own comedy comedian'; the Seaside Girls; the Seaside Serenader with his accordion; the Golfus Crazy Boys, Loretta, 'a clever young dancer' and the 16 Hilly-Billys in 'Home on the Range'.

At the Winter Gardens there were evening performances of their summer show 'Sunshine Parade' and even a personal appearance by Paul Robeson. On Wednesdays and Saturdays, summer afternoon tea dances were held with music provided by John Allen's Colonials (1s). The Wednesday evening dances (2s 6d) at the Winter Gardens from 8.30pm until 1am included what was billed as 'a novel floor show by Fai Robina, the Sherman Fisher Girls and the other members of the 'Sunshine Parade' company. Many new dances are being introduced including the latest novelty dance 'Park Parade'.

At Bognor Regis there was Pierrotland for entertainments and where the Eric Ross Cabaret Company presented their summer season show 'Dazzle' while the Revuettes were playing at the Roof Garden Theatre on the pier.

Brighton Aquarium and Marine Parade in the 1930s.

14

Worthing, Brighton and Hove were always popular with Londoners in the same way as Blackpool was the mecca for holidaymakers from the north. Worthing Pier Pavilion began the 1939 season with vaudeville featuring such delights as Alwright's Comedy Circus, Barney Powell 'Xylophonist' and Harry Jerome 'Complete Wangler' followed by 'Gay Parade' the resident summer show for the season presented by impresario Richard Jerome.

Brighton had the biggest star on the south coast in August 1939. With the exception of George Formby there was really no bigger name than the 'Cheeky Chappie' himself, Max Miller, who played to packed houses on his 'home turf', at Brighton Hippodrome. Audiences were also looking forward to the return of The Crazy Gang (Nervo and Knox, Flanagan and Allen and Naughton and Gold) in the last week of the month.

Along the south coast to Hampshire, where Portsmouth was on a high after winning the FA Cup in April, Southsea had Jack Hylton and his band on the South Parade Pier Pavilion. Bournemouth and the Isle of Wight were both enormously popular holiday destinations. Dorset and Devon offered a run of resorts from Weymouth to Torquay where the Pavilion presented Stanley Holloway, another figure popular across the country for his funny

Plymouth from the Hoe looking west in the late 1930s.

FROM SMEATONS TOWER PLYMOUTH HOE. LOOKING WEST.

34099-

monologues. At The Palace, Plymouth there was popular light music from conductor Henry Hall and his orchestra supported by Walker and Ray, Will Duffy, The Ascot Three, Stainless Stephen and the Three Sparks Brothers. The band of the Royal Air Force College gave three performances a day at the bandstand at The Hoe and the Devonport Alhambra presented Edgar Taylor's 'Lavender Follies'.

On to Cornwall, dubbed 'The Cornish Riviera' with Falmouth, Penzance and Newquay all around the tip of the toe of Britain. Up the west coast to Wales and such delights awaited holidaymakers as 'Bright Breezy, Bracing' Barry, Pwllheli 'for golden sands, mountain scenery and a sun-kissed shore', Prestatyn for 'splendid bathing on a sandy beach', Conway and Colwyn Bay the 'Holiday paradise of the North Wales Coast'.

High on the north west coast of England lies the well-loved resort of Morecambe, but further down is Blackpool, in its heyday the king of all the popular coastal resorts. Described in 1934 by J.B. Priestly as 'That great, roaring spangled beast', Blackpool was where folks from the big industrial towns and cities of Lancashire and the north west traditionally took their holidays. Famed for its Tower, golden beaches, the very best in seaside entertainments, amusements and illuminations, by the late 1930s Blackpool was Britain's premier seaside holiday resort equipped to cater for not just thousands, but hundreds of thousands of visitors during the holiday season. Its biggest venues could seat thousands at a time, businesses wanted to be there and Blackpool wanted to offer the best.

Blackpool Tower c1939.

Littlewoods, having made their name with football pools and mail order clothes opened their first high street store there in 1937 and Woolworth's, once a popular chain of shops found in every major town and city across the country offering goods at sixpence or less, opened its biggest purpose-built shop in Britain at Blackpool in 1938. Spreading around the corner of Bank Hey Street and the Promenade the building was a veritable shopping palace containing three smart and fashionably furnished sales floors and above them two restaurant floors capable of accommodating 2,000 people at a time 'from dawn to 11pm'.

The Blackpool Opera House had been completely rebuilt on a grand scale and decorated in the most beautiful deco style, be it live shows or 'super cinema' it was able to seat a total audience of 2,920. The newly built and fully fitted theatre cost £125,000, an incredible amount for any provincial theatre in the 1930s. Opened on 14 July 1939 by Jessie Matthews the 'golden girl' of stage and screen, at the time the first show could really have no-one else at the top of the bill, George Formby in the revue 'Turned Out Nice Again'.

The week war broke out Bebe Daniels (who went on to record a version of *White Cliffs of Dover*) and Ben Lyon, a stage and screen couple billed as

Publicity photograph for holidays in Blackpool, 1939.

'England's Favourite Americans', were making their annual appearance at the Palace Theatre, Blackpool with Yorkshire comedian Dick Henderson and Ted Ray. There was good clean fun and repartee, humour aplenty, dancing and tricks with Wilson, Kepple and Betty and comedy acrobats Jack and John Bredwin.

The Blackpool publicity advertising for 1939 proudly announced they had invested more money than ever in new entertainments, promised top shows at its venues across the town and great plans were being made to make the Blackpool illuminations even more spectacular when they were switched on in September. Blackpool was offering 'a holiday in a million' and was preparing for a bumper season.

Sadly, it was not to be. The summer of 1939 was variable, there were some spells of glorious weather, but there were also long periods of grey skies and rain. Some people did make an extra effort to have a break away, even if it was just a day trip to the seaside, others hung back under the cloud of war. Concerns over bombing by enemy aircraft were intensifying and there was talk of huge amounts of high explosive bombs dropped by enemy aircraft if war broke out, of 'knock-out blows' destroying cities in days hardly put people in the holiday mood. Those trying to escape the clouds of war were confronted by gaping trenches and construction work as public shelters were built and in a number of areas there was the booming of guns from anti-aircraft training camps.

The August Bank Holiday saw the LNER arrange 1,800 extra trains, but the visitor numbers were dramatically down on previous years. Many Londoners cancelled their holidays and most of Britain's coastal resorts suffered badly, to the degree that a number of local councils, groups of hoteliers and shopkeepers sent deputations and appeals to Parliament for financial assistance.

After the declaration of war on 3 September 1939 the government did not want to risk any large gatherings of civilians in confined spaces, especially in the days when many cinemas and theatres were regularly playing to houses of over 1,000, so an order was made that places of entertainment were to be closed and there was no indication of a foreseeable re-opening date. Under blackout restrictions the coloured lights of the coast would also be turned off and with the limitations of the austere post-war years even the Blackpool illuminations would not be switched on again until 1949.

On the night the war broke out Leo Walmsley walked up to the ridge above his Yorkshire cottage home and looked out along the coastline:

At night in clear weather, while the hills and coastline would have been blurred, I could have picked out every individual farm and village in the landscape, especially in the holiday season, the lights of Whitby and Scarborough would have made a big yellow glow in the sky. Now, although the weather was fine, there was not a pin prick of light anywhere. The black-out of which we had heard so much during the 'war of nerves' and which I had consistently believed would never happen had come.[3]

* * *

The year 1939 had begun under the shadow of war. In 1938 Hitler had ordered his forces to occupy the Sudetenland and major concerns were felt across Europe for what he might do next. In September 1938 Britain stood on the brink of war with Germany and it had only been averted when Prime Minister Neville Chamberlain had flown to Munich to meet with Hitler to see if some form of non-aggression agreement could be reached. Chamberlain returned and before the world's press on the runway of Heston airport held aloft the paper and declared he had secured 'Peace in our time'. Many were not convinced Hitler would stop his aggressive actions but at least Chamberlain had bought Britain some time to prepare for war.

In fact, Britain had been making preparations for the event of a 'war emergency' since the mid 1930s, but they were not as advanced as they could and really should have been. Air Raid Precautions (ARP) committees had been set up for every county since 1935 but it was only after the world had seen the horrors of strategic bombing carried out by the German air force during the Spanish Civil War – notably the bombing of Guernica in 1937 – and the fact that Hitler showed no signs of abating his aggression in Europe in 1938, that more plans were instigated to engage the British public in the event of a war emergency occurring. Extant organisations such as St John Ambulance, Red Cross, Boy Scouts, Girl Guides and the Women's Institute staged ARP courses open to the public, explaining what to do in the event of an air raid and how to use a gas mask, and many members trained as instructors in their own right. Stella Isaacs, the Dowager Marchioness of Reading was asked by the government to form The Women's Voluntary Services which was to act as a support unit for the ARP.

By the time of the Munich crisis in late September there was already a considerable ARP organisation in Britain. Teams of volunteers, in some instances staff from large shops and businesses, members of the Women's Institute and WVS worked in production lines under the supervision of trained ARP staff assembling the various parts of gas masks and packing them into boxes. This was no mean feat, for example, girls from the leading department stores in Eastbourne assembled 60,000 gas masks for the local population. Once the stocks had been made up, ARP workers assembled at their district posts and fitted patient queues of local people with their gas masks. Every household was also sent a copy of *The Protection of Your Home Against Air Raids* which provided homeowners with useful advice on how to protect their home from bomb blast, gas attack and select and equip a 'safe room'. Air raid shelter trenches were hastily dug on public parks and suitable ground in cities, towns and villages.

As Britain teetered on the brink of war men of the 'key parties' of Territorial Army units presented themselves at their headquarters to organise the paperwork and equipment ready for mobilisation. The Observer Corps had had its first general call out and the emergency services had been placed on standby. An assessment was also carried out for a government evacuation scheme whereby areas were classified according to risk of bombing. Evacuation areas were mostly London and industrial areas from which children, pregnant mothers, the elderly and the vulnerable would be evacuated. There were 'reception areas', initially on the coast and in the countryside, that were believed to be safe from bombing and 'neutral areas' where there was some risk of bombing but from which children would neither be evacuated from or to these locations.

Many areas published their provisional evacuation, neutral and reception areas in early January 1939 and local authorities in reception areas began the search for potential foster homes for evacuees. Volunteers described as 'Visitors' interviewed householders and filled in census forms. These returns were to help decide how many evacuees could be billeted in each area. The *Dover Express* published the provisional list for Kent: Chatham, Gillingham and Rochester. Neutral areas – which will neither be evacuated nor become reception areas – were listed as Beckenham, Bexley, Bromley, Dartford, Erith, Gravesend, Margate, Queensborough, Ramsgate, Broadstairs and St Peter's, Chislehurst and Sidcup, Crayford, Northfleet, Orpington, Penge, Sheerness and Swascombe. Folkstone was not mentioned, it being a Channel port and military station. Initially the paper's 'In the Street' column sagely commented, 'It is hoped that foreign bombers will be supplied with copies of the list of neutral towns in Great Britain.'

Much to the surprise of those who knew the history of Dover during the First World War, and to anyone aware of the military significance of the place in 1939, Dover was also listed as a reception area for evacuated children. Realising its vulnerable position, the town had not only dug shelters during the Munich Crisis but went on to prepare an impressive scheme for the construction of bombproof shelters to be sited at a number of locations around the town and air raid tunnel shelters in the chalk hills. The plan was submitted to the Home Office with an estimated cost of £208,245 for the tunnels and £24,200 for

Members of the first Kindertransport of Jewish refugee children from Germany, arrive in Harwich, 1939.

the shelters, but the Home Office refused any grant for the tunnel scheme. It was only after a deputation from the town went to meet officials at the Home Office in March, when the situation was explained directly to them, that the decision to make Dover an evacuation reception area was reversed and they were assured the town would be provided with Anderson shelters.

Britain's coast had also seen ever increasing numbers of emigrants and refugees arriving on its docksides to escape persecution since the Nazi regime came to power in Germany in 1933. Two months after the Kristallnacht pogroms, when the Nazis showed their hands openly by attacking synagogues, businesses and properties, the first parties of unaccompanied German children (predominantly Jewish) fleeing the Nazis arrived at Harwich on 2 December 1938. Thousands more from Germany and Austria followed soon after. The children were initially accommodated at the Dovercourt Bay holiday camp and Pakefield Camp in Suffolk was also used for a short while until foster homes could be found for them. As Czechoslovakia and Poland faced the heel of Nazi occupation forces more and more refugees found sanctuary on

Britain's shores throughout 1939 and 1940. These children were mostly in their early teens, but some as young as five would be known simply as the *Kindertransport*.

Despite the scares of the Munich Crisis in 1938 the British government had not undertaken any immediate schemes for the expansion of any of the armed forces. It was only after Germany breached the terms of the Munich agreement by invading and occupying the remnants of the Czech state on 15 March 1939 that it was announced on 29 March that the Territorial Army was to be doubled in size. Many experienced TA officers were of the opinion that this late expansion was deplorable and really should have been addressed in the mid 1930s when the Nazis began to militarise the German people and rebuild their armed forces on an ever-growing scale.

The renewed German aggression came just as city and town council ARP committees were holding meetings to decide how they were going to collect in all the gas masks that had been issued and where they were going to be stored. Now the ARP services, increasingly referred to as Civil Defence services, would address recruitment and obtain the necessary equipment and supplies for their volunteers with renewed vigour. An order within the Ministers of the Crown (Emergency Appointments) Act 1939 transferred the statutory powers of the Home Secretary, Secretary of State for Scotland and the Lord Privy Seal to the Minister of Home Security and the Ministry of Home Security was created as a result. The ministry is best known for overseeing the Civil Defence Services of Britain, it was an enormous undertaking that had the oversight of central and regional air raid precaution schemes, Civil Defence organisation, supplies and the provision of gas masks and air raid shelters for millions of people.

In April 1939 the Ministry of Home Security set up twelve Civil Defence regions across Britain, each with an appointed regional commissioner to co-ordinate officials of government departments and local authorities in Civil Defence work. In May 1940 their powers were extended under Defence Regulations to direct local authorities in Civil Defence matters and they were empowered to issue orders in, or control entry to, defence areas. Every region also had a secure and bomb proof 'war room' to collect information concerning air raids, report numbers of casualties and request assistance from other regions if required to the central Home Security War Room under the Geological Museum on Exhibition Road, South Kensington, London.

Each regional commissioner headed an impressive a team of personnel too – a deputy and a 'war room' staffed by duty officers, administration staff and telephonists twenty-four hours a day. There would also be specialist officers appointed in the regions for specific tasks or to address particular issues such as refugees, supplies, rehousing of those made homeless due to air raids and the organisation of the clearance and salvage of bomb-damaged buildings. Regional information officers reported to the Ministry of Information and co-ordinated the distribution of government information circulars and public information leaflets. There were also advisers from the Ministry of Works, an inspector from the Ministry of Health, Regional Technical Intelligence Officers and a Regional Security Liaison Officer from MI5.[4]

The regional commissioner's organisation is well exemplified in Region 12 (South Eastern), which had its headquarters at Bredbury House, Mount Ephraim in Tunbridge Wells. Councillor E.S. Oak-Rhind (Broadstairs), chairman of the county council ARP committee announced in May 1939 that 'the Herculean task of setting up an ARP organisation which can operate smoothly across the county of Kent' had been completed. For the purposes of co-ordination and administration Kent had been divided into six divisions – Ramsgate, Margate, Broadstairs, Sandwich and Eastry Rural District which were all included in the No.6 'Cinque' county division which encompassed fourteen local authorities. The chain of command and communication that had been established consisted of firstly, HM Government, secondly the Regional Commissioner (Sir Aukland Geddes) with his council and staff and thirdly the County Controller Colonel J.H. Campbell and his council and staff. The members of his council consisted of Campbell, Major M.T. Kirby (Ashford) and Mr R.W. Rule (Sheerness). The net cost of the scheme was £4,110. Having dealt with the main county organisation within the South-Eastern Civil Defence Region, there was also a sub-division for the part of Kent in the London Civil Defence Region where Major T. Hepburn acted as ARP Controller.[5]

It would have appeared to the general public that the primary function of the regional commissioners was to run the Civil Defence organisation in each area. The duties of regional commissioners, which the Ministry of Home Security did not want to become public knowledge, were that in the event of Britain being invaded, and if communication between government and regions broke down, the primary purpose of regional commissioners was to assume full civil powers in their area.

Britain's regular armed forces were still not authorised to embark on any major recruitment campaigns in the early months of 1939 with advertising focusing on the old mainstay of recruiting boys from both coastal areas and inland for training at HMS *Caledonia* at Rosyth in Scotland and HMS *Ganges* on the Shotley peninsula in Suffolk. Basic training for boys and young men entering the Royal Navy, and for that matter the day-to day training at shore establishments as a whole, remained pretty much unchanged with their mix of drill, discipline, sports and seamanship, but with the addition of training on some of the more modern weaponry, communications and anti–gas courses.

The only other recruits really in demand for the Navy were mature men with experience as mechanics to join as engine room artificers. After years of wrangling with the RAF the Navy had also taken over the manning of the Fleet Air Arm and were looking for 1,000 men between the ages of 17½ and 25 to join the Air Mechanic branch. Senior Royal Navy officers presenting addresses at public events were, however, stressing they would soon be needing more men for the ships they had recently commissioned.

On 26 May The Military Training Act 1939 (often referred to as The Militia Act), Britain's first peacetime act of conscription, was passed by Parliament. It applied to all males aged between 20 and 21 years old and required the 35,000 men in this age bracket from across the country to answer

Boys practising mast manning at HMS **St Vincent**, *Royal Navy Training Establishment, Gosport 1939.*

a compulsory call-up to serve for six months full-time military training, after which they would be transferred to the Reserve for three and a half years during which time, it was pointed out in the terms, they might be recalled in an emergency for full time duty. There was an option for these young men to express a preference for the service in which they were to serve, but it by no means meant they would be placed in the arm of service requested. The Royal Navy and Royal Marines did not require huge numbers of recruits and could only accommodate 500 'militiamen', so they decided they could pick their men and all were required to be passed 'A1' by the medical inspection board. Their arrival at HMS *Drake* was reported in a number of newspapers:

> *Today's assembly at Devonport of the first Militiamen called up for service in the Royal Navy makes history and marks a remarkable step forward from the days of the press gangs…Only a fraction of those who wanted to serve with the Navy have had their wishes granted in their first year of compulsory military service so that every man who reports at Devonport today is tantamount to being a volunteer to the Senior Service.*[6]

24

P5 Class, HMS St Vincent Royal Navy Training Establishment Gosport, March 1939.

Royal Marines at Anti-Gas School, Devonport 1939.

The Navy did not like the name Naval Militia attached to these men, so they were rapidly retitled Royal Navy Special Reserve. Just like their counterparts in the army, they were still in uniform when war broke out and their six months training turned into nearly six years' service through the Second World War.

Territorial Army units had rapidly got into their stride with recruitment for its expansion from April. The plan was that extant battalions of the TA, be they infantry or corps, duplicated themselves using experienced officers and men from the already extant battalions to form the core of the new battalion. A huge recruiting campaign began with public events staged by Territorial units in their towns and cities. Men were urged to join as soon as possible so they would be able to attend summer camp. Keeping true to the tradition that sea air was good for you, all manner of groups from the Boys Brigade to Girl Guides held their summer camps on the coast and many Territorial Army units also followed suit. Regional newspapers were particularly keen to cover the progress of their local units. In 1939 the *Aberdeen People's Journal* headlined a record number of Territorials were leaving Aberdeen for summer camp that year and in a special feature described:

It's a hectic rush. They're working day and night, but I think they'll do it. The scamper is to provide all Aberdeen's latest Territorial recruits with uniform before they leave for camp next week-end. In the case of the 5/7th and 6th Gordons the latest 'battle dress' – light attire that's far from dressy – had to be rushed to some of the recruits on the camping grounds but Aberdeen is struggling hard to avoid resorting to such an expedient. It is hoped the last uniform will be on hand this week, so that the tailors will have a clear week to make the necessary adjustments.[7]

Between the local Territorial lads in the Gordon Highlanders bound for Gailes; Divisional Signals on their way to St Andrews; Royal Engineers at Peebles; the 75th (Highland) Royal Field Artillery bound for Barry Buddon, near Carnoustie and the Auxiliary Air Force contingent travelling to their camp at Tangmere near Brighton, in excess of 3,200 Territorials left Aberdeen bound for their summer camps in 1939.

The *People's Journal* report continued the story of the Gordon Highlander Territorials:

Colonel Philip mentioned to me that about 800 would leave for Gailes at midnight on Friday, July 14. Reason for the sma' 'oors start is that special trains could not be arranged during the day. The Colonel will have quite a family with 50 tons of baggage! Breakfast or any other meal – will be a housewife's nightmare, for among the necessary ingredients for that one 'tuck in' are 125 dozen eggs, 50lb of butter and 150lb of bacon...The midnight trip of the Terriers needn't worry them very much – they'll be well looked after. En route there'll be a generous issue of pies and cigarettes and pies and cigarettes will be the order on arrival about five in the morning.

The men of the 75th (Highland) Royal Field Artillery departed looking forward to showing their best turnout and efficiency at gun drills for inspections by both the General Officer Commanding Scottish Command, Sir Charles Grant and their Divisional Commander (51st (Highland) Division) General Victor Fortune while at Buddon. The Gordons also addressed some of the new challenges that reflected the changing face of modern warfare during their manoeuvres. Low-flying aeroplanes sprayed them with supposed 'liquid mustard gas' and the men enacted the necessary anti-gas equipment drills and defensive tactics in response, including the use of anti-aircraft guns. A selected platoon would also visit Abbotsinch 30 miles away, in full marching order and with the aid of a 22-seater aeroplane would engage in 'emplaning' and 'deplaning' practice.

The 163 (Norfolk and Suffolk) Brigade held their 1939 summer camp at Falmer, near Brighton, East Sussex. The experiences of an un-named new

Army Service Corps Territorials of the 2nd Cavalry Division show and explain their weaponry and equipment to members of the public in South Wales, 1939.

recruit in 4th Battalion, The Royal Norfolk Regiment (TA) written, I suspect with some help from the recruiting officer, but nonetheless an evocative account of the experiences and feelings of new recruits at that time, regardless of regiment, was published in the *Diss Express*:

After parading at the Drill Hall and receiving our equipment we marched to the station, some of us new and very raw recruits, feeling very self-conscious as we met the gaze of some 'old sweats' to whom we were known. By the time the station was reached this had worn off and I realised that for some of us we were on the first stage for a great adventure – camp and what it meant. Some of us had never been away from home on our own before. Now we were all members of a happy party and the trained men of the company did their utmost to make us feel at ease. Punctually at 9.30pm our train drew up and we were all comfortably seated, some in corridor coaches and others, of which I was one, secured places in the saloons. The whistle sounded and we were off. To what? We wondered.

After a time we were issued with a box containing a meat pie, two cakes, a sausage roll and sandwiches. This was to last us through the night. Soon it was dark outside and those who could settled down to get a little sleep, but not me. Everything was so new and so strange. Despite that, the journey became somewhat boring and we were not sorry when Falmer, our destination was reached. Here we formed up and marched to the camp, a distance of about one and a half miles. On arrival we were served out with ground sheets and blankets and detailed to our respective tents, seven to eight in a tent and then we turned in and 'kipped down.'

Sunday was an easy day for us, naturally. We just got up, washed and cleaned up and went to Brighton in the afternoon. I must say that the meals on the first day were not so good, but they have improved since. After turning in on Sunday night we were all soon asleep and reveille at 6am was too early for some of us but there it was and up we had to get out to wash, and here I must say shower baths are provided. First parade is 6.25, when we do a little rifle drill and inspection. Breakfast is at 7.30 and the weekly menu shows a good variety, such as eggs and bacon, bacon and tomatoes and bacon and beans, all washed down with an ample supply of tea.

Our next job is to get ready for parade at 8.40 when the real business of the day starts. We get ready for company manoeuvres, some men being stationed as enemies and others having to rout them out (we are carried in lorries for these). We get back in time for dinner and after a rest we tackle the meal with a gusto. There are always two courses and tea to follow.

Then comes rifle inspection, after which we are free for the rest of the day to do a little cleaning of kit etc. For tea there is as much bread and jam as one

likes after which we loll about or go for a walk, some walking into Brighton.
The NAAFI supplies us with our needs for supper.

Games are played and we have an inter-battalion football match coming off
soon…For our second week the really serious work will commence for us with
Brigade exercises and we are looking forward to it with great anticipation.
A word as to the weather. It has been 'lousy', absolutely 'lousy' but we are
making the best of it and having a darned good time.[8]

The poor weather was unfortunate to say the least, the two weeks the Norfolk
and Suffolk lads had for their summer camp were some of the worst of the
whole summer of 1939; they were not alone and many units suffered training
and camping on ground that soon became cold, wet, muddy mires. Old hands,
however, recalled the Territorial Army summer camps of 1939 were filled with
training that seemed more purposeful than before and those who had recently
joined up were observed for any who showed potential for promotion. Many
a good young soldier came away with his first stripe and by the time of the
outbreak of war some of them had even made sergeant or had been selected
for officer training.

The main responsibility for the Anti-Aircraft (AA) defence of Britain had
been entrusted to the Territorial Army, but rather than allow an expansion
to accommodate this, extant units of Yeomanry, Royal Field Artillery, Royal
Engineers and even infantry battalions had been converted to AA roles as
gunners and searchlight operators as Britain developed its air raid precaution
schemes in the late 1930s. Consequently, a number of infantry training camps
were converted and new camps created specifically for anti-aircraft artillery
training at a number of locations around the British coast.

Doniford Gun Park Range, Watchet, Somerset in the 1930s.

DONIFORD RANGE. (16.)

Commanding officers were keen to win over local people and visitors and it was also with quite some pride that a number of the TA camps did hold public open days. One such was held at the brand new Territorial Army AA Training Camp at Flookborough, near Grange-over-Sands, Cumbria on Sunday, 30 July 1939. The public had the chance to see firing displays and to meet some of the 600 Territorial gunners in camp from Dumbarton, Linlithgow and Edinburgh, belonging to the 54th, 18th and 19th Light AA Regiment R.A. (T.A.) The camps were ideal for gun drills and firing practice, blazing away at targets over the sea, but such sounds were far from popular among holidaymakers attempting to escape the gloomy clouds of war in 1939.

Gunfire was not the only reminder of the situation as local blackout arrangements were tested and ARP services conducted large-scale exercises through the summer months. The first major blackout and ARP exercise carried out over the whole of Sussex and Kent was staged on Saturday, 8 July 1939.

Poster giving the public notice of the ARP exercises and 'black-out' to be staged on 8 July 1939.

The south coast town of Hastings, the scene of the last successful invasion of England back in 1066, provides a typical example of the Air Raid Precautions exercises staged all around the British coast during the summer of 1939. Instructions for the public during the exercise were displayed on posters put up across the town and printed in local newspapers. The problem was some people, especially holidaymakers, saw it as an added attraction and turned up in considerable numbers to watch the proceedings. The *Hastings & St Leonards Observer* published on the day of the exercise was keen to point out:

There will be little alteration in the town's entertainments tonight. All cinemas with the exception of the Ritz will follow their normal routine which allows a brief time in which patrons can get home before 'lights out.'...All three concert parties will finish their shows in ample time and at the White Rock Pavilion the dance will finish at 10.30pm. Dancing at the Hastings Pier will finish at 11.00pm The New Palace Pier will continue its dance until the usual time 11.45. The management state that very little if any light will be seen from the outside.[9]

The following week the local newspapers were pleased to report Hastings had played its part well in the blackout exercise. The public had responded satisfactorily to the appeal for lights out and the ARP services were severely tested by fire and casualty handling exercises, one of the principal objects of the exercise.

The only real glow of light that could be seen at the outset was spotted from the sea front to the west of the town. This turned out to be the street lamps between New Palace Pier and the bathing pool due to the breakdown of the clockwork mechanism in an automatic switch. It was soon realised that under the blackout conditions buses and trolley buses shed conspicuous pools of light and the flashes from overhead wire at junctions were very noticeable. The *Hastings & St Leonards Observer* recorded an evocative account of the exercise:

The shrieking of massed sirens and steam whistles barely audible above the roar of mist-laden wind; the hills of Hastings showing here and there a pin prick of light, dimly silhouetted at times against the beams of distant searchlights; in the streets, hurrying unseen figures blowing whistles, motor cars and vans crawling along under sidelights or suddenly showing a white blaze with their headlights; lorries racing along with rescue party, cars towing fire pumps, knots of spectators sheltering under the lee of buildings or in shop doorways; groups of men and women wearing white tickets on their coats indicating casualties – such were the early impressions of Hastings in last Saturday night's black-out exercises.

The other side of the picture lay in the activities behind screened and shuttered windows at the wardens' posts at the first aid stations and in the hospitals where casualties poured in from the scenes of the various incidents staged about the town and the control room at St Andrew's Square, the focal point of a continuous stream of ingoing and outgoing messages bearing tales of destruction, breakdown, delay and rescue.

For the purpose of the ARP exercises the town was supposed to be the subject of two air raids, one just after 11pm and the second at midnight. As a result of the first raid the imaginary effects of the bombing were to be dealt with by the ARP services:

Lifeboat house and car park wrecked by two bombs. Two casualties under debris, one injured by fragments. YMCA building wrecked by bombs, one casualty under debris, two injured by fragments. Alexandra Park Gates area contaminated by gas, roadway blocked through bombing, casualties, two contaminated. Railway Mission Hall at Portland Place fired by bomb, no casualties. Extensive fire in furniture store in Caves Road caused by high explosive and incendiary bombs, four people suffered from burns.

Silverhill Council School fired and adjoining house damaged by incendiary and explosive bombs. Casualties, three injured and two trapped. Regal cinema water and gas mains damaged by high explosive bombs, roadway contaminated by mustard gas. Small fire at High Bank Ore by incendiary bomb. Casualties two burned. Small fire at St Paul's School caused by incendiary bomb, three people burned. Ore village schools damaged and roadways contaminated by lewisite gas. Casualties, two by fragments, two gassed. Oil depot at Bulverhythe fired by explosive and road damaged and contaminated by mustard gas. Three casualties caused by fragments and two gassed.[10]

According to the scenario a second raid was supposed to occur at midnight, similar incidents were staged and a further twenty-nine 'casualties' had to be dealt with. The nature and location of each incident was unknown in advance to those taking part in the exercises and all were keenly watched by one of fifty roving umpires. A tour of the exercise was carried out by prominent townspeople including the mayor and deputy mayor, town clerk and the chairman of the ARP Committee accompanied by the Chief Constable Mr Joseph Bell, the ARP co-ordinating officer.

Some idea of the size of the exercises may be obtained from the numbers involved in Hastings which were listed as: 350 first aid and ambulance workers, 300 auxiliary firemen in addition to the professional firemen, 280 special constables and 600 wardens. There were also decontamination squads, each consisting of a lorry with anti-gas equipment manned by a crew in anti-gas clothing and masks, as well as mobile squads of technicians for electricity, gas, water, sewer and road repairs. These squads, together with the rescue parties, were provided by 122 volunteers from among corporation employees and 70 volunteers took part to play the roles of casualties.

Four lorries were loaned by local haulage contractors for carrying decontamination squads and seven lorries manned by rescue parties with heavy equipment for shoring up buildings and digging out debris. The fire fighters, in addition to four engines of the professional brigade, mustered 12 auxiliary trailer pumps and 18 cars. A fleet of cars was also on continuous duty throughout the exercises including 80 special constabulary cars, 16 emergency ambulances, consisting of tradesmen's vans fitted with racks and driven by members of the Women's Voluntary Services (WVS). They also provided and drove 16 cars to convey the sitting casualties while 16 first aid party cars were lent and driven by owner volunteers.

There were mistakes and confusion to be expected during the first big exercise of its kind, but it was a great learning experience and overall the exercise was successful, though you can never please everyone. The regular Flotsam and Jetsam column by 'Vigilant' in the *Hastings and St Leonards Observer* discussed the situation:

People who come from London on holiday seek respite from ever-present questions of National Service and ARP which have necessarily to be continually brought to their notice in the workaday lives. They want to forget the whole depressing business for the week or fortnight of their annual vacation. Yet those who have been unfortunate enough to choose their holidays in the early part of July will find themselves plunged into the midst of the very thing they want to avoid. The Observer *cannot be accused of lack of patriotism nor of any reluctance to press the cause of National Service and ARP to the utmost, but it must protest most strongly against the action of the higher authorities in inflicting this hardship on a holiday town at the most unsuitable time. There are many things the public will want to know. Will they be expected to stop at home? Will householders be expected to darken windows and if so how is it suggested this must be done? They have to incur expense by providing dark blinds or curtains that many undoubtedly would not possess in the ordinary way? The whole business is most unfortunate. It may be suggested by the Home Office that their desire is to put Hastings and other resorts to the test under the most stringent conditions. If so, their aim will be fulfilled, for the difficulties seem immense and I am certain that the July black-out will be remembered as the black spot of the 1939 season.*[11]

Similar attitudes were recalled further along the coast by reporter H.P. Twyford:

Some months before the war broke out I was assigned by the Western Morning News *to visit every town, large and small, in the West country to report on their preparedness to meet enemy air attack…I found an amazing divergence of opinion and readiness. In some places there were public men who flatly pooh-poohed the idea of air raid precautions being necessary. 'We are too far away', 'A sheer waste of public money'. Those were some of the remarks I heard. In most places, however, there was some measure of doubt and fear in the minds. 'Better be prepared,' they said. So it was that while some set about their preparedness wholeheartedly, others did so with half enthusiasm and in a few places there was a contented policy to drift.*[12]

Comedian Max Miller, worked a response into such complacency and complaints about time and money being wasted by British authorities making preparations for war in his comedy routine suggesting: 'Perhaps I should write to Hitler, tell him to call the whole thing off?'

The golden sands of the east coast were darkened under the shadow of a German aircraft during August 1939 when the Graf Zeppelin II (LZ 130) flew slowly along the coast. Most of those who saw it, complete with its fins painted with black swastikas on white circles on a red background, were firmly of the opinion that its intentions were malevolent and their suspicions were later to be confirmed. The Graf Zeppelin was reconnoitring any military installations it could spot, paying particular attention to the tall radio towers that had been erected along the North Sea coast from Portsmouth to Scapa Flow. The sites were photographed and the experts on board conducted a series of radiometric tests which suggested the radio towers were involved with some form of radar.

The radio towers were indeed significant because they formed the then Top Secret Chain Home Radio Direction Finding (RDF) system of coastal radar stations. The system, otherwise known as AMES Type 1 (Air Ministry Experimental Station), enabled the long-range detection of aircraft flying over the waters around Britain.

August Bank holiday had been dubbed the 'silver wedding weekend' because many couples who married during the month of the outbreak of the Great War were now celebrating twenty-five years of marriage. The rush to wed on the eve of war was no different in 1939. Registry offices remained open for greatly extended hours to accommodate the rush and many prospective bridegrooms who were expecting a possible call-up notice had to cancel their honeymoons. Mounting international tensions saw many Territorial Army units with anti-aircraft and coastal defence roles mobilized, some of them only just back from their summer camps. Among the many caught up in the war emergency was Territorial soldier Gordon Stout who married Miss Jessie Scott at Whitley Bay on the afternoon of 25 August; but instead of a honeymoon in the Lake District he would have to rejoin his searchlight battalion of the Royal Northumberland Fusiliers the following day. Chief Constables also issued mobilization notices to all members of the Observer Corps on 24 August, the same day school teachers were recalled from their summer holidays and thrown in at the deep end readying preparations for the 'go' signal.

On Friday, 25 August 1939, Hitler cut off all telecommunications beyond the borders of Germany and the invasion of Poland appeared imminent. Over the previous days, holidays were already being cancelled for staff in banks and some of the bigger offices. Many public buildings were belted around with sandbag walls and their windowpanes crossed with rubberised tape or sturdy brown paper to reduce flying glass in the event of a bomb blast.

A military presence was becoming apparent in many coastal areas as defences were manned and docks had sentries posted. It was noted in press articles that policemen were now on duty on the streets wearing their new additions of blue shrapnel helmets with 'POLICE' stencilled in white lettering, carried over the gas mask bags they were now carrying as a matter of course. Territorial Army 'key parties' of battalions not yet mobilised were called to assemble at their drill halls and set about building sandbag blast walls and digging shelter trenches, while the adjutants, senior NCOs and clerks ensured all paperwork was in order and procedures in place for mobilisation.

On 1 September 1939 the Territorial Army was fully mobilised and having received the order 'Evacuate Forthwith' from the Ministry of Health on 31 August, the first trains laden with evacuees began leaving for their reception areas from early in the morning of 1 September. Many of the larger ports and harbour areas, especially those with a strong military presence, evacuated their children and vulnerable people to safe areas. Some 37,000 people left in a total of fifty-four trains from the Medway towns of Rochester, Chatham, Gillingham and Rainham bound for reception areas in Kent. Some 30,000 were evacuated from Southampton and Gosport to various places in Hampshire, Dorset and Wiltshire, and at Portsmouth 3,765 mothers and children (1,338 mothers, expectant mums and 1,478 children) were taken to other parts of Hampshire. A further 949 mothers and children embarked for the Isle of Wight from Clarence Pier and thousands of others would be departing from similar evacuation areas around the country.

The coast also offered what were considered at the time safe haven reception areas for evacuees. A total of 110,000 evacuees were sent to Wales, many of them billeted in homes along the coast. In East Anglia some 11,000 Dagenham children were evacuated by pleasure steamers to Yarmouth, Lowestoft and Felixstowe. Along the south coast train after train brought evacuees to stations along most of the south coast over a period of three days. The numbers of evacuees involved were truly remarkable; Bexhill on Sea received 4,000, Newhaven 2,000, Worthing 12,500 and so on.

Once at their stations of arrival many evacuees would then be taken on a second journey by bus or charabanc to an outlying suburb, town or village. Children would be marshalled by local police, special constables, members of St John Ambulance, WVS and WI volunteers to a suitable public building or school taken over for the purpose. There they would be checked off on the list by the billeting officers and given a brief examination by a doctor or nurse, mostly to make sure they did not have bodily infestations such as nits or lice or communicable diseases such as smallpox, diphtheria, measles, tuberculosis or typhoid. Some of the children were found to be very unclean, Harry Priestley the Chief Sanitary Inspector and Billeting Officer for Blackpool commented that some of those that arrived in his area were found in a condition of 'downright filthiness deeply ingrained'. Some were even given baths or a quick clean up at their reception centres before being presented for billeting.

Once passed by the doctor each child would be handed a paper carrier bag containing perhaps fruit and biscuits or 'energy rations' consisting of the likes of condensed milk, a tin of unsweetened milk, a bar of chocolate and a packet of biscuits. Once they had eaten their food the billeting process would begin. In some cases the evacuees would then be taken to the streets where they were to be billeted and deposited with each household registered to receive evacuees. In other areas the children would be lined up in the main hall where they had gathered and have the indignity of being selected by foster families. Sometimes siblings were split up as some billetors only wanted boys or girls or did not have room to keep all the family together in their house; the children had no say in the matter. Once selected and the necessary paperwork completed, they would then go to their new temporary home with their foster families.

No evacuee forgot the experience. One of the thousands of children involved was Betty Peer who vividly remembered the day she was evacuated fifty years later:

> Us Dagenham schoolchildren sailed from the docks near the Ford Motor Works; there were three boats in total, the Royal Daffodil, Royal Eagle and the Royal Sovereign. All the decks were filled with hundreds of children and we were soon heading down the river and up the coast. We docked at Great Yarmouth that evening and spent the night sleeping on straw-filled sacks in a most beautiful school that any of us had ever seen, I think, so clean, so modern.
>
> The following day we boarded charabancs to who knew where? My sister, brother and I were born at Wells, our school master at King's Lynn and as the miles went by and as sign boards were still up the interest was very keen between us, especially as the person who guessed where we would end up would win a bar of chocolate.
>
> We won because we recognised the destination as we approached, Cley. We disembarked at a hall where people came along to take us off. Some were lucky, ones, two or three girls or boys even were easy to fit but we were three odds [two girls and a boy] getting very left behind. The two Miss Hudsons said they would take my sister and I but not my brother. Mrs Binns from the Town Hall was there, she had had an entire mixed six, all from one family and suggested one more wouldn't hurt. So, off we all went with the Miss Hudsons. They lived opposite the Town Hall at the Post Office and we all loved it there.[13]

Evacuees arriving at Brighton Station, 1 September 1939.

Brighton was due to be the largest reception area in the south offering 30,000 places to evacuees due to be brought to the town in fourteen specially chartered trains over three days, but evacuation was not compulsory and when it actually came down to parting with their children many parents did not let them go, so only around half the spaces in Brighton were actually taken up. A similar story emerged in Scotland where 37,000 had registered to take part in the scheme in Edinburgh but only 26,000 actually left the city; 338 trains had been arranged to carry 237,523 evacuees out of Glasgow over 1, 2 and 3 September but only 118,833 turned up, trains were leaving half empty and thirty-five services were cancelled. Even the biggest reception area of all at Blackpool where over 70,000 places for evacuees were offered, only 37,000 arrived.

Despite the actual numbers being lower than anticipated, the total numbers of people evacuated over three days commencing on 1 September 1939 remain staggering: 825,000 school children, 624,000 mothers with school children under school age, 113,000 school teachers and helpers, 13,000 expectant mothers and 7,000 blind and vulnerable people. Add to them the patients evacuated from hospitals and infirmaries, children privately evacuated or sent abroad, and statistics compiled at the end of September 1939 showed a quarter of the population of Britain had changed their address.

Chapter 2

Phoney War?

I tell you now, every man who helps get rid of these ships will be awarded a house of his own and all the medals that are going

Herman Göring

As September 1939 ended and October progressed, with the British Expeditionary Force (BEF) deployed to France amid huge news coverage and hopes for a swift end to the war, the British public waited. The troops had taken up defensive positions beside the Maginot Line and dug in but the campaign on the Western Front rapidly descended into one of stagnation. The world watched and waited week after week for the next move, but no attack came, and no attack would come until the following year. Thousands of evacuees returned home and the situation was rapidly dubbed by the American press as a 'Phoney War'. The truth of the matter was that there was already an all too real war being fought at sea, but one that was not always shared with the wider public through the press and media. It soon became forgotten as these events were replaced in the 'popular memory' of the war by events in May 1940.

For many months after the outbreak of war Hitler still held on to hopes of Britain 'seeing reason' and entering into a peace settlement, so he was determined that hostilities would not open with a bombing campaign against targets on mainland Britain that might incur civilian casualties. However, on 3 September, the day that war

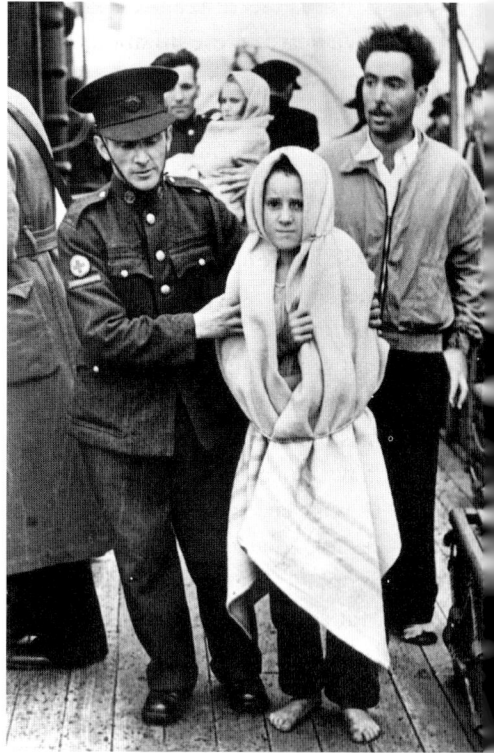

Some of the passengers rescued from the SS Athenia *bound for Canada from Glasgow via Liverpool and Belfast, that was torpedoed and sunk in the Atlantic off the North West coast of Ireland on on 3 September 1939.*

was declared, Kapitänleutnant Fritz-Julius Lemp on *U–30*, sank the passenger liner SS *Athenia* in the Atlantic Ocean, north-west of Ireland after leaving Belfast while en route from Glasgow and Liverpool to Montreal, Canada. Amongst the 117 civilian passengers killed were 16 children, 69 women and 19 crew members. Hitler ordered no more passenger ships were to be attacked but this decision would change (on 29 October passenger ships in convoys could be attacked) but for the time being it meant the only targets left for the German Navy or Luftwaffe to attack were British warships and with these targets came the proviso, in an effort to try and avoid civilian casualties, that they could only be attacked when they were in open water and not while docked in a harbour, dry dock or moored against a pier.

There were still attacks on merchant vessels carrying civilian passengers, but German military commanders erred on the safe side for offensive operations and kept their eyes on the most prestigious targets of significant vessels in the British Fleet at sea such as battleships and aircraft carriers. Most readers will have heard of the infamous British hunt for the *Bismark* in 1941 and similarly the Kriegsmarine and the Luftwaffe hunted the British Fleet in the opening months of the war in 1939 with honours aplenty on offer for the destruction of the most significant vessels.

An attempt to torpedo the Royal Navy's prize aircraft carrier HMS *Ark Royal* when she was off the north-west coast of Scotland on 14 September 1939 had gone badly wrong when a technical defect in the torpedoes fired by the *U–39* exploded before they hit home. *Ark Royal*'s destroyer escort HMS *Faulknor*, HMS *Firedrake* and HMS *Foxhound* located *U–39* on their ASDIC equipment and wasted no time in dropping depth charges that caused such damage to *U–39* that it was forced to surface. The entire crew were taken prisoner and the Kriegsmarine suffered its first loss of a U-boat to the Royal Navy since the outbreak of war. All the destroyers on the scene had helped to recover the U-boat crewmen, who were transferred to HMS *Foxhound* to be landed at the port at Kirkwall on Orkney the following day. Here the first people in Britain got a glimpse of German servicemen in the Second World War as they were marched down the gangplanks and onto lorries to take them to a prisoner of war camp.

A total of nine U-boats would be lost by the end of 1939. There would also be numerous losses of British vessels, among them the aircraft carrier HMS *Courageous*, which would not be as fortunate as *Ark Royal* when torpedoes were fired at her by *U–29* while on anti-submarine patrol in the Celtic Sea on 17 September. She sank with the loss of 518 crew. The losses of such great naval ships had a profound effect on our coastal communities where they had family and friends and the dock towns where they regularly moored. Many had come to know and attached such pride to their local ships over the years. H.P. Twyford captured the atmosphere when he recalled:

...the first awful shock when the aircraft carrier Courageous, *a ship we knew so well at Devonport, was sunk by German submarine on a Sunday evening within the waters of the Western Approaches. Hundreds of Plymouth homes were bereaved by the sinking, it was the first grim incident of the war. I well remember interviewing many of the survivors at the Royal Naval Barracks and the anxious scenes as relatives scanned the lists of rescued as they were posted outside the main gate.*[1]

* * *

If you stand among the battlements atop Edinburgh Castle on a clear day the views of the Firth of Forth, the great estuary on the east coast of Scotland where a number of rivers flow into the North Sea, are truly magnificent. The Forth Bridge, when it was opened in 1890, was the longest single cantilever bridge span in the world, located about 9 miles from the centre of Edinburgh, which links South Queensferry, Lothian with North Queensferry in Fife. The bridge and its approaches span 1½ miles, it is a true engineering wonder and remains one of the iconic symbols of Scotland to this day.

Built to carry a double track of railway over the Forth, in 1939 the bridge was the main link between north-east and south-east Scotland used by hundreds of trains carrying thousands of passengers every day. Passage across the Forth for those travelling by car or any other means at this point was only possible by

The Forth Bridge pictured in 1939 when it was scene of the first German aerial attack on British mainland during the Second World War.

ferry. Two brand new custom-built ferries, the *Queen Margaret* and the *Robert the Bruce,* capable of carrying 500 passengers and 28 cars, had been launched in 1934. At a time when Britain commanded the finest modern navy in the world, the naval dockyard a few miles away at Rosyth saw just about every vessel of the fleet pass through the dock for repair or refit or anchor in the Firth of Forth at one time or another and a Royal Naval Armament Depot at Crombie provided one of the largest munition storage facilities for the Home Seas Fleet.

In 1919 Admiral David Beatty reflected on the role of the Firth of Forth during the First World War describing it as 'The principal base of the greatest fleet that has ever sailed the seas.' Just twenty years later, on 16 October 1939, it would be the scene of the first air raid over the British mainland during the Second World War. Strictly speaking it was not part of the campaign we know as the Battle of Britain and is often omitted from books charting the history of the Second World War, but it should be included, not just because it was the first air raid over British territory, but because it was the opening salvo of the battle *for* Britain during the Second World War.

The story begins on 25 September 1939 when most of the Royal Navy Home Seas Fleet set out on a sortie into the North Sea to provide cover for the rescue of the damaged submarine *Spearfish.* The following morning flying boats of 2/KüFlGr506 were reconnoitring an area of sea in preparation for a Kriegsmarine destroyer action planned for the next day, when a gap in the cloud cover beneath them revealed the battleships *Nelson, Rodney,* the aircraft carrier *Ark Royal* and the screen of destroyers that accompanied them.

Two of *Ark Royal*'s Blackburn Skua aircraft of No.803 Squadron were on patrol and spotted the Dornier seaplanes, radioed warning back to *Ark Royal* which immediately sounded its 'squealers' and hands were piped to Action Stations. As the ratings doubled to their positions pilots and air gunners raced to a further nine Skuas on the flight deck and took to the air to engage the enemy aircraft. Lieutenant Charles Leo Glandore 'Crash' Evans and Lieutenant William Alastair Robertson hammered fire at the Dorniers and Lieutenant Bruce Straton McEwen and his air gunner Petty Officer Airman Brian 'Horse' Seymour delivered the *coup de grace* to Dornier Do18D flying boat ('M7+YK', Werk Nr.0731) causing it to go down in the sea off the Great Fisher Bank, 145 miles east of Rattray Head (at approximate coordinates 57.36N, 02.38E.) It is acknowledged as the first Luftwaffe aircraft to be brought down by British forces during the war. Robertson would later comment that the Dornier flying boat was going so slowly it would have been embarrassing to miss. The Dornier crew consisting of Ff (Pilot): Leutnant zur See Wilhelm Freiherr von Reitzenstein, Beo (Observer): Leutnant zur

41

See Ernst Körner, Bf (Radio Operator): Unteroffizier Walter Heckt and Bm: (Flight Engineer) Unteroffizier Fritz Schmalfeldt were rescued by the destroyer HMS *Somali* and became prisoners of war. The Dornier seaplane, which had remained afloat, was sunk by gunfire.[2]

The remaining two Dornier seaplanes were damaged but managed to limp back to their base and report their findings. As a result, Heinkel 111s from 1/KG26 Löwengeschwader under Hauptmann Martin Vetter and four Ju88A-1s from 1.KG/ 30 Adlergeschwader under Oberleutnant Hans Sigmund Storp, a veteran of the Condor Legion attack on Guernica during the Spanish Civil War, were soon despatched to attack the Royal Navy ships that had been spotted.

After flying for nearly two hours the bombers were over the Royal Navy ship and dived to deliver their bombs. In the melee that ensued bombers screamed down and the battleships and destroyers replied with a hail of fire. In one of the Ju88s Gefreiter Carl Franke fixed the *Ark Royal* in his bomb sight and released his two 500kg bombs at her. As the aircraft climbed back up again the bomb exploded, a huge plume of water climbed skyward and a flash was observed on the bows, but the question remained – was she hit and did she sink? A reconnaissance patrol was sent to look for patches of oil on the sea that might indicate the sinking. These they found but in wartime there are patches of oil to be found on the sea for many reasons. They could only see two battleships and their accompanying vessels, there was no sign of *Ark Royal*, but there was no definite proof the aircraft carrier had gone down or even received a serious hit. Göring was not going to be dissuaded from his conviction that the *Ark Royal* had been sunk. He sent his personal congratulations to Franke, had him immediately promoted to lieutenant and decorated with Iron Crosses First and Second Class. The announcement was also made to the press that the Luftwaffe had successfully sunk an aircraft carrier.

Even after the Admiralty issued a press release to the contrary stating that the *Ark Royal* had in fact returned to her base undamaged, Göring dismissed it as British propaganda in a vain attempt to hide the severity of their loss. It would have been quite a climb down for Göring to admit he was wrong. He did not withdraw the honours he had bestowed on the man who had targeted the bombs, but Göring, when he encountered Franke a few months later, smiled sardonically and pointed out 'You still owe me an aircraft carrier.'[3]

The Ju88s of 1/KG30 claimed ten bomb strikes on Royal Navy cruisers in the action but fortunately none caused any serious damage. HMS *Hood* also had a near miss when a 500kg bomb glanced her port side and detonated in the sea spattering the area with shrapnel shards, springing rivets and caused a port bulge amidships. Flooding ensued and damaged her condensers, but she too returned safely to base at Scapa Flow in Orkney.

The German aircrew had scented blood, a number were decorated for their part in the attack but the pressure was on for a confirmed sinking of a significant Royal Navy vessel by the Luftwaffe. Göring summoned KG 30 Staffelkapitän, Hauptmann Helmut Pohle (Acting Gruppenkommandeur) to join a conference in Berlin. Addressing Pohle directly Göring told him:

> *We have got to score a success! There are only a few British ships that stand in our way: the* Repulse, *the* Renown, *perhaps too the* Hood *and of course the aircraft carriers* [he clearly could not bring himself to even mention the name *Ark Royal*]. *Once they are gone the* Scharnhorst *and the* Gneisau *can rule the waves…I tell you now, every man who helps get rid of these ships will be awarded a house of his own and all the medals that are going.*[4]

Ship movements off Scapa Flow and the east coast of Scotland were already the subject of regular Luftwaffe reconnaissance flights. HMS *Repulse* was at Rosyth to have her boilers cleaned when she was spotted by Luftwaffe reconnaissance aircraft on 15 October who mistook her for HMS *Hood*. When Pohle was telephoned his orders for the attack by Generalmajor Hans Jeschonnek it left him under no illusions when he stated: *I also have to convey to you a personal order from the Führer. It runs as follows: Should the* Hood *already be in dock when KG 30 reached the First of Forth, no attack is to be made.*[5]

Jeschonnek then impressed on Pohle that he made him personally responsible for acquainting the crew with the order pointing out 'the Führer will not have a single civilian killed'. Nor did he wish to be the first to drop bombs on British soil in the conflict.

At 11am on 16 October 1939 twelve Junkers Ju.88A-1 from 1/KG 30, each loaded with two 250kg bombs, took off from Westerland on the German Isle of Sylt – at the time the nearest German air base to Britain – and sped across the North Sea bound for the Forth. Led personally by Pohle with 1/KG 30's Oberleutnant Hans Sigmund Storp as his second in command, the crews were both buoyant having learned the *Royal Oak* had been sunk while in the harbour at Scapa Flow in an audacious raid conducted by Günther Prien in *U-47* less than 48 hours previously; but they were also only too aware the pressure was on and the stakes were high. They were undertaking the first air raid over the British mainland, the rules of the engagement had been impressed upon them and Göring was not only taking a personal interest in the mission, he wanted results.

Initially the raiders were in luck, the Chain Home RDF at RAF Drone Hill had been disabled by a power cut and the Ju88s approaching over the sea remained undetected. By 12.15pm they had reached the outer estuary of the Forth. Flying in loose formation because they had been informed no Spitfires were stationed in Scotland, they were soon passing over Edinburgh and with this act a German bomber unit was flying over Britain for the first time since the outbreak of war. A few heads turned skyward on the streets, but initially no-one suspected anything untoward because no sirens had sounded and they carried on about their business once the aircraft had passed overhead.

In the air Pohle was flying at the head of his formation, his guide the landmark of the Forth Bridge that he had familiarised himself with from reconnaissance photographs. He noted how it visually separated the outer and inner Forth which hove into view and the sight of Rosyth followed soon after. He could see the ship he believed was HMS *Hood* (actually HMS *Repulse*) in the dock, recording later, 'She was a sitting target, but orders robbed us of our prize.' Nonetheless a number of cruisers and destroyers lay at anchor in open water in the roadstead and Pohle put his Junkers into a dive of nearly eighty degrees to aim his bombs at one of the largest, HMS *Southampton*. The local anti-aircraft batteries were opening up on the raiders, *Southampton*'s crew had also been alerted and were at action stations just in time to open up with their machine guns at the raiders with a steady rate of fire.

As Pohle dived – and he was never sure if it was due to being hit by flak or whether these new bombers brought on stream so quickly had reached an untested level of tolerance – the crew of the Ju88 suddenly heard an ominous crack followed by a tearing sound and the roof canopy was suddenly no longer there! Pohle maintained control, targeted and released a 250kg bomb onto *Southampton* at 3,000ft. He had no time to study its effect as he pulled up to regain height and as he did so he received warning that they were under attack from three Spitfires and disengaged.

Meanwhile the 2.30pm train from Edinburgh to Dunfermline had been held at Dalmeny Station, the station closest to the Forth Bridge. Train passenger David Archbold of Dunfermline recalled:

...we were informed that an air raid was in progress and it was left to our own discretion whether we would continue the journey across the Forth bridge. Most of us decided to continue. As the train travelled slowly across the bridge we were able to watch the progress of the raid. Two planes, one near the south shore of the Forth appeared to dive over the bridge. Bombs were dropped a short distance to the east of the bridge. A great column of water shot up.[6]

Another passenger, Miss Hunter of Easter Cottage, Charlestown, a student at Moray House Training College, Edinburgh said that when the bombs exploded in the water the steelwork of the bridge seemed to vibrate from top to bottom.

The second wave of Junkers 88s under Storp had been spotted by members of 603 (City of Edinburgh) Squadron RAF from RAF Turnhouse. The flight consisted of Flight Lieutenant Patrick 'Pat' Gifford, Flying Officer Harold Kennedy 'Ken' MacDonald, and Pilot Officer Colin Robertson who were already in the air on one of their regular patrols. Every one of them had been a pre-war member of the Auxiliary Air Force who learned to fly and the skills of combat pilots part time during the years of peace before the war, in much the same way as the Territorial Army on land. Flight Lieutenant Gifford (29) until the outbreak of war had been an 'Auxie' with a full-time job as a solicitor working in his family firm at Castle Douglas. The account of the action he gave to a reporter from *The Scotsman* was published but did not name him:

They were on patrol over East Lothian and at 3,000ft in weather that was none too good for visibility. There was an October haze between them and the ground and overhead were big patches of heavy cloud with clear sky lanes between. Suddenly he heard the voice of one of his section on his radio. He had spotted a big twin-engined enemy bomber and almost immediately, his grey metal sides gleaming, appeared from a cloud.

He was flying fast and coming head on! Evidently spotting the interceptors the German pilot immediately swung off into a handy patch of cumulus but not before his guns had attempted to rake the approaching fighters. Giving his orders by radio the leader at once put his section into fighting formation and threw his machine into a stiff climbing turn, the other two aircraft following tightly.

He dived away and I stayed above him for a few seconds to recognise him. There was no doubt about his markings. Then I went down in a stiff dive, came up under his tail and pulled out, my other boys following close behind, all our guns firing. Before the others had finished, I regained my height and position and diving after them, gave him a long burst. He was responding with all his armament; tracers were whistling past and I got a glimpse of a gunner behind twin guns. We gave him further long bursts and I saw he was hit forward of the tail as I could see bits of fabric dropping off and I thought I noticed a red glow appear. I broke away as the bomber's guns flashed again and saw one of my other machines coming in at speed from the port side with all his guns firing. We were now over the coast and as the German bomber sought a lower course he was sprayed with bullets, some of which I could see splashing in the water.

So the attack proceeded with the fighters diving alternately and the Ju88's armament in full blast. Then came the end. He was badly crippled and I could see the rear gunner had stopped shooting. As soon as the machines in front of me had broken away after delivering more bursts I went close in all I had towards the controls. He flopped into the sea and as we circled we saw that he was sinking. One man was swimming and some boats were approaching.[7]

The aircraft Gifford had brought down was Ju88A-1 (4D+DH) flown by Oberleutnant Hans Sigmund Storp. It had been observed struggling overhead near Whitecraig, Carberry and Wallyford and finally ditched in the sea off Gullane, about 4 miles north of Port Seton. Flight Lieutenant 'Pat' Gifford of 603 Squadron has the distinction of being the first member of Britain's armed forces to shoot down a German aircraft over British territory during the Second World War.

Storp's rear gunner Obergefreiter Friedrich Krämer had been killed in the combat and went down with the aircraft when it sank; his body was not recovered when the wreckage was salvaged. The rest of the crew, the pilot Oberleutnant Hans Sigmund Storp, observer Feldwebel Hugo Köhnke and Feldwebel Hans Georg Hielscher, the radio operator, were all picked up by a fishing trawler *Day Spring* skippered by John Dickson and crewed by his two sons John and William and brothers Alexander and Andrew Harkess, all of Port Seton, who had been out fishing off May Island. Having recovered the crew, all of whom had been injured, the trawler made full speed for shore where, upon landing Storp gave Dickson his gold ring bearing the Storp family crest, explaining in fairly good English that it was given 'as a souvenir in thanks for saving my life'. The three airmen received treatment at a local doctor's house and were then removed to the military hospital at Edinburgh Castle.

Another young pilot of 603 Squadron told of how his 'team' had intercepted the Ju88s but owing to the heavy clouds they indulged in a grim game of hide and seek which broke up the bomber formation and one of them headed seaward with one of his engines disabled. He then went on to describe a 'second job' that began near the Fife coast as his Spitfire climbed to gain height the pilot could see anti-aircraft shells bursting close to the enemy aircraft on his flank. When the guns stopped firing and he attacked the German dived towards the water. They streaked down together and, making a 90-degree turn, the bomber crossed the land near Bowness. With his rear gunner shooting steadily, the Ju88 pilot flew lower. Meanwhile the fighter had climbed and then diving close in pressed his gun controls and the rear guns of the aircraft were silenced.

The low flying chase continued by way of the shale bings at Winchburgh, along a railway siding and over Turnhouse golf course. In the Davidson's Mains area in northwest Edinburgh the fighter pilot held his fire while over houses and saw residents staring up from their gardens as the aircraft flashed past. When over the open fields the Spitfire pilot gave another burst of fire and thick smoke began to pour out of the Ju88's engines. The bomber was flying at about 300ft when over Leith. The pursuit went on by Portobello and at Musselburgh the bomber was seen to 'waffle about' and after passing North Berwick and Dunbar it headed out to sea and the fighter had to withdraw when he discovered he had expended all his ammunition.

Blue Section of 602 (City of Glasgow) Squadron, consisting of Flying Officer Archibald Ashmore 'Archie' McKellar, Flight Lieutenant George Cannon Pinkerton, and Flying Officer Paul Clifford Webb, engaged the first wave of Junkers bombers. Flight Lieutenant Pinkerton delivered the fatal final blows to Pohle's Ju88 (4D+AK) which ditched in the sea off Crail about nine minutes after Storp had ditched his. Pohle suffered a fractured skull and injured his face on landing and was semi-conscious when he was picked up by a fishing boat his aircraft had narrowly missed when crash landing. From that vessel he was transferred to HMS *Jervis*, where he received initial treatment in their sick berth. Pohle's rear gunner Unteroffizier Kurt Naake was dead, radio operator Gefrieter August Schleiker was also rescued but had been badly wounded and the observer Werner Weise was missing.

On the streets of Edinburgh and in the towns around the Forth people could see the aircraft and hear the pounding of the anti-aircraft guns and steady spurts of aircraft machine guns but could not see the action itself. The belief was that it was only a practice because if it had been an enemy raid the air raid warning sirens would have sounded. Nobody was in the least alarmed and instead of taking cover many rushed onto the streets and looked up to the sky to see if they could catch a glimpse of what was going on. The manageress of the Sealscraig Hotel, South Queensferry had a grandstand view from her balcony:

> *The planes did not stay, she said, they just dropped their bombs, flew off and returned again. I think they came four times. They first appeared from the direction of the Pentland Hills and did not come up the Forth. It was a lovely sunshiny afternoon and watching the attack in the distance seemed so strange. It was just as though somebody was having a game. The streets were deserted as most people sought shelter, but I thought I was quite safe on my balcony.*[8]

People in Linlithgow became aware of gunfire coming from South Queensferry and quite a crowd gathered on the high street to watch puffs of smoke from bursting shells at a great height and shrapnel from exploding anti-aircraft shells spread over a wide area. Some windows were broken through concussions caused by the explosions. The *Musselburgh News* recorded:

It was the same the length of the seaside resort from King's Road [Portobello] to Joppa. There were those people who were as if held in a trance by the thrilling spectacle of a bomber flying low being chased and fired upon by smaller planes. A crash seemed imminent to many people and yet they could not take their eyes away. On the other hand, there were those upon whom this instinct of self-preservation was not lost even for the time being. They rushed out of the open air into shop, close or house when the aeroplanes roared in their direction and the machine gun fire could be heard above the noise of engines. The empty shells [and spent bullets] *were retained by the finders, old and young as mementoes of a memorable occasion.*[9]

Indeed, one enterprising soldier who found a piece of shrapnel near the Hawes Inn at Queensferry sold it for two shillings to a civilian who was particularly keen to obtain a souvenir.

The raid had not been a complete failure from the German perspective. Pohle dropped his bomb on HMS *Southampton* from as low as 490ft. It hit the corner of the pom-pom magazine, passed through three decks and exited through the hull, only then exploding in the water, blowing up the admiral's pinnace and shooting a huge spout of water high into the air. Incredibly there was only one fatality, a former HMS *Ganges* trainee, Boy 1st Class Herbert Michael Bradley (17) of New Fletton, Peterborough. Other vessels suffered damage and casualties were caused by flying shell fragments and splinters aboard HMS *Edinburgh*.

HMS Southampton *whose crew were at action stations just in time to open up with their machine guns at the raiders as they dived to attack on 16 October 1939.*

HMS Mohawk *whose Commander 'Dick' Jolly, despite being severely wounded when the ship suffered bomb blasts during the attack of 16 October 1939, refused to leave the bridge saying 'Leave me – go and look after others.'*

The destroyer HMS *Mohawk* was returning from convoy escort when the Ju88s sped towards her. Those on board did not realise what was happening until it was too late. Two 250kg bombs were dropped and exploded on each side of her creating a deadly crossfire of shell casing and splinters across the upper decks and bridge.

Among the wounded was the ship's captain, Commander Richard Frank 'Dick' Jolly (43). He had been on the bridge when the bombs detonated and was severely wounded in the stomach. Jolly repeatedly refused to leave the bridge or accept treatment saying 'Leave me – go and look after others.' The 35-mile passage back to Rosyth lasted an hour and twenty minutes during which his orders became so faint that he spoke them to his navigating officer, who was also wounded, who then repeated them. Having brought *Mohawk* back to port, Jolly rang off the main engines and immediately collapsed; he died five hours later. Commander Jolly was awarded a posthumous Empire Gallantry Medal which his family were invited to exchange for a George Cross when the award was instituted the following year.

An overall total of 44 sailors were wounded and 16 died as a result of the raid. The majority of casualties were on board HMS *Mohawk*. Below is the roll of the dead, all others have the name of their ship included after their name:

Commander Richard Frank 'Dick' Jolly, GC RN
Lieutenant Eugene Joseph O'Shea
Gunner George James Mitchell (HMS *Edinburgh*)
Boy 1st Class Herbert Michael Bradley, (HMS *Southampton*)
Petty Officer Alfred William Coward
Chief Petty Officer Frederick Alfred Dent *
Ordinary Seaman Henry George Gallett
Able Seaman George William Hatcher *
Able Seaman Cecil William George Hawkes (HMS *Edinburgh*)
Ordinary Seaman Ernest Holt
Able Seaman Lewin John Jones *
Ordinary Seaman Charles Thomas Mason *
Ordinary Seaman Bernard Roebuck *
Able Seaman George Frederick Rogerson
Ordinary Seaman Gerard Traynor
Able Seaman Charles Victor Whatley *

* Buried at Douglas Bank Cemetery, Dunfermline

Despite early official announcements published in the press claiming there had been no civilian casualties, over the ensuing days Scottish newspapers revealed there had been a number of civilian casualties as well as some very near misses. Shrapnel from the anti-aircraft shells fell all over the area where the aerial battle was fought and there were many narrow escapes from injury recorded at Blackness, Philipstoun and at Baldie-tap where people of all ages suddenly had to rush for cover as the shells burst above them. Not all the shells exploded either, such as the one at Linlithgow where an unexploded shell was discovered buried 3ft in the ground at Cockleroi.

There were numerous instances of aircraft machine gun bullets being found to have penetrated houses and embedded in walls and furniture in the Joppa area and a piece of shrapnel smashed the window of a busy tramcar as it proceeded through Portobello. Even the home of Lord Provost Henry Steele caught some of the machine gun fire and he made sure he lodged a formal complaint about the failure of the sirens to sound a warning. Peter McGowan had been injured by falling shrapnel as had Mrs Milne who was injured by shrapnel when it fell through the roof of her farmhouse in Aberdour. Mrs Forgan, of 26 Morton Street, Joppa also had a narrow escape when a bullet smashed through the woodwork of the sash window in the bedroom she was dusting and landed on her eiderdown quilt.

A number of civilians suffered minor injuries caused by flying splinters from exploding anti-aircraft shells. Mrs Julia Hargreaves of Bradford was visiting her daughter Mrs Emma Riddell at her home on The Green at Davidson's Mains and had her right arm cut by flying glass. It could have been worse, she was sitting at a table knitting and the bullet that shattered the glass came through the back of her chair; had she not been leaning forward she might have been killed. The bullet finally lodged in the doll's pram her grand-daughter had been playing with just moments before. John Ferry who lived in Granton was struck in the thigh by a machine gun bullet while walking along Ferry Road. He was taken to the Western General Hospital and made a successful recovery.

The most serious injury was suffered by Joseph 'Joe' McLusky (28) of Guthrie Street, Edinburgh who was working with his pal Francis Flynn of Tron Square painting a house at Abercorn Terrace, Portobello. Flynn was at the top of the ladder when a plane flew over. McLusky, who was at the bottom, called to his pal saying 'Something has hit me' as he crumpled up. Flynn climbed down the ladder to see what had happened and saw blood coming from McLusky's waistcoat. Flynn called to the lady of the house and she went for the doctor who lived next door. The doctor stabilised McLusky, who had received a bullet in the abdomen. An ambulance was summoned and he was rushed to Leith Hospital. The surgeons treating McLusky thought it best not to remove the bullet, but he did make a good recovery and was granted a pension of 18 shillings a week, making him the first civilian war pensioner of the Second World War.

Storp, Pohle and the other injured German aircrew were treated at the military hospital at Edinburgh Castle where they were visited by both Gifford and Pinkerton. Once they had recovered sufficiently, they were removed to prisoner of war camps.

The attack on the Forth may have been the first but it would be far from the last visit the British coast would receive from enemy aircraft in 1939. On 17 October, the day immediately after the attack on the Forth, Ju88s of 2./KG 30 set out on a mission to attack the British fleet further north at Scapa Flow. They were spotted by watchers on the north coast as they crossed Duncansby Head at 10.30am and a warning was flashed to Orkney. The Orkney and Shetland anti-aircraft defences were already on a high state of alert and gave the intruders a hot reception. Bombs from the raiders were seen to fall near a Belgian trawler in the Pentland Firth and the passengers and crew of the little steamer *St Ola*, which regularly transported mail between Kirkwall and Scrabster, had a terrible shock as bombs dropped in the water and fragments of anti-aircraft shell fell from the sky as she steamed towards Scrabster. Fortunately, neither vessel was damaged but passengers on *St Ola*, including several women, were ordered below to take cover.

The bombers reached Scapa Flow only to find the fleet had departed (withdrawn to the Clyde after the sinking of the *Royal Oak* while defences were improved) and all that remained was the base ship, the old dreadnought HMS *Iron Duke,* flagship of the Grand Fleet during the First World War, which was moored at the mouth of Ore Bay. No direct hits were achieved but two bombs fell either side of *Iron Duke* which caused such damage she had to be beached to avoid sinking. The press release from the Admiralty, widely reported in both local and national newspapers, proclaimed there were no casualties, but in reality a number of sailors had been injured and Petty Officer Stoker Arthur James Davis (29) and Frederick George Steele, were killed aboard HMS *Iron Duke* during the raid.

During the attack Ju88A-1 (4D+EK) was brought down by the 4.5″ guns manned by men of the locally recruited 226 (Caithness & Orkney) Heavy Anti-Aircraft Battery RA (TA) on the islet of Rysa. The battery fire blew the nose off the Ju88 causing the rest of the aircraft to plummet to earth with most of its bomb load still intact. It exploded on impact at Pegal Burn on the island of Hoy, becoming the first German aircraft to be brought down by anti-aircraft fire over British territory during the Second World War.[10]

The pilot Oberleutnant Walter Flämig, observer Gefreiter Hans Attenburger and gunner Unteroffizier Rudi Faust were all killed, only wireless operator Unteroffizier Fritz Ambrosius managed to release the upper escape hatch and bale out. The bodies of his crew mates and the wreckage of the plane spread over a wide area and what body parts that were recovered could not be identified and were buried in two graves at Lyness cemetery marked with headstones inscribed *Ein Deutscher Soldat.*

Dornier Do18D (8L+ DK) from 2/KüFlGr606 made a reconnaissance mission to assess the damage inflicted during the raid, and perhaps see if any of the downed crew were bobbing around in rubber dinghies. When reports were received of the German aircraft being spotted off the coast in the early afternoon B Flight 'Blue' section, No.607 Squadron consisting of Flying Officer Dudley Craig and Pilot Officer William 'Nit' Whitty under Flight Lieutenant Johnnie Sample, were scrambled in the Gloucester Gladiator biplanes from RAF Acklington. They engaged the Dornier and inflicted such damage the aircraft had to ditch 26 miles NE of Berwick. The pilot Feldwebel Paul Grabbet and observer Oberleutnant zur See Siegfried Saloga were both badly injured, but helped by their radio operator Oberfunkmaat Hilmar Grimm they managed to land the plane on the water and get into the rubber dinghy. They were soon picked up by HMS *Juno* which was a short distance from where the Dornier ditched, however, the mechanic Unteroffizier Kurt Seydel died of his wounds.

On 20 October Rosyth echoed to the sound of naval deck boots as the solemn cortège of naval personnel passed along the streets in slow march transporting six of the sailors who died in the action to Douglas Bank Cemetery where they were buried with full Naval honours. Pohle's observer August Schleicher died of his wounds and was buried along with Kurt Seydel with a full honours funeral the same day. The streets of Edinburgh were packed to catch a glimpse of the two swastika-draped coffins as they were driven through the city on a flat-bed trailer with an RAF escort to Portobello Cemetery. To modern eyes this may appear incongruous, but it should be remembered that the tradition had been established during the First World War that each side should provide military honours for the burial of those who died in the opposing side's territory. The bodies of Schleicher and Seydel were removed in the 1960s, along with most of the bodies of German aircrew who had been buried in British civilian cemeteries, to the *Soldatenfriedhof* that was created for German war dead of both wars at Cannock Chase.

The raid on the Forth and the subsequent military funerals were covered by Pathé news and shown in cinemas all over the UK. It was also dramatised in the GPO film unit of the Ministry of Information short movie *Squadron 992* (1940) that told the story of the attack, how it caused an immediate reassessment of the anti-aircraft defences of the area and how future threats would be tackled by the deployment of a mobile barrage balloon column or 'squadron' to the Forth – No.992 (Barrage Balloon) Squadron, RAF. Although there was some dramatic licence in the retelling, the practical efforts were factual and the first anti-aircraft barrage balloon was flown over the Forth on 18 October 1939. Within days John Colville, the Secretary of State for Scotland also announced North and South Queensferry and Inverkeithing were to be added to the list of areas covered by the government evacuation scheme.

Elsewhere on 17 October Konteradmiral Günter Lütjen aboard his flagship Z21 *Wilhelm Heidkamp* led the destroyers Z20 *Karl Galster,* Z16 *Friedrich Eckholdt,* Z17 *Diether von Roeder,* Z18 *Hans Lüdemann* and Z19 *Hermann Künne* and set off from Wilhelmshaven, heading north. The direction of their passage, however, was a sham and as dusk descended and they changed tack and made for the mouth of the Humber for these vessels were laden with sea mines and under the cover of darkness in the early hours of 18 October they laid a deadly minefield between the Humber Estuary and the Withernsea light and then steamed home completely undetected. The 300 mines they laid also remained undetected and were responsible for the sinking of seven ships. After another mine-laying mission on the night of 12/13 November a further 288 magnetic mines were laid in the Thames estuary that also lay undetected and caused the loss of the destroyer HMS *Blanche* and a further twelve merchant ships. These were some of the worse losses, but they were not isolated incidents, throughout the later months of 1939 up to the spring of 1940 German ships and aircraft carried out regular mine-laying missions around the coast of Great Britain.

Both Kriegsmarine and Luftwaffe also kept up the offensive attacking all manner of vessels from fishing boats to merchant shipping. The sound of gunfire became familiar to anyone living on coastal areas on the north, east and south coasts of Britain as anti-aircraft batteries kept up regular practices or blazed away at enemy intruders. So too did many fishing vessels that were now armed with twin Lewis guns on anti-aircraft mounts and the RAF fought them off in the skies above.

On the same day the attack was launched on Scapa Flow (17 October), Heinkel He 111H-1 (F6+PK) from 2./Aufklärungsgruppe 122/72 was on its second reconnaissance sortie that day looking for Royal Navy vessels along the north east coast when it was engaged by the Spitfires from No.41 Squadron, RAF Catterick and was damaged to the degree it had to ditch in the sea. Observer Leutnant Joachim Kretschmar and Unteroffizier Hugo Saur were both dead, only Oberfeldwebel Eugen Lange and Unteroffizier Bernhard Hochstuhl survived. Hochstuhl, the radio operator/gunner, had suffered a shrapnel wound to his leg but nonetheless the pair managed to inflate and launch the rubber dinghy carried on the aircraft for such emergencies and weathered a bitterly cold night on a rough sea. Lange was suffering from shock and exposure, so it fell to Hochstuhl to paddle ashore, landing at Whitby, where he hauled both dinghy and semi-conscious comrade up the beach and then pulled himself up 40ft of shelf rock from the shore to the railway line to seek help.

Railway Special Constable George Thomas was on duty at Sandsend tunnel and was just returning from one of his patrols to the Kettleness side when he spotted Hochstuhl standing near the line in his flying kit. He explained in broken English that he was German aircrew and that he had a comrade who needed medical assistance below. Sadly, there was something lost in translation and a struggle ensued when Hochstuhl would not leave with Special Constable Thomas until he had been given assurance help would be coming for Lange. He was allowed to return with help from other locals and the group used the dinghy as a stretcher to carry him back to Whitby police station where he was given a warm bath. Both were then removed to Whitby War Memorial Hospital where they made good recoveries and were then handed over to become prisoners of war.[11]

Germany maintained the offensive and on Saturday 21 October nine Heinkel He115B seaplanes from 1/KüFlGr406 flew out from their base on Sylt aiming to attack a shipping convoy off the east coast of Britain when they were intercepted about 35 miles east of Withernsea and scattered by Hurricanes of A Flight, No.46 Squadron from RAF Digby, Lincolnshire. Three of the Heinkels were brought down and two ditched in The Wash, their crew were rescued and became prisoners of war.

The third, (K6+EH werk no.1876), came down 5 miles east of Spurn Head, Yorkshire. All crew lost their lives and their bodies were carried on the tide until one of them was washed ashore at Mundesley and a further two at Happisburgh. They were given a full honours funeral at Happisburgh on 2 November 1939. The pilot, Oberleutnant zur See Heinz Schlicht, observer, Leutnant Fritz Meyer and mechanic Unteroffizier Bernhard Wessels were carried in coffins, draped in swastika flags by RAF bearer parties for a funeral service inside St Mary's Church. Afterwards they were formally borne to their graves in the churchyard where they were laid to rest. The event drew local and national press interest and was featured, with photographs of the funeral, in *The Times*. The body of an unidentified Luftwaffe Unteroffizier was also buried alongside them.

The first plot of an enemy aircraft over Norfolk by the Observer Corps occurred on Wednesday, 6 December 1939 when a Heinkel He115 float plane (S4+BL werk no. 2081) from 3/KüFlGr406 on a mine-laying mission flew across the Wash to Sheringham. It was dark and while flying at low level the Heinkel collided with the Chain Home radio-location mast at West Beckham, narrowly missed the Sheringham gas holder and at 3.15am finally crashed onto the seashore on the West Beach, a short distance from the lifeboat house.

Despite the hour a number of local people went to investigate, some earnestly advising their wives and children to stay inside and lock the door 'in case there are Germans about' as they departed. A couple of fishermen were determined to take a few souvenirs, the plane's compass and the pilot's seat were the first to disappear and did sterling service as useful additions to fishing boats for many years afterwards. A military guard arrived soon after and remained on the site to prevent further losses and most of the wreckage was removed. Upon closer examination the plane's fuel tanks were found to be protected by a rubberised material that the Aircraft Research Establishment at Farnborough tested and found to be both fire and puncture resistant and it proved to be of interest and value to British researchers.

The first body from this crew to be washed up on the shore was that of the observer, Oberleutnant zur See Emil Rödel (29) who was buried in Great

Bircham churchyard with full military honours on 9 December. The coffin was draped with two swastika flags and there was a large wreath inscribed, 'A tribute to a gallant airman from the officers, NCOs and airmen of the RAF'. Three volleys were fired, and the Last Post sounded. The bodies of Obleutnant zur See Wolfgang Wodtke and Oberfeldwebel Karl Ullman were washed ashore later in the month and were also given full military honours funerals at Sheringham cemetery attended by a number of representatives from the town including the Urban District Council, fire brigade and the British Legion who dropped a Flanders poppy on the coffins.

After the war the remains of Wodke and Ullman and the aircrew buried at Happisburgh were exhumed and re-interred at the *Soldatenfriedhof* German War Cemetery at Cannock Chase, only Rödel remains in the military section of the cemetery at Bircham Newton where he was originally buried.

* * *

The winter of 1939–40 was one of the coldest on record; an Arctic current from Siberia ensured it was certainly the coldest since 1894. Troops were delayed returning on home leave for Christmas due to freezing fog, 16 degrees

The frozen sea at Tankerton, Devon, January 1940.

of frost were recorded in Edinburgh and the upper reaches of the harbour at Leith docks were covered by ice. The coldest period was during the last two weeks in January 1940 when buses and cars could not make it through roads, some bus services had to be suspended, trains were delayed up to eight hours and some country areas were cut off due to snowdrifts. Scottish lochs iced over, as did the Fens and there were ice floes on the Tay, Thames, Humber, Mersey and Severn.

Ships were frozen at their moorings as docks iced over. One of Southampton's biggest docks was frozen over and even the Ocean Dock had a sturdy fringe of ice. Grimsby had a foot of snow and both the fish docks and Royal Docks were thick with ice. The low-lying foreshore in the Hamble area, Hampshire, Herne Bay and Whitstable in Kent, Felpham near Bognor Regis in West Sussex and Cromer and other areas on the Norfolk coast had large expanses covered with frozen sea water. Hundreds who could make it to the beaches went to see the phenomena for themselves. Spare a thought for the soldiers deployed on the coastal defences where many of those in wooden barrack huts were limited to a single solid fuel stove per hut to keep warm and even the water in their toilets froze over.

This winter of bitter cold provides the backdrop for one of the most tragic and worst instances of losses of life suffered by Trinity House during the war. Often one of the forgotten organisations that does so much for the safety and welfare of those at sea in peacetime and during the war, Trinity House had about fifty crewed lightships around the coast of Britain in 1939. Those who operated the service were determined they would continue to shine their lights that warned of maritime hazards in wartime. Although they were uniformed, the men of the service did not consider themselves combatants and initially none of the lightships were armed or defended in any way, nor was there any plan to change the status quo because they shone their lights for all shipping irrespective of its ownership be they a friendly or a hostile power.

The problem began with German suspicions that the crews of lightships were observing and reporting German shipping movements to British Naval authorities and as a result they became targets with the first attack directed at the Smith's Knoll lightship on 11 January 1940.

The East Dudgeon Lightship (No.63) had shone its light for decades to warn of a dangerous shoal in the North Sea off the Norfolk coast. On 29 January 1940 it was attacked by a German aircraft and as a result out of a crew of eight men only one man, John Sanders (31) of Great Yarmouth survived to tell what happened:

One of the fifty crewed lightships that warned shipping of hidden dangers in the waters around the coast of Britain in 1939.

It would be about 9.30 on the Monday morning when we saw a German plane coming from the direction of the English coast. It was a Heinkel. The plane circled round and the next thing we knew the crew had opened fire on us with machine guns. Then still circling round, they started to bomb us. The ninth bomb hit the ship and at the same time damaged one of the two ship's boats. The ship heeled over and seemed to go right under. The decks were awash and we were floundering about waist deep in water. One of the crew was ill in his bunk and we had to get him on deck and then we took to the small boat. Although badly knocked about, the ship remained floating. The plane circled round but dropped no more bombs.

We then started rowing shorewards, as there was no ship in sight. We still continued to row after darkness had set in and it would be about two o'clock the next morning when we heard the sound of waves breaking on the shore. We dropped anchor and it was then that waves capsized the boat. We were flung into the sea and I could hear my mates shouting all around me. Someone grabbed hold of my life jacket but he was shot right over my head by a wave. I am a good swimmer but realised it was useless to attempt to swim in my heavy clothes. I turned on my back and hoped for the best.

Soon I found I was in calmer water and, on turning over, discovered it was like a shallow pond. I must have remained on my hands and knees in that

*water for ten minutes, until I had regained some strength, and then I crawled
ashore. I heard one of my mates shouting as the waves carried him ahead of
me, but in the darkness I could not find any of them.*[12]

Sanders and his comrades had landed on a beach near Mablethorpe on the
Lincolnshire coast. Soaking wet, freezing cold, suffering from exhaustion
and exposure he stumbled along the beach until he found a house. He broke
in, removed his clothes, wrapped himself in blankets and lay down on a bed
where he was found later that morning. It was not long after daybreak that the
dead bodies of his crewmates were found washed up on the sands. They were:

- Roland Robert George (53), Senior Master and Skipper, Gorleston, Norfolk
- James Malcolm Scott Bell (31), Master Mechanic, from Hornchurch, Essex
  (native of Dundee, Scotland)
- Bardolph Basil Boulton (41), Fog Signal Driver, Great Yarmouth
- Horatio Davis (51), Lamplighter from Gorleston
- George William Jackson (31), Seaman, Lowestoft, Suffolk
- Richard Edward Norton, Seaman, Great Yarmouth
- Herbert Rumsby (46), Lampman, Belton, Suffolk

The story was told in both national and local newspapers and questions were
raised over the future plans for the protection of the crews of lightships.
Their story, which moved the nation and caught something of the way
ordinary working people were being dragged into the war, was turned into a
film made by the Crown Film Unit for the Ministry of Information in 1940.
Released as *Men of the Lightship*, an edited version was produced under the
supervision of Alfred Hitchcock and released in the United States as *Men
of Lightship 61*.

Tragically, despite some lightships being moved or removed from service
altogether there would be further attacks and losses of life on lightships around
the British coast during the war. It was unusual that such a story was released
when many others were withheld or sanitised by censors. The situation as far
as the British public were concerned at the time, when some international
newspapers were still speaking of a 'Phoney War', was summed up eloquently
in a short piece of reportage in the *Yorkshire Post*:

*A curtain of silence, of distance and censorship, hangs over the North Sea but
sometimes events can break through that curtain. Residents on the East Coast
catch a glimpse of war at close range. They see a German aeroplane loom
swiftly out of the mist and batter with bombs or machine-gun bullets a ship
within sight of shore. They see our fighters go up and watch the dizzy course*

of an air battle overhead. On Saturday, near Whitby, they saw a German raider hunted inland until it crashed, bullet ridden, close to a farmhouse.

On any day they may see a lifeboat go out and return with survivors from a ship sunk by a bomb, U-boat or mine. But they are still only on the fringe of the North Sea battlefield. Further off, beyond the horizon, that battlefield stretches over mile after mile of wintry waters under sodden grey skies. Here, unceasingly, the struggle goes on – cargo ships nosing their way through stormy seas, while men on windswept bridges keep watch against danger from below and danger from above; minesweepers about their hazardous unending task; destroyers and patrol vessels searching for submarines; aircraft on the same errand circling overhead.

This is the battlefield which sends out its messages day by day – men rescued from rafts or found there, frozen to death; empty boats and fragments of wreckage drifting idly; bodies of seamen or airman washed up along the coast. Those who live by the North Sea find these messages; the rest of us read them in newspaper paragraphs. Let us keep in thought the men who are fighting for us on that hidden battlefield, by day and by night, and pay tribute from our hearts.[13]

At a time when good news from the war at sea was so desperately needed there had been great news coverage of the sinking of the *Graf Spee* at the Battle of the River Plate. The British warships and crews that returned to our shores from that engagement were given heroes' welcomes, such as the return of the cruiser HMS *Exeter* to her 'home' dock at Devonport on 15 February 1940. H.P. Twyford vividly evoked the day when he wrote:

She was in many ways our own ship. Apart from the fact that she bore the name of the 'ever faithful' city capital of Devon, she had been built at Devonport by Devonport hands and she was manned by a West Country crew… Every point of vantage from Mount Batten to Devonport Dockyard was black with people and the early morning air was filled with their cheers, the music of bands and the answering cheers of the Exeter's *ship's company as the ship slowly passed up harbour…when the ship steamed past the South Dockyard, past the cradle in which she had been fashioned. The dockyardsmen who built her dropped their immediate work to join in the welcome. They cheered as they had when she had slid down that slipway at the launching and high up on that 'cradle' in which her hull had rested their message of welcome was boldly displayed.*[14]

But despite the best efforts of the crew to 'patch up her wounds' HMS *Exeter* still bore the scars of battle, hundreds of them from holes through her funnel to grim repair patches on her hull. Curiously her guns appeared unscathed, when reporters were permitted aboard the truth was apparent, as Twyford recalled he was told 'Don't lean on them' very shortly after he arrived:

Yes, with one exception they were magnificent dummies. The ship's carpenter, the artificers and the painters had accomplished a striking piece of make-believe.

When asked why this had been done one of the officers replied:

Well, we had to make a show in case we met anything [as they made their way back], *we had to look business-like even if we were not.*[15]

Other vessels from other incidents over the months to come would return in far worse states, tragically, others would not return at all.

During the first seven months of the Second World War 402 British, Allied and neutral ships were lost amounting to some 1,303,000 tons. The biggest killer by far were German submarines that accounted for the loss of 222, while mines claimed 129, aircraft accounted for 30, warships sank 16 and 5 were lost to other causes.

Those who died in Britain or in 'home waters' around our coast between 3 September 1939 and the end of March 1940 while serving in the armed forces, merchant navies of a variety of nations, in the lighthouse and pilotage authorities and civilians commemorated by name on the Commonwealth War Graves Commission Debt of Honour register, number over 6,500. Sadly, not all fishermen nor all civilian passengers who lost their lives due to enemy action while aboard passenger ships or merchant vessels are recorded. Some rolls exist of those lost with the sinking of specific vessels, while others, especially fishermen, remain known only to their families and communities because reporting restrictions did not allow their loss of life due to enemy action or sea mines to be recorded in newspapers. Their names are not usually recorded among the war dead on local war memorials either. The total number of fishermen and civilians lost at sea during 'The Phoney War' remains uncounted.

Chapter 3

Front Line Coast

*I would sum up the German character best by saying that
they are the best of losers and the worst of winners.*

General Edmund Ironside

As the Nazi threat in Europe became more acute over 1938–39 the number of refugees fleeing to Britain escalated from hundreds to thousands and a number of the extant holiday camps around our coast were utilised to accommodate them. The problem that rapidly emerged over the first months after the declaration of war as thousands of men and women were mobilised, volunteered or conscripted for service, was where they were to be accommodated.

The Militia Act of 1939 which called 35,000 young men for military service had pushed the accommodation and facilities of military barracks and camps to their limits and many old barracks that had been in stasis for years had been reactivated. The number of tents for the creation of new camps only went so far and it would take time for the production of wooden barrack huts to be expanded to meet demand. Guest houses, hotels and private homes around the coast were being used as billets and many larger houses and hotels were requisitioned to become accommodation for military units. This meant the men were often dispersed over a number of locations and it was far from ideal when it came to discipline, morale or building a unit's *esprit de corps*.

It was at this time of flux that the emerging holiday camp entrepreneur Billy Butlin approached the War Office with a mutually advantageous proposal whereby his holiday camps could be used as military training camps for the duration. His camps at Skegness and Clacton could be used straightaway and the War Department was to organise the completion of his camps that were under construction at Filey, Ayr and Pwllheli. A rent of 25 per cent of the previous year's profits was agreed with Butlin and he agreed to buy them back at the end of hostilities.

Butlin's camps would become training centres for all three branches of the armed services. The first opened at Butlin's first ever holiday camp at Ingoldmells near Skegness which was commissioned as the Royal Navy 'stone frigate' (shore establishment) HMS *Royal Arthur* on 22 September 1939.

Sailors on parade at HMS **Royal Arthur,** *a former Butlin's Skegness holiday camp, handed over to the Royal Navy for the duration of the war.*

Capable of accommodating some 4,000 Royal Navy personnel, *Royal Arthur* became one of the main training bases for both Royal Navy ratings and Wrens entering the communications branch of the service as signallers, telegraphists, wireless operators and coders.

Butlin's camp at Clacton had been destined to become Internment Camp 4 for 'enemy aliens' and was surrounded with barbed wire and floodlights, but when the assessments of 'aliens' considered potentially hostile were far less than anticipated, the camp became the main training base for the newly formed Auxiliary Military Pioneer Corps (AMPC) in October 1939. The AMPC had been created from a core of older reservists aged 35–50 from infantry and cavalry reservists who were not deemed A1 for front line service but still considered ideal for pioneer work such as labouring digging trenches, building defences both at home and abroad, as well as constructing the desperately needed military camps in the UK.

First World War Victoria Cross recipient Donald Dean was recalled for service in the Second World War and appointed as a group commander in the Auxiliary Military Pioneer Corps centre at Clacton. He recalled:

The centre was very well housed in a Butlin's Holiday Camp there and I found large numbers of officers already on the spot. Practically all were middle aged or elderly and all wore the uniform and badges of their former units. I found also a very mixed bag of other ranks, all except the staff being privates, mostly over military age or of low medical category, but nearly all volunteers and therefore keen.[1]

After many of the Territorial battalions had been deployed in the defence of airfields in anticipation of the much-vaunted aerial attacks that did not emerge, they were redeployed to coastal defence duties through the bitterly cold winter of 1939–40. Up to May 1940 there did not appear to be any impending threat of invasion so there were few resources directed towards these units. Many roadblocks and defences had to be improvised based on instructions from the field engineering manual, with some useful practical additions drawn from the memories of those who had served in the First World War. One innovation often seen was empty tin cans strung on barbed wire that would clank a warning if there were surreptitious attempts to cut or interfere with it under cover of darkness.

Many of those serving at that time would recall that it all seemed such a sedate period where, although they had been deployed to a war footing, nothing much had changed in the day to day running of barracks and camps. There seemed, especially to the younger men, a lot of officers, some lifelong soldiers, others recalled from the Army Reserve who were very much of 'the old school' with gentlemanly manners who proudly wore their medal ribbons of the First World War, and who had their own way of doing things from an older age of soldiering. NCOs would be instructed to make sure the men carried out tasks such as filling sandbags 'by numbers', insisted on beginning their day with 'gunfire' (tea and biscuits) being brought to them at reveille by their batman (officer's servant from the ranks who would clean, iron and polish the officer's kit as required, ensure his meals were delivered and run errands) and who would refer to the Germans as 'The Local Boche' or 'The Common Hun'.

Veterans would reflect on these times decades later as being 'a different world', a world that ended abruptly when Hitler unleashed his Blitzkrieg and German forces invaded France, Holland and the Low Countries on 10 May 1940. The BEF were rapidly knocked back into a fighting retreat. In the wake of the advance of German forces into Holland, British national and provincial newspapers carried stories, allegedly relayed to them by reliable witnesses, of how German parachutists had disguised themselves in civilian clothes when they made their landings and spread confusion ahead of the attack. Despite such accounts later being proved wildly over exaggerated and highly inaccurate, they were believed credible at the time and led to widespread scares and even alleged sighting of paratroopers being dropped at numerous localities across Britain.

Troops were put on a heightened state of alert across the country and those on the coast were deployed to guard places vulnerable to invasion, especially piers. In East Anglia, for example II Corps HQ ordered the immediate fortification of Great Yarmouth, Gorleston, Weybourne and Lowestoft on 11 May. Orders also stipulated 'Special watch is to be maintained for enemy parachutists.' All companies of the 5th and 6th Battalions, The Royal Norfolk Regiment were ordered to battle stations on a front from High Kelling and Sheringham to Overstrand and stringent works were carried out installing road blocks, digging weapons pits, sandbagging and reinforcing defensive emplacements at vulnerable points across the area and on the main roads. The men of the 4th Battalion, Royal Norfolk Regiment improvised roadblocks consisting of herring barrels filled with sand and lashed with timber, constructed all around the perimeter of Great Yarmouth and Gorleston. Great ingenuity was also shown by young officers, NCOs and men as they installed cunningly prepared tripwires, klaxon horns and bell alarms in the vicinity of their section posts; these, however, caused inconvenience to senior officers unaware of their existence when visiting the posts at night.

The high-profile newspaper reports of the deployment of German parachutists during the invasion of Holland, especially those of parachutists being dropped in a variety of civilian uniforms and clothing, led to both the police and military authorities being inundated with reports of sightings of enemy parachutists dropping to earth all over Britain. In some areas unofficial groups took matters into their own hands and raised armed foot and horse patrols of their local areas. Government and local authorities were not comfortable about these unregulated armed bands roaming coast and countryside and with so much valuable military and police time being taken up by mistaken reports of enemy parachutists, it was decided to create a new officially sanctioned organisation to specifically deal with what was becoming commonly known as 'the parachute menace'.

Matters moved apace, Chamberlain had resigned on 9 May, Winston Churchill was appointed Prime Minister and entered the House of Commons on 13 May to the cheers of his colleagues.

The morning papers of 14 May carried headlines of a 2,000 tank clash north of Liège, bundles of enrolment forms began to arrive at police stations and it was made known an important announcement would be made on the BBC Home Service that evening. Just after 9pm on 14 May 1940 Anthony Eden, the newly appointed Secretary of State for War, made the appeal for men not in military service between the ages of 17 and 65 to come forward and offer their services in a new force to be known as the Local Defence Volunteers (LDV).

The place for enrolment into the Local Defence Volunteers was announced as the local police station and many men set off to join immediately, some volunteers arriving at police stations even before the broadcast had ended, setting out with all speed with the intention of being the first to volunteer only to find a queue had already formed in front of them. Many of them turned up in their work clothes, bank clerks in smart suits, bus drivers in their uniforms and workmen in their overalls. The announcement had been like a pistol shot at the start of a race and the volunteers poured in, not in hundreds as anticipated but in their thousands through the night and following day.

As one might imagine, the response around coastal areas where the danger of invasion would be far more immediate was outstanding. At Dover over twenty names had been given in before 8am on Wednesday and throughout the day a steady stream of volunteers made their way to the police station. Volunteers there also came from a real cross section of society and included a general, captains and several musketry instructors. By 17 May the number of names stood at over 400.

At Portsmouth Guildhall police station and sub-stations applications averaged one a minute and by 9am on 16 May 615 forms had been signed; by Saturday 18 May the number stood at 1,045; on 31 May it was reported 1,500 had registered. In Fareham 350 had registered within 24 hours, 215 at Droxford and 164 at Gosport, where classes of men ranged from retired army and navy men of high rank to assistants in various local trades including dress designers, brewery machine minders, bank clerks, dockyard fitters and even members of the clergy. Among the Gosport volunteers was the Vicar of Elson, the Rev. F. Flintoft Wood, who was of the belief that every able-bodied man should be made familiar with the use of a rifle. He went on to point out he felt it would be a good thing if volunteers were allowed to use the firearms with which they are most familiar stating:

I have been big game shooting in Africa. The gun I favour and the one I hope they would let me have would be a Winchester repeater. I understand it thoroughly and I know what it can do.[2]

Within a few minutes of the broadcast several men presented themselves at Brighton and Hove police stations and from the early hours of the following morning they included men of every class, retired Indian Army officers and a man in a top hat (only in Brighton!). Nearly 200 had registered at Newport by the evening of 15 May. The volunteers of the morning and afternoon were those in a position to make a call through the day, but large numbers enrolled on their way home from work and after tea there was a fresh influx by those who had gone home from work first.

At Plymouth a steady stream came to volunteer at Greenbank Police Station. Mr L.W. Ford of Hotspur Terrace told a *Western Morning News* reporter that he and a number of his ex-servicemen workmates at the dockyard had all sworn that they would volunteer when they heard of the appeal. Both Mr Fred Taylor of King Gardens, another veteran of the First World War, and his 17-year-old son also volunteered. Mr Taylor senior summed up the feelings of many of those volunteering, pointing out:

> *We could see the enemy was taking the upper hand wherever he was not meeting military opposition. So it is very necessary for us in this country to be ready. I am an old soldier and I am tired but I feel this is my job at home.*[3]

By the morning of 17 May 350 had volunteered at Plymouth, 533 at Plympton, 529 at Totnes, 358 at Torbay and 700 in the Exeter Police Area. Scores joined at Sidmouth, including Mr Percy Baron, the well-known all England and Bisley shot. In Tavistock they had 125, among them retired admirals, generals, colonels and majors and ex-servicemen of all ranks, some with service back to the South African War.

In Penzance the first to join was the Town Clerk Mr Alfred Robinson who had shot at Bisley and was very keen to see the formation of a corps. Another early volunteer was Alfred Robinson, 64 years old, who had been a member of the Penzance Volunteer Rifle Corps in 1895. At Eastbourne the first to enlist were both First World War veterans – Alexander Henry Lewis, a hotel employee who had been an ambulance driver in the ASC and Richard W. Lewis an employee at a bicycle shop on Terminus Road who had served in the 20th Battalion, The Manchester Regiment – a Manchester 'Pals' Battalion. The third man to register was the Right Hon. Lord Tollemache of South Cliff Avenue, also a First World War veteran who had served in armoured cars and the heavy artillery. By the following day such were the numbers volunteering to join that the supply of enrolment forms was exhausted before all the names were taken.

At Worthing in Sussex well over 1,000 youths and men volunteered for the LDV in the first twenty-four hours, the first men arriving at the Union Place police station just minutes after the speech. Registration was resumed at 6am on Wednesday morning and the rush increased as the morning went on. By 10am there was a two-deep queue waiting to enrol. They continued arriving up to midnight on Wednesday 15th, some of the last men to arrive being bus drivers and conductors coming off late duty. The men were of all types; labourers and bank clerks, errand boys and professional men. Several town hall workers also enrolled. At one time those waiting to join included the borough treasurer and the manager of Martin's Bank. A well-known local professional man who was an excellent shot reduced his age to 62 and hid his ARP warden's badge to make sure he was accepted.[4] This was because full time ARP workers were barred from serving in the LDV, but part time workers could volunteer and problems arose when ARP workers resigned in considerable numbers to join the new force.

Concurrent with the Eden broadcast a telegram was sent by Eden to the lord lieutenant of every county stating, 'I am sure that we may count on your co-operation and help in connection with the Local Defence Volunteer Force.' Each lord lieutenant was expected to begin the county structure of the LDV by appointing an area commander with overall command and organization responsibility for the county. Each county was divided into zones; some simply using the extant police division areas as frameworks to define their zones. In each zone a headquarters was established to administer the number of groups within it.

An unpaid volunteer organiser was to be put in charge of each zone and each group. The numbers involved were not quite like the army; whereas a regular army platoon consists of thirty men the LDV equivalent could range between ten and fifty men. Most of those appointed to command positions

Members of Cromer Home Guard ready to use Molotov Cocktails against an 'enemy tank' during an exercise. Note the anti-tank blocks and rails of the road block.

in the LDV had previous military experience, but it was not essential as those with respected managerial, organizational and leadership skills from civvy street equally found themselves in positions of command. There were many instances of bosses proudly falling in with all ranks of the LDV, indeed some retired senior officers and NCOs in areas such as Eastbourne where there were a lot of their kind, were happy to do their bit as private soldiers, especially when the man appointed commander of Eastbourne's LDV was Brigadier Edmund Costello VC, a name already familiar in the town as chief warden and the organiser of the town's ARP scheme.

The duties of the Local Defence Volunteers were three-fold. First and foremost it was for observation, to spot paratroopers or invasion forces and report back. These duties gave rise to the nickname of the unit based on its LDV letters – 'Look, Duck and Vanish'. In fact, so synonymous were the LDV with this duty in many of the early reports of these units they were often referred to as 'parashots'. Secondly, they should help stop the free movement of any invading enemy by blocking railway lines and immobilising cars and other motorised vehicles. Thirdly, they were to patrol vulnerable spots such as railway bridges, gas, electricity and water works to prevent damage or sabotage. The first patrols of the local LDV units were often covered in the local press, such as this account published in the *Worthing Gazette*:

> *Worthing's first 'Parashooters' – members of the Local Defence Volunteers – went on duty for the first time in the rural areas around the town. They were armed. Armed pickets will now be sent out every night. Only a fraction of the 1,400 men who have volunteered will be required. As they are selected they will be issued with their uniforms. They will only carry arms when on duty. Worthing was divided into three sections for the purpose of the patrols. Company headquarters at the old Connaught Theatre are open day and night.[5]*

The *Eastbourne Herald* also published a poem in the style of Jack 'Mind my Bike' Warner (based on his popular song 'I'm a Bunger Up of Rat Holes' in tribute to the new defenders of our land:

> *I'm a popper off of parachutists,*
> *I'm a parachutist popper-off, I am.*
> *I've got a lovely lot of pops*
> *For every parachute that drops*
> *And I shan't be slow to lay the blighters out.*

At night I'd like to be upon the Downs perhaps,
Or at any other place upon the maps.
If there's Nazis to be shot
You'll find me on the spot,
'Cos I'm a popper-off of parachutists, Yes, I am![6]

The LDV would remain the subject or witty and jocular remarks, but over in France by 20 May the situation had declined to the degree that Churchill informed the War Cabinet he had suggested to the Chiefs of Staff that they should consider a scheme for the withdrawal the British Expeditionary Force. Deep in the galleries below Dover Castle Vice-Admiral Bertram Ramsay, Flag Officer Dover began planning what would be codenamed Operation Dynamo and the Admiralty began to amass suitable shipping from Dover, Portsmouth, Thames Estuary and along the east coast. Originally planned as an evacuation from three ports after the fall of Boulogne and Calais, only Dunkirk remained when the War Cabinet sanctioned the BEF's march north to Dunkirk on 25 May. The following day the Cabinet despatched a signal sent via the Admiralty to Ramsey that simply stated: 'Operation Dynamo is to commence.'

The problem was that 26 May was a Sunday and many of the men of the coastal craft, such as minesweepers, had been given a few hours of shore leave and had to be sought out by local police and told to return to their vessels. Wilfred Walters, Yeoman of Signals aboard Minesweeper HMS *Ross*, was one of them. Having recently returned to port at North Shields, way up the east coast in Northumberland, he was spending the few hours of shore leave in an evening out with some of his crew-mates in Whitley Bay when he was told to return. They thought it was an exercise to see how long it would take their ship's company to get back on board in the event of a sudden call to sea. When they arrived back their captain told them they were sailing as soon as they were ready and off they steamed to Harwich. When they arrived at the port an officer came aboard to enquire how many boats they could tow across to Dunkirk to which their captain was heard to enquire 'What's happening?' to which the officer replied: 'Don't you know?'

Most of the ratings of the Royal Navy who would crew evacuation vessels did not know what was planned for them when they received instructions that they were to make ready to leave their barracks. Those who were loaded onto coaches or lorries recall it was fine, sunny weather as they motored through the countryside; some were told where they were heading while in transit, others were still wondering when they had reached their destination, Dover Castle, after nightfall. Told they would be required at any time at short notice they kipped down as best they could, where they could, in the areas of the complex allotted to them, most ending up sleeping on floors. After a few short hours of sleep the call came for crews in the early hours of the morning to form up into boat crews of three, draw three days rations and they were sent to man any boat tied up alongside the inner breakwater of the harbour. Once ready, each boat's skipper would report to the officer in charge, present him with a list of the names of crew and receive orders to rendezvous outside the breakwater. Once assembled groups of these boats were then towed out to sea by tugs and were given their course to steer by the skipper through a megaphone. They were on their way to Dunkirk.

Troop transport ships, hospital ships and a host of Royal Navy and Merchant Navy vessels made their way to Dunkirk, but if the evacuation was to be as quick and successful as possible more ships would be needed. On 27 May 1940 the small-craft section of the Ministry of Shipping undertook the massive task of contacting boatyards around the east, and south coasts and along the River Thames asking them to collect all boats with shallow draft: pleasure boats, private yachts and motor launches. The call was also answered by the owners of paddle steamers, pleasure steamers, tugs, fishing vessels and barges all around the British coast including Scotland and Wales, in fact just about any vessel capable of carrying passengers that could make the journey across the Channel would be needed. Experienced seamen would also be required and appeals were soon put out by telephone and word of mouth across fishing ports and harbours, even films were stopped to flash up notices requesting fishing trawler crew to report to their local Admiralty office.

Some vessels were taken with permission with numerous owners insisting they wished to sail their own vessels, others were requisitioned and crewed by naval personnel, ex-naval personnel or experienced volunteers. After checks being made that the vessels were seaworthy and some of them fitted with machine guns for defence from aerial attack the 850 'little ships' were fuelled and then made their way to Ramsgate, Sheerness and Harwich. On the night of 29/30 May the first organised convoy of 'little ships' consisting of eight motor launches with their escort left Ramsgate, the first on the evening of 29 May for La Panne and at 1am on 30 May nineteen launches led by the Belgian Ferry *Yser* left bound for Dunkirk. On 30 May a further call was made to the Royal National Lifeboat Institution (RNLI) to ask if they would send their boats too and nineteen lifeboats from stations over hundreds of miles of coastline from Gorleston in Norfolk to Shoreham Harbour, Sussex answered the call, that simply requested the boats proceed to Dover at once 'for special duty under the Admiralty'.

The *Hastings and St Leonards Observer* recorded:

Throughout Wednesday and Thursday an endless procession of small craft,
mostly fishing boats and yachts could be seen making up Channel past Hastings
on their way to join in the great task of rescue. The Hastings fishing fleet,
consisting of the boats Industry, Boy Billie, Boy Bob, Henry Harris, Good
Luck, Edward and Mary, Leading Star, Little Mayflower, Mayflower *and*
Oritara *arrived on Thursday and the next day they were taken over by naval*
authorities.

Another *Observer* reporter described the scene at Dover:

The port of departure had the appearance of a regatta day, both ashore and
afloat with a grim reminder now and again that something more serious was
afoot. Fishing boats from every port on the south and east coast crowded
the harbour. The fleet of lifeboats added a gay touch of colour. There were
pleasure boats, paddle steamers, 'sixpenny sick' craft from Southend complete
with drinking bars, Thames barges under sail and under tow…Ashore the
crews swarmed about the naval headquarters discussing the job ahead, the
weather, the tides and their chances. Old shipmates from distant ports met
with a handshake. It all seemed much more like a regatta than a war! Until
one saw the destroyers that came limping or hurrying into the harbour, their
decks a solid mass of waving khaki. Wounded men and wounded ships sharply
cancelled the regatta atmosphere.

The men in khaki, French, Belgian and British tramped wearily along the
jetties where they landed, almost – but not quite – too exhausted to smile. The
heroic deed performed by the Navy could be read by those who knew how to
interpret the signs at the port. Officers wearing soaked uniforms, hollow-eyed
through lack of sleep. Bluejackets tumbling cheerily into small, unfamiliar,
commandeered craft to set out on the 45-mile crossing to the opposite coast.
Destroyers, funnels, bridges and boats riddled with bullet holes, listing
dangerously through flooded compartments, running to and fro five or six
times a day and perhaps more, just as though they were on a ferry service.[7]

Those who made the journey to evacuate troops from the beaches were also
shocked at just how bad things were when they arrived as they saw the flaming
ruins of Dunkirk and the black pall of cloud that hung in the sky from the
huge burning oil storage tanks. Ordinary Seaman James Woodhams of Battle
was one of the Royal Navy crew of the paddle steamer *Brighton Queen*:

We first arrived off the beaches early last Friday morning. I went as one of the
crew of our lifeboat and we made seven trips ashore fetching off troops. Once
our boat capsized and once it was holed against an improvised embarkation
pier made from lorries driven into the sea, but not a man was lost. Bullet holes

or any other kind of holes were soon plugged up. Once we had picked up our complement of men we towed off another vessel crowded with men which was stranded…

When we returned to Dunkirk on Saturday we went into the harbour and this time they got us with a second salvo. One of the bombs missed me by a few feet only. I was knocked off my feet but was uninjured. The ship sank quickly and most of us swam for it. Owing to the shallow water the masts and a few feet of the funnel still remained above water and many men clung to these. After about an hour a tug came along and picked us up. By the time we were landed in England I felt little the worse for the adventure.[8]

Rather than carrying out runs back and forth between Dunkirk and the reception ports on the south east coast, many of the 'little ships' ferried troops from the beaches to the larger evacuation ships capable of carrying thousands of men at a time in the deeper water off the coast. When they eventually made their return journeys to England after days at the beachhead they filled up with as many personnel as they could safely carry back. Thousands of men also boarded some of the larger vessels direct from the East Mole of the harbour under the supervision of the indefatigable Captain William 'Bill' Tennant

Troops evacuated from Dunkirk on a destroyer about to berth at Dover, 31 May 1940.

who through his remarkable skills of personal leadership, organisation and improvisation kept the men rolling along the East Mole to the evacuation ships.

Worthing soldier, Corporal T.A. 'Andy' Clifford wrote of the beaches being like 'Hell let loose on earth' in a letter recording his experiences when he reached the Dunkirk sands:

The beach at last. What a sight. Troops, troops everywhere and out in the bay what remained of some boats…one hour, two hours, three, four, five, six hours waiting there on the beach. At last we were moving. Yes! Yes! Towards the Mole. 'Make your way to the pier head along the Mole in batches of 50.' At last! Suddenly a high-pitched whine and a shell smashed into the Mole, right in a bunch of fifty men. Then the order 'Forward the Regiment.' Slow, slow but each step bringing us nearer home and to that mangled mass there left on the Mole. The fifties stopped. We were to wait there in the open until the next boat came up to the pier head…We lay there once again towards the boat. At last we were on board and then they started to shell once again but they dropped the other side of the Mole thank goodness…[9]

All were vulnerable to regular machine gunning and dive bombings from enemy aircraft. Some men were unfortunate enough to board a vessel only to have it sunk beneath them, for some lads this happened on more than one occasion. During the nine-day period between 27 May and the fall of Dunkirk on 4 June 1940, 338,226 troops (139,097 of whom were French) were successfully evacuated back to England from Dunkirk.

There was also a solo arrival – Second Lieutenant Timothy Stoyin Lucas of Queen Victoria's Rifles. Having been taken prisoner at Calais on 2 June he had escaped from the large group of prisoners he was part of as they were being marched down the St Omer Road. After walking some distance away, he dived into bushes and went to sleep until the following morning. As soon as it was light he ditched his greatcoat and threw a sack around his shoulders and walked across country to the coast, where after walking some way up the beach he found a dinghy and oars near Wissant. An elderly French fisherman helped him launch the boat and Lucas rowed out to sea near Cap Gris Nez under cover of darkness and rowed himself across the Channel 'like a Brighton boatman', guided by the sun and the wind. Starting at 10pm, at 7am he reckoned he was halfway across and could see the white cliffs of Dover and he kept his boat on course for them. Lucas was spotted half a mile outside Dover where he was picked up and brought in by a minesweeper.

After the evacuation from the Dunkirk beaches there would be further evacuations of allied troops and civilians from the continent from ports

Troops on the quayside at Falmouth after being evacuated from France, June 1940.

further along the coast. There were still plans for a counter offensive and fresh troops were landed in France, but it never emerged. Terrible numbers of casualties were sustained, their stocks of ammunition ran out and a naval evacuation for these men proved impossible. As a result the majority of the remaining troops of the 51st Highland Division were taken prisoners of war after the division surrendered at St-Valery-en-Caux on 12 June 1940.

Under Operation Cycle the main rescues were from Le Havre up to 13 June and Operation Aerial evacuated from ports in Western France such as St Nazaire and Nantes from 15 June to 25 June when official evacuations ended to conform to the terms of the German–French armistice. It was also during these later evacuations the former Cunard liner HMT *Lancastria* was attacked and sunk in the Loire estuary on 17 June 1940 with the loss of an estimated 3,500 evacuated personnel and crew. It remains the greatest loss of life in a single British ship, in peacetime or war.

It should not be forgotten that there were also thousands of British and allied troops who had not escaped and would spend the duration of the conflict as prisoners of war. Over 100 'Little Ships' did not make it either and took their place in the toll of 236 vessels that were lost during the evacuation. However, it could have been a lot worse and it was far from in vain. Operations Dynamo, Cycle and Aerial resulted in a total of 558,032 British and Allied military personnel and civilians being successfully brought back to Britain.

The majority of those evacuated from Dunkirk landed at one of the three main reception ports of Dover, Ramsgate and Margate. Generally, Dover acted as the main port for Royal Navy and transport ships and some 200,000 British and allied troops were landed there, among them 4,500 seriously wounded soldiers removed to hospital trains or taken to the nearby Buckland Hospital for emergency treatment. Ramsgate was the main hub for the 'little ships' where an estimated almost 43,000 evacuated troops were landed. Some 47,772 British and allied servicemen and refugees – one seventh of the entire number of those evacuated – landed at Margate Jetty in ninety-six vessels over the eight days of the evacuation. Ramsgate General Hospital treated 250 and Margate 100 casualties, but it was the emergency hospitals that dealt with the greatest number. The Royal Sea Bathing Hospital at Margate dealt with 436 cases and hundreds were also treated at the two emergency hospitals at Ramsgate. Newhaven in East Sussex provided a base for several hospital ships. Other ports around the coast such as Harwich, Deal, Sheerness and Southampton also sent vessels to help and received landings of evacuated troops.

The entire operation was controlled from a small room at Dover Castle, Vice Admiral Bertram Ramsay, who was awarded the KCB for his leadership in the operation, explained:

We set aside a room here with about seven telephones and 15 or 16 fellows working in it. Most operations are given a name nowadays and it was known as a Dynamo Operation. If anything could have been better named I should like to know it. The room which was the hub of operations was called the dynamo room. After three or four days the men working in this room were so tired that they were just lying down behind their chairs, on beds, on mattresses or even on the floor and falling fast asleep. As they woke up they would carry straight on with their work…It became clear that this was a bigger show than anybody had imagined. The numbers we were going to get off were going to be bigger than had been thought possible.[10]

During the evacuation Dover was directing in the region of 200–300 shipping movements every twenty-four hours. The work involved in making the evacuation happen was relentless and behind the dynamo room there were

Some of the Women's Royal Naval Service despatch riders who worked round the clock and often against the clock to back up Operation Dynamo, 1940.

also teams of men and women military personnel in the Dover tunnels and casemates, from coders and cypher clerks to teleprinters, telegraphists, switchboard operators and a remarkable team of Wren motorcycle despatch riders, who all worked round the clock and often against the clock to back up the operation.

With the Royal Navy focused on getting the troops off the beaches, the organisation of refreshments and facilities provided for returning troops fell to the Royal Army Service Corps (RASC) and local Civil Defence organisations with help from local troops, off duty Wrens, WAAFs and ATS and hundreds of civilian volunteers. Once off the boat, troops who were not in immediate need of medical attention were provided with a snack to eat as they moved along. In some instances the uniforms worn by evacuated troops had been reduced to rags, or had been ditched so they would not sink as they waded out to the boats, and these men were provided with clean, dry clothing. They would then be put on trains to the larger army depots such as Aldershot, Tidworth, Warminster, Bovington and Blandford so they could be rested and re-equipped and the process of rebuilding shattered units could begin.

With the numbers of troops running into tens of thousands, swift and efficient movement from docks to trains was essential and the railways were magnificent. At the height of the evacuation a 'Dunkirk Special' train was leaving Dover Marine station every twenty minutes. To speed up the process and avoid delays caused by stragglers and the opening and closing of doors, the majority of the carriage doors were locked so if the men were to have drinks and snacks their food had to be brought to the open windows of the carriages. It was no mean feat, but this was achieved as volunteers brought buns, sandwiches, fruit and cups of tea by the trayload to the men. The Ramsgate Harbour Fund for Dunkirk Evacuation raised money and received gifts for returned troops from the people of Thanet that enabled food and clothing to be handed out throughout the evacuation. On one day alone members of the Ramsgate Women's Voluntary Service and volunteers cut up 3,000 loaves of bread ready to feed the troops and hundreds of garments were handed out to those who needed them.

Two Kent stations stand out for their work in supplying refreshments for the train loads of evacuated troops, one at Paddock Wood near Tunbridge Wells and the other at Headcorn near Maidstone. Their roles were not created by design, more that fate decreed that these were the most suitable stations on the train lines carrying the 'Dunkirk Specials' to have an eight-minute stop for refreshments to be distributed. Paddock Wood was the larger, it served a

Meat patties being handed and fed to soldiers returned from France by an ATS volunteer helper. One of the soldiers is wearing a souvenir too, 31 May 1940.

town and the local canning factory provided helpers and crates of tin cans to act as receptacles for drinks. The doors of the carriages were locked so local male and female military personnel and civilian volunteers including Scouts and Guides worked in two-hour shifts helping to deliver refreshments and clean socks to the troops through carriage windows and doors.

The Weald village of Headcorn, usually a quiet place with a station staff of three, a station master and two porters, had never known such excitement and activity before or since. Between forty and fifty local women volunteers worked round the clock in eight hour shifts boiling thousands of eggs and cutting up 2,500 loaves of bread to make sandwiches each day. A Royal Army Service Corps unit supplied food and kept nineteen stoves running to provide a constant flow of snacks, tea and coffee distributed to returned troops during their short stops at the station. On one evening 5,000 meat pies, 5,000 sausages and 5,000 rolls were delivered to Headcorn and all had been given away to evacuated troops by the following afternoon. In fact, 6,000 bananas, 6,000 apples, 6,000 oranges, 8,000 eggs, a million tinned sardines were consumed and 100,000 cups of tea were given out over a period of three days. It was estimated that Headcorn provided refreshments for an incredible 145,000 troops during the Dunkirk evacuation.[11]

The troops were also handed postcards at the stations where they boarded or when the train stopped so that they could write a message to their loved ones to let them know they were home safe. These cards were then collected by willing helpers at the stations where the trains stopped and were then sent on. Some soldiers simply threw their cards with written messages out of windows as they passed crowds and these too were carefully collected up and sent on. Many other stations and the communities around them clubbed together, or had donated, gifts of sweets, chocolate and cigarettes for the evacuated soldiers when the 'Dunkirk Specials' stopped at their station.

Many of those who returned from Dunkirk had done so fearing they would be shunned and blamed for the defeat, but the kindness shown to these men, the people who lined fields and roads or stood in their gardens to wave as the trains passed and the slogans painted in whitewash on walls facing the railway such as 'Welcome Home BEF Boys' did so much to lift the mood of the returning troops. Recalling these kindnesses would often bring a tear to the eyes of Dunkirk veterans for the rest of their lives.

Every soldier had his own story from the evacuation, a number were told in local newspapers across the country, the same papers that were soon carrying lists of local men known to have returned, appeals on behalf of families for information about those who were missing, or the sad news of local men who had been killed.

One of the most grateful mothers on the entire south coast was Mrs Earthrowl of Brampton Road, Hampden Park, Eastbourne who had four sons on active service in the same unit of Royal Engineers in France. All made it back home again, not one of them suffering any injury, just blistered feet from their trek to Dunkirk.

Chapter 4

Britain Alone

The whole fury and might of the enemy must very soon be turned on us. Hitler knows that he will have to break us in this island or lose the war.

Winston Churchill, June 1940

On 27 May 1940, the first full day of the evacuation of BEF troops from the beaches of Dunkirk, General Edmund Ironside was appointed Commander-in-Chief, Home Forces with the heavy responsibility of the defence of Britain.

Ironside was always immaculately turned out when in uniform and struck an imposing figure standing 6ft 4in and weighing-in at 17 stone. A former rugby international for Scotland, while at school he had gained the nickname of 'Tiny' and it stuck among his friends for years after and was frequently used as verbal shorthand for the man among his peers in the War Office.

David Low's poignant cartoon **'Very well, alone'** *first published in the* **Evening Standard** *on 18 June 1940, that perfectly captured the mood of the British people as they faced invasion.*

'VERY WELL, ALONE'

Ironside also had an impressive military service to match his stature dating back to the South African War where his adventures behind enemy lines are believed to have been one of the inspirations for John Buchan's fictional hero Richard Hannay in such books as *The Thirty-Nine Steps* (1915). Ironside had risen up the senior ranks of the British Army during the First World War and was given his first brigade command of 99 Infantry Brigade (33rd Division) on the Western Front in 1918. As an old boy of St Andrews and Tonbridge School, he was well suited to lead. His commands included the 17th (Empire), 22nd (Kensington) and 23rd (1st Sportsmen's) Battalions of the Royal Fusiliers and the 1st Battalion, King's Royal Rifle Corps, where there still remained a significant number of former public schoolboys among their officers and non-commissioned officers. He was given his first independent command as part of the Allied Expeditionary Force fighting Bolsheviks in Northern Russia a few months later. The mission, although far from successful, showed Ironside was capable of making the best of a bad job which earned him a knighthood and substantive promotion making him one of the youngest major generals in the British Army.

Having anticipated being appointed commander-in-chief of the British Expeditionary Force (BEF), much to his surprise, Ironside had been appointed Chief of the Imperial General Staff (CIGS) in September 1939. As the BEF fought its retreat to the beaches and began to evacuate in late May 1940 maintaining morale would be the key to success as we prepared to defend our country from invasion.

The view held among many British people at that time was grave but not desperate or defeatist. Reports from Mass Observation correspondents spoke more of the indignation of the British people at the impudence of Hitler and his forces daring to threaten them. It was spirit well evoked by the David Low cartoon published in the *Evening Standard* on 18 June 1940 showing a strong jawed, fully-equipped British soldier wearing a tin hat with rifle in one hand and raised fist in the other facing a raging sea from the shore entitled 'Very well, alone.' The problem was many people were wondering, in the light of the complacency during the 'Phoney War' were we actually too late to do anything to effectively stop an invasion force. H.P. Twyford, the war correspondent of the *Western Morning News* caught the mood of that time well when he wrote:

Anxiety grew and we began to look around. We saw the sandbags with which we had barricaded public and other buildings at the start of the war – what feeble protection they would have been – had begun to rot and were spewing their contents around sodden bases; the trenches which had been dug were crumbling in. These things which seemed sufficient when the war was far away were no longer adequate, something more concrete had to be done and done quickly.[1]

Troops from 15th Scottish Infantry Division filling sandbags on Southend beach with Marine Parade in the background, May 1940.

How right Twyford was, in so many ways. Ironside's predecessor as Commander-in-Chief Home Forces was General Sir Walter Kirke who, along with most other senior military commanders in all forces in 1939, was of the opinion that France would not fall if she was attacked by German forces, and if there were to be attacks on British shores they would come in the form of raiding parties of paratroopers, or troops landed from seaborne assault craft and not a full blown invasion.

A review of the threat was carried out by the Chiefs of Staff (Air Chief Marshal Sir Cyril Newall, Chief of the Air Staff; Admiral of the Fleet Sir Dudley Pound and General Sir John Dill, Vice Chief Imperial General Staff for CIGS) and was presented in a report to the War Cabinet in November 1939 in which it was stated:

…we reached the conclusion that small scale raids, although a possibility, did not constitute a serious threat and that so long as our naval and air forces remained in being and provided the necessary precautions were maintained

effectively, the invasion of this country by means of a combined airborne and seaborne expedition did not constitute a serious threat to our security.[2]

The situation was re-examined in the wake of the German invasion of Denmark and Norway in April 1940. As British troops began to depart from the coast of Scotland for Norway, and mindful of the impact a successful invasion of Holland would have on any potential invasion attempt, a Chiefs of Staff report presented to the War Cabinet in early May recognised the danger now posed by German forces in possession of harbours and airfields in Norway to the north and east coast of Britain, specifically:

Since the German cannot expect to attain complete neutralisation of our naval and air forces it seems improbable that they would attempt airborne or seaborne landings in strength outside the area in which the full weight of their short range bombers and fighters could be brought to bear. Moreover, it is within the area covered by these types of aircraft that German forces could be transported by the shortest sea routes and could land within striking distance of the most vital area of the country – London. We consider the most vulnerable area is between the Wash on the east coast and Folkestone on the south coast.

On this coastline the Thames Estuary is difficult to approach and sufficiently strongly defended to act as a considerable deterrent to a surprise landing. Owing to the necessity of passing through the Straits of Dover and the longer passage from the German or Dutch ports, attacks appear much less likely on the south than on the east coast. Initial landings at Yarmouth, Harwich and Dover are unlikely as these ports are defended, but there are numerous beaches on the east and south east coasts which are suitable for landings.

The area in which the attack is most likely lies between The Wash and Newhaven but the possibility of landing on the east coast further north must be taken into account.[3]

In fact, their greatest concern at that point in time was the vulnerability of the Shetland Islands. Just 230 miles from Stavanger aerodrome and garrisoned by just one Home Defence battalion it was considered:

With this insufficient Garrison a raid might succeed in gaining control of the main islands since only a small force would be needed to effect this, it might land with sufficient supplies to last for some time and might thereafter by supplied intermittently by sea and air transport relying on evasion…The effects on our prestige of enemy troops in occupation of British soil would be serious and far reaching. In addition, the enemy might succeed in destroying the air facilities which would be a serious inconvenience. We think it is not impossible that this landing might be attempted before the main attack as a diversion to distract our attention to the north. We therefore consider that an adequate garrison should be maintained in the Shetlands and in particular at Lerwick and Sumburgh.[4]

General Kirke remained obdurate that an invasion remained unlikely and it was only under some duress that he drew up an anti-invasion scheme dubbed the Julius Caesar Plan, a name some would view as hardly appropriate – after all, Caesar was one of the few to successfully invade and conquer Britain. The warning code 'Julius' was issued to regional commissioners and military commanders in the event of a credible threat of invasion being detected. At that point all armed forces' leave would be cancelled. The counterpart of 'Caesar' would only be issued in the event of imminent invasion, all troops would be issued with live ammunition and placed on alert and parties for the immobilization of harbours and cranes would be placed on stand-by by harbour authorities.

The Julius Caesar Plan was based on a notional enemy invasion force of 20,000 troops landed from seagoing vessels, 4,000 paratroopers and 6,000 trained air landing troops in gliders. If Kirke's plan was to be viable he would require no less than one division in both the Scottish and Northern Command, two in Eastern Command and three divisions to form a reserve. Assuming the invasion force would be expected a good eight hours in advance of landing, troops from Aldershot and Southern Commands would be deployed to aerodromes and potential landing grounds to deal with the paratroopers and gliders as they descended. Any troops establishing themselves after landing would be contained within a military cordon or broken up by armoured troops or mounted cavalry.[5]

The advance troops dropping from the air would be given the task of capturing a suitable port to enable the landing of the bulk of the combat troops from seagoing vessels, along with the necessary supplies of weaponry and ammunition to support them. Particular emphasis was given to the defence of the Humber and Harwich.

Additional artillery batteries from Scottish Command armed with 18 pounders were to provide artillery for the defence of Aberdeen and Dundee and Eastern Command was to provide similar for Lowestoft and Ramsgate. Troops from Scottish, Northern and Eastern Commands were also ordered to allot infantry for the protection of ports and the fixed defences in their respective areas.[6] The plan was confident the ports themselves were protected from attack from the sea by fixed defences; indeed Kirke ordered the construction of 400 concrete pillboxes in key defensive positions along the coast to take place over the next six months from October 1939.[7] Kirke, however, remained convinced any such attack would never arrive as it would be intercepted in the air by the Royal Air Force and cut up at sea by the Royal Navy.

The problem was, even up to May 1940, most ports were not equipped with their allocated firepower. Defence works were sometimes carried out without much forethought, with the embrasures of some of the coastal pillboxes only facing seawards whereas an additional side embrasure would enable a deadly crossfire over any troops attempting to run up the beach. Other defences such as roadblocks were often inadequate or could be simply driven around off road in a tank or tracked vehicle. Critically, since the creation of the Julius Caesar Plan in late 1939, further troops had been deployed abroad, including five of the best trained and equipped Territorial infantry divisions. The 1st Armoured Division had been deployed to France and the 1st Cavalry Division to the Middle East. Of the troops left at Kirke's disposal many had not completed their training or were inexperienced, they only had limited supplies of heavy weaponry and artillery, not to mention a lack of army trucks to transport them. This latter matter was however being addressed with hire arrangements being put in place with local bus companies.

General Kirke had also shown great innovation helping to redress the deficit in home defence manpower, with particular emphasis on tackling the menace of paratroopers. In doing so he also mobilized an armed organisation to keep an eye out for Fifth Columnists, especially those believed to be signalling to the enemy by flashing lights or attempting to engage in sabotage activities, by arguing the case for the creation of Local Defence Volunteers in early May 1940.

Kirk was joined in his efforts by General Sir Robert Gordon-Finlayson, Vice-Chief of the Imperial General Staff. Together they tapped the martial enthusiasm of many old soldiers too old to serve in the armed forces to create an armed organisation. The original idea had been for Kirke to announce the scheme through a radio broadcast but Anthony Eden, the newly appointed Secretary of State for War, who had also taken a personal interest in the creation of the LDV, wanted to do this personally and drafted the text of his broadcast from notes collated by General Kirke on 14 May 1940.

Under the Julius Caesar Plan a number of the Territorial Divisions Kirke had himself helped to raise as the storm clouds of war gathered in the 1930s were deployed to coastal areas. While on the coast these units soon settled into a regular round of parades, inspections, call-outs to deal with mistaken reports of German paratroopers, sightings of enemy troops in the countryside, scares over Fifth Column activities, the construction of improvised road blocks and defences and the guard duties, observation and manning of said defences. While the troops were engaged in these duties it meant there was little or no battle training, nor major exercises being undertaken to train them to fight as part of large combat formations.

If the Phoney War had never become real perhaps the Julius Caesar Plan would have sufficed to satisfy the needs of the War Cabinet and ultimately the country as a whole, but those who had seen the offensive German actions through Poland and Czechoslovakia were convinced Hitler was not going to stop there and felt like banging their heads against the wall when they saw the stasis in the training and the lack of military hardware for home defence units to not just meet, but counter any such attack.

Sir Auckland Geddes, brother of Sir Eric Geddes who had overseen the British government spending cut-backs in the years immediately after the First World War, was also a man who abhorred wastefulness. As a former commissioned officer who had seen active service during both the South African War and the First World War, he was also a skilled politician and diplomat and one of those who were deeply concerned about the state of readiness of Britain's forces and defences. He had good reason too because he was regional commissioner for the South East Region, which included the parts of Britain closest to mainland France. His feelings were articulated in a remarkably frank minute of February 1940:

> *This army business is worse than could have been believed. These second line Territorial divisions are more than a menace. The rubbish we have got here is appalling, and the officers! My God! But the really frightening thing is the way the conscripts are being rotted. No discipline, no training, apparently no equipment. I had no idea Walter Kirke was so bad and the C.I.G.S* (Chief of the Imperial Staff, General Ironside) *doesn't seem to be much better.*
>
> *The spirit of the conscripts is deplorable. They have called us up – now what are they going to do with us?...This phoney war stuff is likely to end with the spring and then look out for squalls...*[8]

The chips were down as the BEF began to evacuate from Dunkirk, Kirke was near retirement, it was felt it was time for a change at the top for military strategy and for the sake of the morale of the nation. Ironside was far better known to the British public, his name alone struck a much-needed chord of confidence among the public much in the way Kitchener had during the First World War when the war leader hero 'KofK' (Kitchener of Khartoum) was appointed Secretary of State for War upon the outbreak of war in 1914. That precedent had not been forgotten by those who had appointed Ironside as

Britain faced invasion in 1940. Times had changed though, Kitchener had been appointed at a time when the people of Britain had never experienced modern warfare, nor had they suffered the huge losses of battles like the Somme and Passchendaele. In 1914 Britain was on a high and was marching confidently to war when Ironside was passed the baton of commander-in-chief Home Forces, in 1940 Britain was a country that had just suffered a major defeat, severe losses and now faced invasion. Let us not forget either that despite Churchill being appointed Prime Minister on 10 May there were still those in government like Lord Halifax and those in positions of influence and power in Britain who were pushing for a peace agreement with Hitler.

The public and media were willing to give Ironside their support, but if high morale and a drive to defend Britain from invasion was to be maintained among its people it would be crucial for Ironside to be proactive in undertaking anti-invasion measures that were visible to the public as soon as possible. Ironside and his team of advisers rapidly got to work, and Britain was soon feeling like it was on an anti-invasion footing as soldiers were set to work filling sandbags and digging rifle pits and trenches all around the coast. The 251,000 coils of Dannert concertina wire and 100 tons of standard British barbed wire issued in May also kept wiring parties busy on the defences.

A rolling programme installing heavy anti-boat booms at the entrances of important ports such as Harwich, Dover, Plymouth and Rosyth and at the mouths of rivers such as the Thames or the Humber, was begun to prevent penetration by enemy vessels. Anti-shipping booms of wire netting were also installed off many beaches and sea minefields were laid off-shore by the Royal Navy. On 31 May orders were given for all signposts to be taken down, milestones uprooted and all names of streets, railway stations and even notice boards bearing the name of the town or village had to be obliterated in an attempt to confuse any invading enemies. In many coastal areas the sale of maps and guides was prohibited too, many people turned out their old maps and burned them to make sure they did not fall into enemy hands.

A number of parishes buried their irreplaceable historic records along with the church plate with tragic results when they were recovered later and discovered to have been damaged by water or damp. Even after many places thought they had taken every precaution to delete any indication of their place name from public areas, they would be foiled in their efforts when they looked down and saw the name of a local builder or company, including the place name on drain and manhole covers in the locality.

Throughout the period of the Dunkirk evacuation Sunday church services were receiving some of their largest congregations in living memory, the British people knew only too well they would be next in Hitler's sights for invasion. Churchill knew the situation was critical and was also only too aware Britain needed strong leadership to crystallise their resolve to carry on. It was no time to waiver and he delivered what had proved to be one of the most powerful speeches, not only of his career, but in British history on 4 June 1940, the crux of the speech being:

> We shall go on to the end. We shall fight in France, we shall fight on the seas and oceans, we shall fight with growing confidence and growing strength in the air, we shall defend our island, whatever the cost may be. We shall fight on the beaches, we shall fight on the landing grounds, we shall fight in the fields and in the streets, we shall fight in the hills; we shall never surrender…

Evacuations, Aliens and Restrictions

Ironside's primary concern was to ensure the coast was defended against invasion. He began this process by attempting to clear his canvas in preparation for this by instigating a new round of evacuations of children, pregnant mothers and vulnerable people away from coastal areas considered

Waving off evacuees from Vauxhall Station, Great Yarmouth as the country faces threat of invasion, 2 June 1940.

liable to enemy attack or an invasion attempt. The bulk of children, some 47,000 in number, were evacuated from eighteen towns and 'danger areas' along the east coast aboard ninety-seven specially chartered trains bound for reception areas in the west of England and the Midlands on Sunday, 2 June 1940. Children were also evacuated from southern England and many of those who had returned home from their first evacuation in 1939 had to be evacuated again. By the end of July over 200,000 children had been evacuated, some towns in Kent and along the East Anglian Coast had evacuated 40 per cent of their populations.

As the situation deteriorated in France, Britain was increasingly gripped by fears of a so-called Fifth Column of enemy agents, saboteurs and collaborators who were spying on Britain's defences and military activities and reporting what they saw back to their German masters. A further concern was that the members of the Fifth Column would rise up to cause havoc among the British forces and do all they could to assist German invasion forces.

The concern was far from a new one. In the late 1930s newspapers and magazines had run a variety of stories of Nazi infiltration in Britain from German Hitler Youth bicycle tours of Britain being a cover for intelligence gathering – dubbed in the press as 'Spyclists'[9] to thousands of German women being specially trained to become 'servant girl spies' in high class hotels, restaurants and the households of military officers in Britain so they could listen in to gossip to glean intelligence about morale and whatever information they could that would benefit Nazi intelligence. Then, as people began to flee the Nazi heel in Europe and arrived in Britain as refugees, further concerns were raised that spies were entering Britain mingled amongst them.[10]

A particular problem was spotted by the Chief Constable of Devon in September when shortly after war was declared 250 so called 'aliens', 60 of whom were 'enemy aliens' (people of German or Austrian birth) had moved into the Torbay area. The number was rapidly increasing too with 400 arrivals, 120 of whom were 'enemy aliens' arriving within a few more days. Perturbed by this concentration and their close proximity to the coast, the chief constable alerted MI5. Guy Liddell, head of MI5's B Branch (the branch concerned specifically with home security) offered the suggestion that he simply refuse them permits and pointed out the chief constable was also empowered to prevent them taking up residence at any vulnerable points. Liddell was also able to reassure him tribunals were being established to assess the danger each 'enemy alien' residing in Britain might present.[11]

That same month the Aliens Department of the Home Office established some 120 tribunals to consider the risk presented by the 73,353 German and Austrian 'enemy aliens' aged over 16 in Britain at that time. The levels of risk were broken down into three categories. Category 'A' were considered the most dangerous, of whom there were 560, who were interned within days of the outbreak of hostilities. Category 'B' covered 6,782 people who were not considered an immediate threat and exempt from internment but subject to restrictions, specifically:

1. They should report daily in person to a police station
2. They shall not make any use of a motor vehicle (other than public transport) or any bicycle.
3. They shall not be out of doors between the hours of 8pm and 6am.

They were also forbidden to have in their possession a camera, film camera, sketch book, wireless transmitter, telescope, binoculars, a bicycle, nautical charts or maps and were also forbidden to keep carrier pigeons. Category 'C' was applied to 64,200, most of them refugees who had fled Nazi Germany, were judged harmless, retained their liberty and initially were subject to no different laws or controls than any other UK resident.[12]

A Home Security meeting on the subject of naval bases as protected areas held on 10 November 1939 agreed the ports of the Firth, Harwich, Humber, Dover, Plymouth, Portsmouth, Medway, Clyde, Portland, Blyth, Dundee, Falmouth, Mersey, Milford Haven, the Thames and the Tyne were all to be declared 'protected areas' with immediate effect.

This meant that the residence of aliens in category B was to be prohibited unless a permit had been granted for the individual by the local chief constable. If any category C aliens caused concern they could be placed in category B at the discretion of the chief constable and no new alien residents were to be allowed unless they had a special permit. Chief constables could also apply for an order to have resident aliens removed from their district if they deemed it necessary.[13]

In response to the mounting concerns over invasion scares and in an attempt to destroy the Fifth Column, male 'enemy aliens' (those of German or Austrian nationality) in Category B, residents in coastal areas between Scotland and Hampshire were rounded up and interned on 11 May 1940. This was extended yet further to all Category B aliens in Britain on 17 May.

Churchill shared Ironside's concerns, decisive action was required so internments under Defence Regulation 18b were further extended on 27 May to include 'enemy alien' women. A concession was made that permitted them to take their children with them and they would soon be shipped over to detention camps on the Isle of Man.

Ironside was also deeply concerned by the reports he had received, and the widely held belief among the military, police and civilian population, that despite all the internments a shadowy Fifth Column was still active in Britain and ready to spring into action in the event of an invasion. He was not alone, the Eastern Command area, covering the eastern seaboard of England from Norfolk to Essex believed at that time to be the most likely to be targeted for invasion, was understandably particularly sensitive. MI5 B Branch head Guy Liddell recorded on 27 May:

Brigadier Hawes of Eastern Command called late in the evening, the GOC Eastern Command [Lieutenant General Sir Guy Williams] *is apparently extremely worried about Fifth Column activities in his area. He picked up a map which was given him by the Lincolnshire police which seemed to indicate some plan for parachutists in the area of the Wash. GOC thinks it is of paramount importance that the Fifth Column should be interned immediately…He himself is prepared to go to the Prime Minister if necessary.*[14]

Even lovers' signs and the marks made by Boy Scouts and Girl Guide trackers on telegraph poles became viewed with suspicion during the Fifth Column scares, concerns that rattled up the line to General Ironside, Commander-in-Chief, Home Forces who wrote on 31 May 1940:

Fifth Column reports coming in from everywhere. A man with an armband on and a swastika pulled up near an important aerodrome in Southern Command. Important telegraph poles marked, suspicious men moving at night all over the country. We have the right of search and I have put piquets on all over the place to-night. Perhaps we shall catch some swine.[15]

On 5 June 1940 an order was made with the intention of clearing the last Germans and Austrians out of any area of potential invasion. Any 'aliens' who remained in Folkestone or Margate were given three days' notice to leave those towns under a new Home Office Order which prevented their presence within 20 miles of the coast. A Ministry of Home Security Order was also passed at the same time prohibiting holiday camps anywhere within 10 miles of the east coast of England and Scotland, on the south coast east of Hengisbury Head, Hampshire and in the Isle of Wight. The order also empowered chief constables to prohibit any camp within a mile of naval, military or air force establishment, aerodromes and aircraft, munitions and explosives factories.[16]

When Italy declared war on Britain on 10 June 1940 Churchill was in no mood for procrastination and it is said he simply barked 'Collar the lot!' and the 4,000 known members of the Italian Fascist Party resident in Britain were arrested and interned, along with Italians aged between 16 and 30 who had lived in the UK for less than twenty years, regardless of their political affiliations. In seaside areas this included many perfectly innocent Italians who had run ice cream shops, worked as chefs and serving staff in some of the top hotels or worked as circus entertainers. They included the famous Blackpool Tower Circus clown Charlie Cairoli who had appeared at Circus Krone in Munich in a special performance for Hitler early in 1939, after which he was personally presented with a watch by the Führer. When he heard the news of the outbreak of the war just a few months later he walked to the end of the North Pier and threw the watch in the sea; he wanted nothing to do with war but like all the other aliens who had not lived in England long enough and were in the age catchment Charlie was interned too.[17]

Despite the internments Fifth Column scares continued, the problem now was identifying suspected members of the Fifth Column who were still at large. Guy Liddell noted:

Some of the units appear to have prepared a kind of Black List of their own. When the balloon goes up they intend to round up or shoot all these individuals. The position is so serious that something of a very drastic kind will have to be done.[18]

Through June and July the Eastern Command security officer and his team of intelligence officers, backed by the GOC, contacted the chief constables across the Eastern Command area to acquire information about local people who the police considered likely to be involved in Fifth Column activities and to collaborate with the enemy in the event of an invasion.[19] Arrests soon took place, in one instance they arrested a man who turned out to have served as an officer with a fine record during the First World War and kept him and his wife under detention for seven days without any justification except he had a German sounding name. The problem Liddell faced was Prime Minister Churchill had the Eastern Command lists brought to his attention and was enquiring why the people had not been arrested already.[20] A compromise was reached and on 24 August 1940 a Home Office circular authorised all regions to undertake the compilation of their own suspect lists.[21]

On 13 June 1940 it was announced that the Control of Noise Defence Order banned the ringing of church bells and henceforth they would only be rung by the military or the police to give warning of invasion to the civilian population. Three days later fifteen million copies of the leaflet '*If the Invader Comes*' were ready for distribution to every household. The leaflet offered practical suggestions for members of the public to help foil invasion forces such as not to believe or spread rumours, be observant and report anything suspicious to the nearest police station with details of time and place. They were to be aware the enemy might send paratroopers disguised in police and

ARP uniforms and, if unsure of the uniformed person giving orders, to check with officials they knew before acting on them.

An appeal was also made for the public not to make pleasure trips to a number of locations along parts of the east coast, a request that rapidly spread from the Wash to Sussex and was extended to include much of the coast in an unbroken line up to Berwick-upon-Tweed soon after.

Ironside's 'Coastal Crust'

As the new round of evacuations and weeding out of 'enemy aliens' was taking place Ironside and his staff toiled long hours to assess and update the defences of Britain and just one week after his appointment as C-in-C Home Forces he was able to report to the War Cabinet on 4 June 1940 that the preparations for defence against airborne and seaborne attack were proceeding as rapidly as possible in all commands.

A reconnaissance had been completed of all beaches on the east, south-east and south coasts from Fraserburgh to Southampton. On beaches considered suitable for the landing of troops and vehicles work had commenced on the construction of pillboxes, wiring and contracts had been placed with contractors for the construction of anti-tank obstacles. The civil contractors employed in this work were in close touch with chief engineers of all commands

Men of the Royal Navy Coast Watch manning a Lewis Gun emplacement on a cliff top in Devon, 1940.

and through the latter with experienced Royal Engineer officers who were supervising the work being undertaken. A total of 50,000 anti-tank mines had been issued and orders placed for a further 200,000. A supply of beach lighting sets that would illuminate the enemy attempting to make a landing under the cover of darkness had been arranged and defensive measures covering the immobilisation of facilities at ports on the east and south coasts from Peterhead to Newhaven were also established.

Potential landing grounds for gliders and aircraft had also been reconnoitred and assessment of how best to render them unusable had been completed. Work started on 90 per cent of possible landing grounds within 5 miles of certain ports between Yarmouth and Newhaven and 40 per cent of such grounds between the Tyne and Humber. Contracts had also been placed for similar work to commence in Scottish and southern commands. The Air Ministry were carrying out similar work within 5 miles of all aerodromes in the eastern counties. Preparations for demolition of bridges on roads providing access from selected ports on the east coast from Aberdeenshire to Kent were 90 per cent complete and temporary roadblocks were 80 per cent complete.[22]

The Royal Navy supplied 150 6-inch guns that had been removed from First World War cruisers and stored in its arsenals. The guns needed to be reconditioned but they provided the much-needed firepower for a further forty-seven batteries, each consisting of two 6-inch guns that were installed on the east coast from Amble, Northumberland to Newhaven, East Sussex. Sixteen of these batteries at the time of Ironside's report were already completed, the remainder would be completed approximately a week later. Extra guns were also supplied for the defences on the rivers Tyne and Humber as well as at the ports of Lowestoft and Harwich.

Roadblocks were also being prepared in every command, some constructed in concrete, some improvised from locally available materials enhanced by defensive posts or rails and a further 291,000 coils of Dannert wire and 2,000 tons of British wire. In addition to roadblocks aimed against vehicles, work was carried out in conjunction with the Ministry of Transport on many stretches of wide arterial road on which hostile aircraft might land, to render them unusable by the erection upright posts with wires stretched between them or by blocks on alternate sides of the road some 300 yards apart.[23]

That was the positive news about the efforts that had been made about the fixed defences, but when it came down to fighting an invader the news was not so good, for the British Army was left woefully short of weapons after so much had been lost at Dunkirk. Fifty thousand Mills bombs had been distributed to commands on the basis of 3,000 per division.[24] This may sound impressive but consider that the British Army had fifteen infantry divisions on home service in June 1940, eight of these were allocated to anti-invasion defences between The Wash and Hampshire. Each division was made up of three infantry brigades with three battalions in each brigade and approximately 900 fighting men in each battalion – that would mean that only one in three soldiers would be armed with a hand grenade.

Ironsides' memorandum reported twenty 6-pounder guns were available to be mounted on 30cwt lorries; 3-pounder, 12-pounder and 4-inch guns were also mounted on lorries and issued to all commands, seventy-six of which would be available in the next two weeks. Some of the stop gap measures put forward under anti-tank weaponry were frankly embarrassing, Ironside tagged on his report: 'Instructions for making Molotov Cocktails [petrol bombs] have been issued to all commands.'[25]

In the summary of Home Defence forces of 13 June 1940 the news was no better, revealing that the British Army was left with just 163 medium and heavy guns, 50 2-pounder anti-tank guns, 37 armoured cars and 500 tanks to defend these shores.[26] All munitions factories were working flat out but it would take time, weeks and months for these deficits to be made up.

Royal Artillery crews manning 9.2 inch coastal defence guns on the seafront at Felixstowe, 1939.

The Dreyer Survey of Coastal Defences

The distinguished Royal Navy officer Admiral Sir Frederic Dreyer, one of the foremost experts in naval gunnery in the early days of HMS *Dreadnought*, the man who instigated the Royal Naval Tactical School at Portsmouth and former deputy chief of the Naval staff, was appointed to Ironside's staff to survey the British coastline and to identify, from a naval perspective, which beaches would be most suitable for invasion landings. Special attention was paid to extant defences and beaches that could sustain crossings by enemy tanks and armoured fighting vehicles.

British military commanders were confident the English Channel and Dover Strait were well mined and German commanders were well aware of that fact too, and with the Royal Navy still in good shape and working in co-operation with the Royal Air Force a German invasion fleet would have been neutralised before it made landfall on the south coast. Following this train of thought, British military strategists believed if an invasion force was going have any hope of gaining a toe hold on the British coast it would be launched from one or more of the big ports in the occupied Netherlands and would aim to make landings on the most viable beaches on the coast closest to them – somewhere on Britain's east coast between the Wash and the Thames Estuary.

Admiral Dreyer was despatched to conduct his survey with a small team of two staff officers on 27 May 1940. They kept Ironside updated with regular interim reports and completed their preliminary survey from Lyme Regis in West Dorset on the south coast, to Berwick-upon-Tweed on the borders of Northumberland and high up on the north east coast of Scotland less than a month later on 18 June.

Dreyer's survey provides a fascinating account of the coastal defences of Britain in late May and June 1940 and it is worthwhile revisiting some of the points he raised from the borders to East Anglia, remembering that these are the front line 'crust' defences we had to stand against a potential invasion force.

The last harbour Dreyer surveyed at the top of the north east coast was Berwick, which he concluded was sufficiently protected by the two naval 6-inch guns on the north end of Spittal beach. The Holy Island area surrounded by rocks and difficult channels could, however, compel tanks and AFVs to make their landing at the more accessible Ross Links golf course to the south, or at Cheswick golf course in the north to attack Berwick.

The coastline from Berwick to Blyth did have some vulnerable areas such as the beach under Bamburgh Castle, Embleton Bay and it was recommended barbed wire entanglements should be installed and mined. However, these locations were judged to be such a distance from any significant objective that the combination of rocky coastline, where landings by small boat parties would only be possible in some areas, beach defences and natural obstacles such as the rivers inland would hinder the progress of forces to such a degree an attempted landing made there was considered highly unlikely. The only significant numbers of troops Dreyer recommended should be deployed in this area were two battalions of infantry with artillery support for the defence of Druridge Bay.

Blyth's northerly beach area was judged vulnerable to tank landings as far north as the River Blyth, but the sand banks would have proved an admirable natural obstacle. There were two 6-inch naval guns on Amble golf links, but it was noted the field of fire was limited by Coquet Island, a slag heap and a colliery so it was suggested the guns be re-sited further north. Fears over enemy seaplane landings on the Rivers Aln and Coquet could also be tackled with the installation of machine-gun posts.

In his survey of the submarine base and its surrounding defences at Blyth Dreyer noted two 6-inch guns were mounted in a small concrete fort manned by the Royal Artillery. The submarines in Blyth harbour were under the protection of two newly installed 2-pounder anti-aircraft guns. The crews were expected to become proficient by regular gun drills, at a rate of fire of between 6 to 8 rounds per minute, and he suggested competitions should be staged between the local gunners to help achieve this.

The defences at Seaton Sluice beach consisted of a sandbag emplacement for two sections of riflemen and two machine guns on the bluff to the north of the sluice. To the south the beach was impassable for landing due to rocks. There was also an anti-tank rifle to cover the coast road. Two 6-inch naval guns were also sited in the centre of the beach under Lieutenant Barty RNR who respectfully requested an issue of khaki battledress for his ratings from the Royal Navy Barracks at Devonport who had been deployed there to operate the guns. Dreyer agreed and recommended that all ratings manning coastal guns should have the khaki battledress. He also supported the lieutenant's request for more ammunition for his forty-seven rifles, which at the time of the survey only had 100 rounds each and the sixteen pistols that had been supplied with just thirty-six rounds a piece. A further frustration was that the Seaton beach outpost was out on a limb; there was no field telephone and messages between its officer in charge and the Tynemouth defences were having to be driven to and fro by the beach unit truck.

Further south Dreyer considered the beaches at Whitley Bay and Cullercoats and the Long Sands at Tynemouth which were all suitable for enemy landings. They had 'good tank country inland', but he duly noted all three were covered by the fixed defences at Tynemouth and the southern fort at Blyth but would require anti-personnel wire and anti-tank obstacles and at their exits.

The problem envisaged by Dreyer at South Shields Bay was the mile long sandy beach which had neither cliffs nor dunes behind it and could easily fall prey to enemy armoured vehicles making a landing there and then using the macadamised coast roads that ran parallel with the beach or the nearby railway line to make rapid progress inland. Dreyer recommended the beach be thoroughly wired and mined, the ramps blocked and further mines and wire installed on the beach roads and promenade. He also suggested the installation of 20mm Hispano-Suiza guns at each end of the beach for the dual purpose of attacking aircraft or enemy armour. These were in addition to the seven 6-inch guns at the Tynemouth gun batteries, a 4-inch gun and two 12-pounders.[27]

Dreyer was very much of the opinion that most of the beaches of the east coast would benefit from the entrances being blocked, wire entanglements installed and minefields laid. In his comments regarding the north east coast harbours such as Seaham, Sunderland, Scarborough, Hartlepool and the mouth of the Tees and Humber, Dreyer suggested these could be protected by booms and coastal artillery. Harbour entrances could also be blocked, in the event of an invasion emergency, by ships sunk for that purpose and explosive charges placed on piers and similar facilities ready to be blown up to prevent use of the docks by the enemy. He did, however, express particular concern that the port of Bridlington had two stone and concrete piers and a heavy-duty crane that could prove invaluable to invading forces if they fell into enemy hands before they could be destroyed.

Dreyer's greatest area of concern was the coastline of East Anglia: Norfolk, Suffolk and Essex down to the Thames Estuary. Areas of the coast where there were natural or man-made harbours with beach surfaces suitable for tanks and AFVs, that also had high water six hours after high water at Dover, offering the crucial window of opportunity to enable the landing of significant invasion forces, were identified at: The Broomways, Foulness Island, Southend-on-Sea; Harwich, Essex; south of the pier at Felixstowe; Bawdsey; Slaughden near Aldeburgh and Lowestoft in Suffolk; Great Yarmouth, Weybourne Hope, Stubborn Sands in the Heacham area and King's Lynn in Norfolk and the coastline across the Wash from Gibraltar Point to Donna Nook in Lincolnshire.[28]

In this latter area Dreyer encountered a misunderstanding between a staff officer representing GOC Northern Command and a naval officer representing Flag Officer, Humber whereby the misapprehension had occurred that the beaches between Mablethorpe and Grimsby were unsuitable for tank and

AFV landings. Dreyer corrected the misunderstanding by detailing how enemy armoured vehicles could easily be landed there for the period of an hour either side of high water. He also recommended that this 25-mile stretch of 'very vulnerable beach' should be protected by four 6-inch guns; two mounted at Mablethorpe and two at Gibraltar Point. Mindful that supplies of the naval guns were rapidly becoming depleted – they were really supposed to arm merchant vessels – he suggested field guns could be obtained from the field artillery and deployed in sandbag emplacements on the beaches or even for mobile deployment, mounted in lorries.[29]

Dreyer's greatest concerns were expressed about the beach landing areas of the Norfolk coast, the nearest point of contact for enemy landing craft approaching from the Netherlands. His observations were recorded in his memorandum for the east coast from Great Yarmouth to The Wash submitted to Ironside on 3 June 1940:

Passing North of Great Yarmouth. The beach of which is wired, there is a gap opposite to Ormesby St Margaret and there is another opposite Hemsby and a third opposite Winterton. These must be blocked with concrete obstacles and mined.

Passing North towards Cromer there are a large number of gaps in the sand dunes which should be completely blocked with concrete obstacles, dannert wire and mines. These gaps exist between the Hundred Stream and Mundesley.

Inland the road crossings of the North Walsham and Dilham Canal about 5 miles inland should be prepared for instant demolition.

Passing north of Bacton Green the beach itself is suitable for the landing of infantry and light vehicles, but the cliffs vary in height from 20 to 100 feet and it would appear that thoroughly filling the gaps therein will meet the situation, particularly in view of the large number of German mines laid out to seaward in the Would and the Haisborough Gat.

There is also a gap in Overstrand which must be filled in.

The small pier at Cromer should have a large section removed and the exits from the beach for vehicles or pedestrians should be blocked with concrete and dannert wire.

Between Cromer and Sheringham there are two gaps in the cliffs which must be filled in as above.

Between Sheringham and Cley, which includes Weybourne Hope, there are 7 gaps in the cliffs or dunes. These must be completely blocked as above.

Major Crofton-Diggins who had taken part with Col. Spicer R.M. in the very valuable reconnaissance of the coast between Lowestoft and King's Lynn and whose advice I have had the great advantage of having, informs me that during their reconnaissance they consulted local opinion. A retired

Major living at Stiffkey who has spent years in small craft off this coast and in wildfowling, stated that the weather could change on this coast from a flat calm to a very nasty sea inside an hour with practically no warning.

Other local opinion obtained entirely corroborated this. All also agreed that the marshy hinterland would necessitate the use of light bridging equipment by any invader as the channels are numerous, steep sided and deep.

The sands of north of Wells-next-the-Sea would at low water provide very good landing grounds for aircraft.

With regard to landing of tanks on the beach between Weybourne Hope and King's Lynn the reconnaissance has shown that there are 3 areas where this could be done.

1. *Weybourne Hope to the Hood. The blocking of gaps would greatly impede this.*
2. *Stubborn Sand off Heacham. The blocking of the two roads to Heacham must be very completely carried out with concrete and mine and dannert wire*
3. *King's Lynn is vulnerable to attack. The navigational marks in the channels have been removed, but local information is to the effect that up to September 1939 a Dutch company ran small steamers to King's Lynn on a regular service. The officers were changed frequently and thus a large number must know the channels.*

The Harbourmaster was of the opinion, however, that even the local pilots would not attempt to enter at night as the lights are extinguished. In this connection it is also of interest to note that a German cable ship was observed before the war to be cruising inside the Sheringham Bank off Weybourne. This calls attention to the fact that the Norwich Command (18 Div) must close all gaps and roads mentioned in this memo and at the same time be prepared for an infantry attack on any portion of the coast.[30]

The value and respect for well-informed local knowledge is well demonstrated by the reaction of Nore Command immediately following the initial reconnaissance when Commander Burton RN, Resident Naval Officer, King's Lynn was sent a letter by Captain W. Croucher DSC, the Lynn dock master on 2 June 1940 with reference to his recent interview regarding the possibility of landing enemy troops at King's Lynn in which he stated:

I have had a good opportunity of studying the various types of Dutch built vessels…The vessels are shallow draught with an average speed of 10 knots and fitted with every modern device for accurate navigation and the masters know every little channel from Cromer to King's Lynn and Boston. With this knowledge I do not think any attempt would be made to land troops on the river front until they had taken the town by surprise, by landing troops along the coast line from Cromer to Hunstanton and thence to King's Lynn...'

The concerns over the expertise of German steamer captains and their knowledge of the Norfolk coast was also voiced in a letter from another man who had been interviewed during the reconnaissance, Mr A. Palmer of the shipbrokers Garland and Flexman of King's Lynn. Commander Burton passed the letters directly to the Flag Officer in Command, Harwich who took the comment very seriously and wasted no time arranging the extension of the auxiliary patrol to the Wash using Lowestoft Auxiliary Patrol vessels based in King's Lynn, minuting the decision on 8 June 1940.

Admiral Dreyer returned to the east coast defences on 13 June and was met at King's Lynn by Major Crofton-Diggins and they undertook a further inspection from the Wash to Bacton. Dreyer asked that an experiment be conducted to see if a tank could be landed on the west shore of The Wash between Boston and Gibraltar Point. If this was possible, he concluded, tanks would also be able to land at Heacham and New Hunstanton either side of high water. The beaches from Brancaster to Cley could stand a tank landing, but the marshy background to the beaches would scupper any chances of a major tank advance. In fact, large areas of these marshes between the coast road and the sea had been allowed to flood as an anti-invasion measure shortly before his visit.

Dreyer concluded his reconnaissance report with an invasion scenario and his suggested methods to counter such a threat:

The Wash is in my opinion a dangerous area which we must be prepared to deny the enemy. Without indulging in 'the painting of pictures' it is not unreasonable to consider the case of the enemy landing on the beach North of Skegness and simultaneously on the Southwold reaches and rushing the Wash with large bodies of troops in fast motor boats, landing at King's Lynn and Boston and opening the Boston sluices to flood the country in a southerly direction thus impeding lateral movement of the defenders. The situation to be still further complicated by a diversionary landing well to the northward.

I strongly recommend that the Admiralty may be asked to consider the taking of immediate action to remove all navigational marker buoys and Lightships in the Wash and the laying of a minefield and also 'Table Cloth Nets' (latter to impede fast Motor Boats). I understand that at present the use of the Wash by shipping is practically nil...An enemy landing in the Wash would be a difficult operation but it is feasible. It is more probable that the operation would be a raid or a diversion, than the Wash area would be the main objective of an expedition.

A minefield was laid and a boom placed across the wide Lynn Deeps channel that leads into the Wash on 5 July 1940. This left only the narrower Boston Deeps where from that time all traffic would enter and leave the Wash and a pilot became necessary.

In Dreyer's summary submitted at the end of his survey on 18 June he suggested a scenario whereby German invasion forces could attempt their invasion using foul weather to evade detection by RAF and Royal Navy sea patrols. Speed would be the key and a lot would depend on getting tanks off the beach before air attacks could be launched against them. Dreyer also reflects the deep concern at the time over the Fifth Column by suggesting that enemy agents ashore would immobilise all telephone communications and overpower Royal Naval coast watchers and coast guards. He also pointed out it was possible that invasion forces in armoured vehicles and tanks could just roll over barbed wire entanglements, but the mines and fire from pillboxes would delay them. Dreyer advised that beach artillery should not open up too soon lest they give their positions away to enemy aircraft and guns. He also suggested there was a pressing need for a supply of instantaneous fuses for high explosive shells and shrapnel shells to attack German aircraft landing on the beaches.

At the same time that Dreyer was undertaking his survey of the English coast the Commander Royal Engineers, Scottish Command was conducting the beach reconnaissance north of the border and began issuing instructions for the implementation of the construction of beach defences commencing with the high priority sections of coast at Wick and East Lothian in early June. The scheme, using the combination of pillboxes, defended ports, coastal batteries, anti-tank cubes, minefields and wire, very much mirrored the defences employed on the English coast. The construction of the fixed defences was to be placed in the hands of civilian contractors appointed through local authorities. If there was any hint of tardiness by local authorities the military had authority to bypass local bureaucracy, the message from Scottish Command being: 'The essential thing is to use common sense and get on with the job as soon as possible.'[31]

By the time Ironside received Dreyer's first full survey France was just days away from signing an armistice with Germany on 22 June. Ironside was faced with possible invasion attempts on both the east and the south coasts and, armed with Dreyer's reports of the coastal reconnaissance, believed he was leaving nothing to chance. On 20 June the coastal strip from the Wash to Rye extending 20 miles inland was declared a 'defence area'. Those who resided in the catchment would be subject to a curfew between the hours of 5pm and 5am. Regional commissioners were given the power to control movement within defence areas in their regions to avoid blockages caused by non-essential traffic. All persons entering the area would be liable to be stopped and questioned by the police or military authorities as to their reasons for being there; holidaymakers, pleasure journeys and stays in holiday bungalows were banned. The official notices for this order took pains to point out that if those who were stopped were unable to produce evidence of their being engaged on business or other similar good reasons they would be asked to leave.[32]

In early July a government order declared that in the event of invasion no private cars or motorcycles would be allowed on the roads in the districts affected. Furthermore, in the event of an invasion all vehicles not involved in war service, or for the benefit of the community in the area invaded, would have to be put out of action by the removal of working parts which should be handed over to the appropriate authorities. Notices warned: 'If this order is disobeyed drastic measures will be taken to enforce it.'[33]

The defence area was further extended along with its draconian restrictions from Bexhill-on-Sea in East Sussex to Portland, Dorset on 6 July.[34] Restrictions were extended further still on 8 July when the Southern Regional Commissioner ordered the closing of the sea beaches of Hampshire and the Isle of Wight and the Dorset beaches from the Hampshire border to Lytchett Bay, Poole including Southsea and Bournemouth, to all except those in possession of military passes. A curfew from 10pm to 4am was also imposed on Eastbourne sea front. The public notices of the new defence areas did, however, take pains to point out:

These steps do not imply that there is any intention of evacuating the resident population, nor is it desired that residents should evacuate South Coast towns. On the contrary, the Government are anxious that people should remain in their homes, particularly in defended ports such as Portsmouth and Southampton. People in the defence area can best assist the defence of the country by carrying on with their ordinary occupation.[35]

As the coastal strip locked down Ironside began the construction of a defensive 'crust' from the south east coast and up along the east coast. This was a massive undertaking whereby miles of barbed wire defences were uncoiled and fixed, tens of thousands of mines were laid and thousands more were on order. Behind the minefields were evenly spaced lines of 13-ton anti-tank blocks designed to impede enemy tanks and steep anti-tank ditches.

Sir John Dill, Chief of the Imperial General Staff, had also placed a paper before the War Cabinet on 15 June that argued the case for the use of poison gas against enemy forces landing on British beaches. Any decision to deploy chemical weapons even in the defence of Britain against invading forces would not be taken lightly. Dill himself pointed out the world view of Britain's high moral standing and the sympathy Britain was receiving would be diminished, especially our relationship with America, if we resorted to chemical weapons.[36] The pro and con debate was nipped in the bud by Churchill who minuted to the Chiefs of Staff on 30 June:

> *Supposing lodgements were affected on our coast, there would be no better points for application of mustard [gas] than those beaches and lodgements… Everything should be brought up to the highest pitch of readiness, but the question of actual deployment must be settled by the Cabinet.*[37]

Emergency gun batteries were to provide the most formidable component of the fixed defences along the coast. Many of these consisted of twin batteries armed with 6-inch naval guns, further 4-inch gun batteries were installed to protect beaches and 12-pounder Q.F. (quick-firing) guns to cover harbour entrances, very much as per Dreyer's recommendations. Admiral Dreyer visited a number of the new batteries established along the east coast in late

A crew from 177 Heavy Battery, Royal Artillery, Fort Crosby near Liverpool firing a 4-inch gun, August 1940.

summer 1940. After expressing his satisfaction at seeing these emplacements, in his report Dreyer emphasised his view that their best location is among sand dunes where they could be completely and carefully camouflaged from aircraft and surface vessels. He was, however, concerned about the lack of fire control apparatus for the gun emplacements on the beaches.

He also expressed his opinion that the batteries did not offer enough protection to the gun crew and that there should be overhead as well as all round vertical protection against the splinters from bombs. This situation was soon rectified with covered casemates.

Around these batteries were also created series of infantry defences consisting of barbed wire, weapons pits, slit trenches and pillboxes. At the height of construction during the summer of 1940 some 18,000 pillboxes were built in key positions for the defence of Britain.[38]

To maximise the effectiveness of pillboxes it was believed they should have an element of surprise and those on sea fronts and coastal areas that could be subject to off-shore survey by enemy vessels and reconnaissance aircraft came in for particular attention from the army camouflage teams. With instructors like the surrealist artist Roland Penrose, the author of *The Home Guard Manual of Camouflage*, who had made a study of colour combinations and structure based on various natural surroundings, and Oliver Messel (who ran the Eastern Command Camouflage School at The Assembly House in Norwich) who had years of experience in theatre and film set design and creation, there were some highly original and effective approaches to the work.

Pillboxes were disguised as a host of structures to blend in with the surroundings, using such methods as covering their exterior with cladding of local stone to painting them to look like petrol stations, cottages, summerhouses, florists, newsagents, public toilets and bus stops, fairground attractions and ice cream stalls.

By late June so much cement had been used in the construction of fixed defences there was a national shortage and contractors were advised by the War Office to use more sand in the mix or replace it with other materials where possible. There was also a great deal of ingenuity shown when official supplies were lacking in the construction of roadblocks.

Troops in Brighton deployed beach huts filled with shingle across roadways to frustrate enemy vehicular access. Rows of cars, redundant agricultural machinery and even old traction engines from wreckers' yards were also used and lined up across open fields to prevent glider landings and hinder enemy armoured fighting vehicles. Areas of open ground and sea marshes had anti-glider posts erected across them.

Beach huts filled with shingle used as anti-invasion road-blocks in Brighton, 1940.

After pointing out the enemy might use seaside pleasure piers as landing stages for troopships Admiral Dreyer recommended all piers should at least have charges and detonators placed upon them with a sentry so that in the event of invasion they could have gaps blown in them to foil the enemy. The commands on the east and south coasts went further and ordered the majority of piers to be disassembled or have sections removed to prevent passage of the enemy across them. In Great Yarmouth a gap was blown in Britannia Pier and torpedo warheads were installed in the seaward end of the pier to deal with any enemy ship attempting to dock there. The idea was undoubtedly good, but the switch for the electrical firing connection to fire the torpedoes was installed beside the switch that operated the beach floodlights. Consequently, it was always a tense moment when orders were received to test the floodlights in case the NCO in charge of the post closed the wrong switch!

When conducting his survey of Cromer Admiral Dreyer had expressed his dismay that the pier was still intact directly to the local commander, but he was assured there would soon be 'a very large gap made in it'. A section of Royal Engineers were assigned to the task; eager to please they set charges and blew a large section out of the pier. The problem was they blew it out using so much explosive that some of the debris, including an iron girder, ended up in the town centre. Fortunately, no one was hurt. The problem that was soon pointed out to the military authorities was that now there was no way for the Cromer lifeboat crew to reach the lifeboat house of their No.1 boat at the end of the pier. It was a fair point, and a single man width gangway was soon in place to bridge the gap.

Ironside deployed more 'second line' Territorial Army units to the coast from inland to man coastal defences, as were partially trained troops unfitted for mobile operations and some corps troops, such as the RASC at Cromer on the east coast, who were being employed to hold sectors of the beaches. With so many soldiers being dedicated to the construction, camouflage or disguise of fixed defences, concerns were raised among senior officers about the lack of time being spent on training these men to fight enemy invasion forces if they actually landed.

Ironside's plan for inland Britain behind the coastal crust relied on defensive 'Stop Lines' being constructed, each one to stop or slow down the progress of enemy invasion forces. The most significant and longest of these was the 'GHQ Line', intended to be a formidable anti-tank obstacle that used natural features and waterways (both natural and man-made) combined with man-made defences of pillboxes, anti-tank ditches, anti-tank obstacles, mine fields, barbed wire entanglements and trench systems.

Planned to bisect Britain for over 800 miles from the River Forth near Edinburgh, through Northumberland and East Yorkshire to the Humber, it would run down eastern England passing Cambridge and on to the Thames, skirting the south of London to the Blackwall Tunnel and down to Maidstone where it would run east to west across the south of Britain to Highbridge, Somerset. The intention of this huge scheme was to create Britain's version of a 'Maginot Line' barrier between the east and south coasts, where the invasion landings were considered likely to take place, and London and the factories and coal fields of the industrial heartlands of the North and Midlands.

A further GHQ line was also constructed around Plymouth, which was considered a particularly vulnerable port eminently suited for the landing of enemy troops and supplies. The Taunton stop line was very much an extension of the GHQ Line running north to south for nearly 50 miles from Pawlett Hill near Burnham-on-Sea (not far from Highbridge) in Somerset, through Dorset to Axmouth harbour in Devon. The original scheme had plans for a stop line consisting of 293 pillboxes, fifteen gun emplacements, anti-tank blocks, anti-tank ditches, anti-tank posts, rail blocks and bridges with built-in demolition chambers which combined to present a formidable continuous anti-tank obstacle for enemy forces landing on the south west coast of England.

In Scotland they were to have anti-tank stop lines too, the largest of which known as the Scottish Command Line across Fife and Perthshire was given the go-ahead in mid-June. There had also been concerns raised about a German invasion of Eire which could then be used as a base to launch raids or an all-out attack on the west coast of the British mainland. Although not considered a major threat, it would have been foolhardy to ignore the scenario, so some 31,000 troops backed up by 15,000 Home Defence troops were stationed in Northern Ireland and Britain's defences on the west coast left predominantly in the hands of the Royal Navy Western Approaches Command and the Royal Air Force.

The British coast was divided into defence sectors. Concentric rings of anti-tank defences and pillboxes were also built in and around London. In eastern and southern counties the stop lines were constructed using the same methods, including defending towns and villages with the intention that they would become buffers for holding up the advance of enemy forces if they managed to penetrate the coastal crust. Bridge crossings over the rivers along forward stop lines formed a 'demolition belt' of key structures that would be blown up to frustrate the advance of enemy invaders. Over fifty major stop lines were planned or under construction across Britain by the summer of 1940.

Ironside envisaged a central corps-size mobile reserve would be based at the rear of the anti-tank line to act as a rapid reaction force in the event of a major enemy penetration. It was also planned that the anti-tank obstacle running down the east centre of England would be manned by Local Defence Volunteers and mobile columns would be created and dispersed between the coastal crust and the anti-tank line to deal with localised attacks and parachute landings.

When Ironside revealed his plans at a meeting of Vice-Chiefs of Staff on 25 June 1940 criticisms were swift and were written up as a memorandum to be brought to the attention of the chiefs of staff as a matter of urgency at the War Cabinet meeting the following day. Senior officers representing all three services: Air Marshal Richard Peirce, Vice Chief of the Air Staff; Vice Admiral Tom Phillips, Vice-Chief of Naval Staff and General Robert Haining, Vice-Chief of the Imperial General Staff expressed their gravest concern at these dispositions pointing out:

...it appeared that the main resistance might only be offered after the enemy had over-run nearly half the country and obtained possession of aerodromes and other vital facilities. They added their further concern: '*Very little mention had been made in the Commander-in-Chief's plan for the defence of the South coast, which was now quite as liable to attack as the East and South East Coasts.*

Peirce, Phillips and Haining also stated, that in their view:

> ...the only policy was to resist the enemy with the utmost resolution from the moment he set foot on the shore. Once he established himself firmly on land experience had shown that the German was extremely difficult to dislodge. The enemy would use their best troops for the initial landing and we should have to face the fact that their training and equipment would be superior to that of our own troops. For this reason, we should have to dispute every inch of the ground at the landing places themselves. It had always been recognised that the most hazardous phase of an opposed landing was the disembarkation on the beaches.[39]

Churchill disliked the lack of aggression in the plan and knew only too well that beach landings and advances could be repulsed from the bitter lessons he learned from the Gallipoli debacle during the First World War. Churchill and some of the senior military commanders had also become frustrated at the regular engagement of troops on building defences rather than training them to fight. Having seen the memoranda and papers of the vice-chiefs and chiefs

Men of 7th Battalion, The Green Howards on an exercise at Sandbanks near Poole, Dorset, July 1940.

of staff, Churchill outlined his own ideas and observations for the scheme of Home Defence and had them placed before the chiefs of staff committee on 28 June 1940:

[I] *It is prudent to block off likely sections of the beaches with a good defence and to make secure all creeks and harbours on the East Coast. The South Coast is less immediately dangerous. No serious invasion is possible without a harbour with quays etc. No one can tell should the navy fail, on what part of the East Coast the impact will fall. Perhaps there will be several lodgements. Once these are made all troops on other parts of the coastal crust will be as useless as those in the Maginot Line. Although fighting on the beaches is favourable to the defence, this advantage cannot be purchased by trying to guard all the beaches. Process must be selective. But if time permits defended sectors may be widened and improved.*

[II] *Every effort should be made to man coast defences with sedentary troops, well sprinkled with experienced late-war officers. The safety of the country depends on having a large number (now only nine but should soon be fifteen) 'Leopard' brigade-groups which can be directed swiftly, i.e. within four hours, to the points of lodgement. Difficulties of landing on beaches are serious, even when the invader has reached them; but difficulties of nourishing a lodgement when exposed to heavy attack by land, air and sea are far greater. All therefore depends on rapid, resolute engagement of any landed forces which may slip through the sea control. This should not be beyond our means provided the field troops are not consumed in beach defences and are kept in high condition of mobility, crouched and ready to spring.*

[III] *In the unhappy event of the enemy capturing a port, larger formations with artillery will be necessary. There should be four or five good divisions held in general reserve to deal with such an improbable misfortune. The scale of lodgement to be anticipated should not be more than ten thousand men landed at three points simultaneously, say thirty thousand in all. The scale of air attack not more than fifteen thousand landed simultaneously at two or three points in all. The enemy will not have strength to repeat such descents often. It is very doubtful whether air-borne troops can be landed in force by night; by day they should be easy prey to air attack.*

[IV] *The tank story is somewhat different and it is right to minimise by local cannon and obstacles the landing places of tanks. The Admiralty should report upon the size, character and speed of potential tank-carrying barges or floats, whether they will be self-propelled or towed and by what craft. As they can hardly go above seven miles an hour they should be detected in summer-time*

111

after they have started and even in fog or haze the RDF stations should give warning while they are still several hours from land. The destroyers issuing from the sally-ports must strike at these with gusto. The arrangement of stops and blocks held by local sedentary forces should be steadily developed and anti-tank squads formed. Our own tank reserve must engage the surviving invader tanks and no doubt is held in a position which allows swift railing to the attacked area.

[V] Parachutists, Fifth Columnists and enemy motor-cyclists who may penetrate or appear in disguise in unexpected places must be left to the Home Guard, reinforced by special squads. Much thought must be given to the trick of wearing British uniform.

[VI] In general I find myself in agreement with the Commander-in-Chief's plan but all possible field troops must be saved from the beaches and gathered into the 'Leopard' brigades and other immediate mobile supports. Emphasis should be laid upon the main reserve. The battle will be won or lost not on the beaches but by the mobile brigades and the main reserve. Until the Air Force is worn down by prolonged air fighting and destruction of aircraft supply, the power of the Navy remains decisive against any serious invasion.

[VII] The above observations apply only to the immediate summer months. We must be much better equipped and stronger before the autumn.[40]

Having heard the disquiet among the chiefs of staff Churchill was not about to risk the disruption and damage to morale that sacking Ironside might cause, however the C-in-C Home Forces was not being as proactive in re-addressing the home defence plans as Churchill would have wished. Churchill regularly toured the defence areas of the country to see for himself and talk candidly with divisional commanders who would be 'at the sharp end' if an invasion attempt was made. During recent visits and correspondence Lieutenant General Bernard Montgomery, then commanding the 3rd Division – the only fully equipped division in Britain at the time – and V Corps commander Lieutenant General Claude Auchinleck, both expressed their concerns to Churchill. Montgomery bluntly stated that he was *'in complete disagreement with the general approach to the defence of Britain and refused to apply it'*.[41]

Ironside's position was not helped by his close association and the trust he was known to place in Major General J.F.C. 'Boney' Fuller. Fuller was a prolific and visionary theorist in the dynamics of modern warfare during the inter-war years, but he had been a prominent figure in the British Union of Fascists before the organisation was outlawed. More problematic still was that Fuller's name had cropped up in a number of security service investigations into subversive pro-Nazi groups that had been operating in Britain in 1940.

On a visit to Southern Command Churchill toured the area in a motor car with its GOC-in-C Lieutenant General Alan Brooke during which they held a long conversation discussing counter-invasion strategy. Brooke clearly shared Churchill's ideas about the value and viability of mobile troops and a more aggressive approach to repelling the enemy. The conversation crystallised the need and viability of a new approach in Churchill's mind and, just as importantly, he had just found the man who would implement it. On 19 July 1940 Ironside was called to the War Office and was informed he was to be replaced by General Sir Alan Brooke as Commander-in-Chief Home Forces. There would be no hand-over period.

Brooke took over at a time when the Ministry of Information daily summaries showed there was a widely held belief among the British public that the date earmarked for the invasion of Britain to commence was Friday 19 July. Of course, the invasion did not emerge, instead Hitler made a speech

Coastal Artillery Observation Post overlooking the shore at Rock-a-Nore, Hastings, East Sussex, July 1942. Note the rows of anti-tank blocks on the beach below.

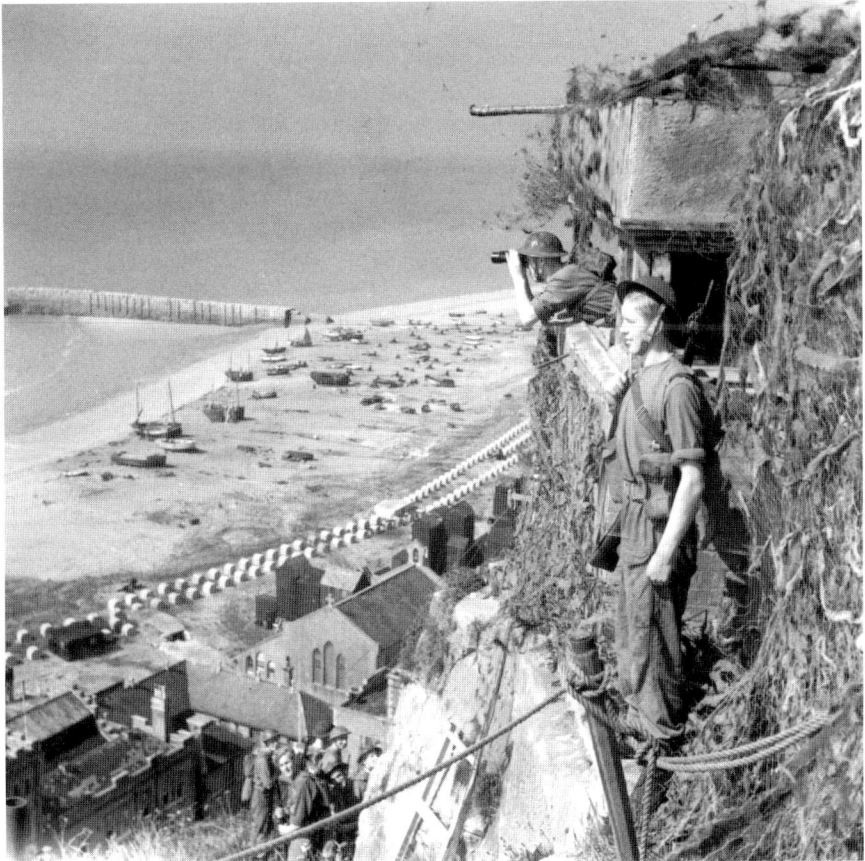

to the Reichstag in which he outlined a final offer of a negotiated peace to Britain which was refused in a BBC broadcast by Lord Halifax on 22 July. Soon after Luftwaffe bombers dropped transcripts of the speech translated into English onto Britain. Each leaflet had the bold headline *A Last Appeal to Reason by Adolf Hitler*. In some areas local police were criticised for the over-zealous collection of these leaflets before people had the chance to read them.[42] In other areas they were collected up and sold as items of curiosity in aid of war charities, but like most air dropped propaganda, after being seen as an item for derision and humour they became a handy firelighter or were found to be pleasantly absorbent in the outside toilet.

Brooke called an immediate halt to many of Ironside's defences and implemented a greater emphasis on offensive action to repel any attempted invasion. Under his new scheme Brooke introduced an intricate system of anti-tank islands and three categories of defended localities known as 'nodal points' were rapidly developed across the country: Category A: Locations not more than 15 miles from the coast, provided good anti-tank defence localities and commanded the nexus of roads; Category B: Defended towns and villages on routes of re-enforcing formations; Category C: Defended villages of military and/or tactical significance such as road junctions and bridging points.

Brooke replaced linear defence with mobile offensive action and improved response time by replacing Ironside's six to twelve-hour reserves with local mobile reserves within striking distance of the coast. The problem that still remained was the dearth of transport to actually get the troops to the coast in the event of an invasion emergency. Two main forms of transport were available after so much had been committed to France and left behind in the wake of the Dunkirk evacuation. Battalions with coastal patrol duties were frequently equipped with bicycles. The dignity and duties of the more senior officers were efficiently maintained with the purchase of civilian cars out of battalion funds or even the officers' own money.

Troops in the mobile reserve battalions further inland were reliant on dedicated civilian buses and drivers supplied under army contract. Yes folks, never fear, having imagined 800 soldiers in battle order with loaded rifles ready to fight off the Hun invader queuing up at the bus stop behind intractable local ladies heading out for their shopping, our brave lads were not reliant on the vagaries of timetabled local bus services. This was all well and good until there were invasion alarms. Sidney Nuttall was serving in the Royal Army Service Corps and was stationed near Newcastle-upon-Tyne, he recalled his unit had Midland red buses and drivers from Birmingham supplied as their company transport and experienced a common problem:

We had a stand-to when we had to dash to the coast in the middle of the night. These drivers had been living the life of Riley, they had money for food, they had accommodation in hotels and lodging houses. But when it came to the night when we were going to move off to fight, they refused to drive the buses. 'We didn't come here to get killed,' that's exactly what they said to us in real Brummie accents. We threw them off the buses and anybody that could drive climbed in and I drove a Midland red bus up to the coast. We got there and deployed but of course it was a false alarm.[43]

There would be a host of changes for the LDV too. Winston Churchill had never liked the cumbersome and somewhat ridiculed title of Local Defence Volunteers (and the corruption of its title letters that appeared on their arm bands such as 'Look, Duck and Vanish' or 'Last Ditch Volunteers') and saw it formally announced that the organization be re-named Home Guard on 23 July 1940. This was not only a change in name, Churchill ushered in a new

A lookout scans the horizon outside one of the coastal batteries between Hastings and Eastbourne, July 1942.

raft of improvements including structured training, 37-pattern battledress uniforms exactly like every army unit, supplies of P.14 and P.17 rifles were issued and the affiliation of Home Guard units to their county regiments which allowed the Home Guard to wear their local regiment's cap badge were set in motion for Home Guard units across the country.

Brooke redefined stop lines and created nodal defence points to hold the enemy at bay rather than deliver a decisive blow against him, buying enough time to establish the direction of the attack.

The units originally earmarked for this task were Home Defence battalions, but due to insufficient troop numbers to hold a second or reserve line in strength, Home Guard units in nodal point towns would be deployed into this role along with any available local troops. With the Home Guard under operational control, the local soldiers were organised into garrisons for towns where the local officer commanding troops of each town would have his defence scheme planned. In villages and other localities the defences would be also manned by the available military forces and Home Guard. Divisional military commanders were in no doubt of the dedication of the Home Guard, particularly in the forward areas on and near the coast; the well uniformed and equipped units felt they had more purpose than ever before, their country needed them, a mood reflected in many official reports and anti-invasion plans which stated confidently when mentioning the deployment of the Home Guard that *'they would, if required, fight to the last round and the last man'*.

Codeword Cromwell

No-one on the coast of Britain, be they part of the military forces or civilians, who lived through what became known as 'The Invasion Summer' of 1940 would ever forget the atmosphere of those tense months of June to September when German forces were expected to make a landing in an attempt to conquer Britain. Those guarding the coast in both the armed forces and the Home Guard also remember the chronic shortages of weaponry to do the job. Peter Erwood was a member of a Royal Artillery anti-aircraft battery on the coast near Ramsgate in May 1940. Shortly after their arrival he recalled they were informed they were the only troops between Pegwell Bay and Dover at that time:

> *In the event of an invasion the defence of that line was down to us as well. With six rifles and a dozen or so pickaxe handles, the chances of any spirited resistance seemed rather on the thin side. Our officers instructed us that should paratroopers land, we were to rush at them with pickaxe handles, stun them and grab their guns.*[44]

Members of 6th Battalion, Black Watch on anti-parachutist patrol on the Isle of Wight, 19 August 1940.

The 8th Battalion Durham Light Infantry, along with the 72nd Field Regiment and 151 Brigade anti-tank company, took up positions east and west of Weymouth from Osmington Mills to Abbotsbury on the Dorset coast. The situation recounted in the history of the 8th Battalion Durham Light Infantry was echoed along the entire invasion coastline:

> *The field Regiment had not a single gun of any sort and without any anti-tank guns was made up of one rifle company…The 14-mile front was divided into two halves for tactical reasons…14 miles of vital coast defended only by riflemen. It was only one stage removed from bows and arrows and there is no doubt that only the Channel and courage of the British people stood between England and Nazi Germany.*[45]

No wonder General Claude Auchinleck, commander of V Corps in Southern Command was moved to write his famous comment on the shortages in late June: 'I am making bricks without much straw.'[46]

That said, the lads of 8DLI soon settled down into the typical routine on the coastal defences, their battalion history records:

117

It meant much hard work: weapons pits and command posts had to be constructed along the whole front and barbed wire erected. In that memorable mid-summer of 1940 with the ever-present danger of invasion, the forward companies 'stood to' at 10.30pm and again at 4.00am, just before dawn. There was little time for sleep between stand-to periods for almost every night brought a scare of some sort such as flashing over the Channel. Whether the scare was false or not it meant that the Battalion had to stand-to until dawn showed all was well. Then a hurried breakfast was followed by another hard day's work on the beach defences.[47]

In the air the Royal Air Force and Fleet Air Arm flew regular sorties over the occupied ports on the continent on the look-out for concentrations of shipping and barges capable of carrying invasion troops. For those on the coastal defences, be they Army, Royal Navy Coast Watch or Home Guard, it was a matter of waiting and watching day and night peering across the sea to the horizon to spot enemy vessels or an invasion armada at the earliest possible opportunity.

The old debate over where any potential invasion force was likely to land still rumbled among the chiefs of staff. Those who remained from the old school tended to favour the east coast and the good tank country of East Anglia as the most likely area for where the main thrust of the attack would fall, whereas General Alan Brooke favoured the south coast that offered far shorter crossing points from occupied France.

On 25 July concerns over the potential invasion danger to Scotland were renewed after a well-researched paper on the possibility of German air and seaborne landings in northern Scotland was presented to the War Cabinet Chiefs of Staff Committee by Admiral Sir Reginald Drax, Commander-in-Chief at the Nore. The salient features of the scenario he proposed were:

(a) The operation would consist of a powerful diversion against northern Scotland with the object of striking at the Home Fleet and drawing a part of our metropolitan air force North into Scotland.

(b) The essential first step in this plan would be the capture of the majority of the Scottish aerodromes near Wick and in the Shetlands by a force of parachutists This would be followed by the landing of some 50,000 airborne troops as rapidly as possible.

(c) Based on the capture of these aerodromes, a strong force of bombers and fighters would then attack the Home Fleet in Scapa Flow, destroy it, or at least drive it south. Rosyth would also be rendered untenable.

(d) The Home Fleet having been disposed of, larger seaborne forces would them capture in succession the Shetlands, the Orkneys and Scapa Flow.

Seaborne and airborne troops would then secure an ample foothold in Scotland down to Edinburgh, or perhaps as far as Inverness.

(e) *Having accomplished all this, the German plan would develop according to circumstances either against Ireland, or a full-scale invasion landing in East Anglia and Kent.*[48]

Drax's paper gained added weight in early August when credible intelligence reported troop concentrations and even the embarkation of German troops in Norway on 11 August.[49] Brooke immediately sent reinforcements to Scotland and embarked on a fact-finding tour in the north east coast of Scotland[50] to assess the state of the defences for himself on 27–28 August.

August, however, had been a month where RAF aerial reconnaissance photographs picked up an increased concentration of invasion barges and support vessels in ports from Texel to Cherbourg. Military intelligence had picked up on troop movements to French ports and Luftwaffe squadrons moving to the coast of the Low Countries and France. British meteorological and hydrographic experts had also analysed their charts and identified a narrow window of time offering the optimum combination of moon and tides for an invasion force to cross the Channel. In their estimation if a Nazi invasion was to have the best chance of success it would come between 8 and 10 September.[51]

The look of all our east and south coast towns as they prepared to repel the invader was captured in this narrative published in *Front Line Folkestone* (1945):

From August 1940 onwards long range and coastal guns were installed along the coast in the vicinity of Folkestone; on the Leas a battery of great naval guns was placed. In and about the town concrete blocks, tank traps and all manner of obstructions were built. Just below the crest of the Downs to the north of the town miles of tank ditches were dug; at the entrances to the town road barriers were prepared from all sorts of material, long derelict cars, old lorries, disused builders' material and so on. Long lines of square concrete blocks formed a defensive belt through the centre of the town, Castle Hill Avenue became a miniature 'Siegfried Line'; barbed wire was everywhere. Along country roads tank obstacles were placed by the verges ready to be set in position instantly.[52]

For those manning the defences along Britain's invasion coast during the summer of 1940 there were many hours of quiet and boredom in many areas, but this would be punctuated with the sighting of enemy aircraft and vessels at sea. For some the early stages of the Battle of Britain were played out in front of them as German aircraft attacked shipping at sea off our coast and our lads on the coastal defences would often give a cheer, shouting 'Give 'em hell!' as the RAF fighters sped in to intercept. They also watched the squadrons of German bombers streaming overhead to targets in Britain as our anti-aircraft guns blazed away at them. If the infantry units had sufficient ammunition,

ATS girls and gun crews of 177 (Mixed) Heavy Battery, Royal Artillery rush to 'take post' at Fort Crosby near Liverpool, August 1940

they would also open up with small arms fire from their Lewis and Bren guns on anti-aircraft mounts, watching their red tracer bullets zip skywards.

They would also see the glow in the sky when the bombs of the same raiders got through and hit their targets setting nearby docks and towns ablaze. For some it was their hometowns and even their own homes; for others deployed to the coast from other parts of the country it was often a place they had visited and liked and shared a pint or two with the locals when they were on leave. Either way those who saw those fires felt the dull, empty thud of anxiety in their guts and be moved to say 'some poor sod's got it tonight'.

Men of those same coastal units may well have also been sent to the scene of the fires to help with the clearing up, seaside places they had seen just hours or days before now scenes of wrecked buildings and roads torn up by bomb craters, strewn with bricks and shattered glass. For some involved in this work it would be the first time they had sight of a dead body and casualties during the war. Other soldiers would remember spending hours guarding the wreckage of crashed enemy aircraft during the Battle of Britain to ensure local people did not take any part of it away as a souvenir – just in case that was *the* vital component or clue to the weak spot in the aircraft design the military intelligence boffins were looking for.

Action stations! Crews rush to their guns at Fort Crosby, Liverpool, August 1940. Note the covered casemates recommended for all the coastal batteries by Dreyer to protect crews from bomb splinters have now been built.

At night the eyes of those who watched from the defences around Britain's coast would peer into the darkness for hours on end. A known phenomena were what were believed to be German U and E boats flashing their lights in an endeavour to draw our fire and reveal coastal batteries and fire positions, as described by the men of B Company, 10th (Torbay) Battalion, Devonshire Home Guard:

> *Their method of attack took the form of exposing a variety of lights close inshore for a few seconds and then moving rapidly to another close in position and repeating the performance. Very lights fired horizontally, a globular pink light and sundry white and coloured flashes. We couldn't make out the slightest sign of a vessel of any type in the murky darkness but down from Thatcher Post, close to Hopes Nose and under a lee rock, we clearly heard the engines of departing enemy craft.*[53]

After all the fears of a Fifth Column and enemy agents making landings, probably the greatest coup of all for the army coastal forces in 1940 was the capture of the first German spies to land in Britain. It happened a year to the day after the outbreak of war – 3 September 1940. At approximately 4.45am Private Sidney Tollervey, D Company, 6th Battalion, Somerset Light Infantry was on patrol at Romney Marsh, Kent. It was still dark when he was near the road at the Dymchurch Redoubt, a few yards from the beach when he heard rustling and suddenly saw the figure of a man silhouetted against the sky as he ran across the road towards the sea wall and flung himself onto it. Private Tollervey challenged the man with 'Halt! Who goes there?' and ran down some nearby steps and, despite not asking for a password, he heard a voice call out 'I do not know your code word.'

Tollervey asked if he had any means of identification to which the man replied he did not understand what he meant. Tollervey told him to advance and be recognised, this the man did with his hands up. The man was dressed in civilian clothes wearing white shoes, with another pair of shoes slung around his neck along with a pair of binoculars. The man appeared very keen to point out he was a Dutch refugee and asked to see one of Tollervey's officers to whom he would explain his case. He did not know it at the time but Private Tollervey had just earned himself the distinction of capturing the first German spy to land in Britain.[54]

Under questioning the captured spy revealed his name was Charles Albert Van Den Kieboom. He had not landed alone and his fellow spy, Sjord Pons, was captured a short while later and their radio equipment recovered from where they hid it. Meanwhile another pair of spies had made their landing on the Lydd side of the Dungeness peninsula. They were also soon in custody after one of them walked into The Rising Sun pub at Lydd for a drink. The man clearly was not familiar with English opening hours for pubs and he was asked to call back later. He was tall, well dressed and yet his clothes appeared wet.

Landlady Mabel Cole didn't like the look of the man when she told him the drink and biscuits he had ordered would be 'one and a tanner', slang for one shilling and sixpence. The money parlance clearly threw the stranger and he had to proffer the cash in his hand so she could take the requisite coins in payment. Mrs Cole had alerted customers Horace Rendal 'Rennie' Mansfield, an inspector of the Aeronautical Inspection Directorate (AID) and his friend, insurance adviser Ronald Silvester, to the suspicious character. Mansfield and Silvester followed the man outside, Mansfield approached the stranger, showed him his AID photo identification, pointed out he was in a restricted area and challenged him to produce his identity card. All he had to offer was a Dutch passport in the name of Karl Meier. He agreed to accompany Mansfield and Silvester to Lydd police station. Silvester recalled as he entered the car he said: '*You've caught me, I guess and I don't mind what happens to me but I refuse to go back to Germany.*'[55]

Meier's fellow spy José Waldberg was also captured by the following morning, along with his radio equipment in the bushes near Boulderwall Farm, Lydd where he had remained hidden for the last 24 hours.

The police handed the spies over to MI5, they were then interrogated, the summary included the revelation:

The demeanour of the spies was such that they were convinced invasion would take place before the middle of September. The spies work in pairs and were provided with food and £60 in British currency for expenses to last fourteen days. There was no German contact in England. The spies gave the information that the contact was unnecessary as the Germans would be here within two weeks.[56]

They would, of course keep on waiting as no invasion emerged. Three of the spies ended up on the gallows, only Pons evaded the rope; it was hoped he would be useful to counter espionage.

There were a number of localised invasion scares brought on by 'jitters' and mistaken sightings of invasion craft on the horizon but there was only one night when the 'Cromwell' code word was given.

The day of 7 September 1940 will go down in history as the first day of the blitz on London and late that same afternoon British chiefs of staff met to consider a report on the increasing likelihood of German forces making the invasion assault on Great Britain. What happened next has been the subject of speculation over the understanding of what the Cromwell code word was actually intended to mean; some accounts state it was issued as a warning for troops to be placed on alert, while others receiving the warning believed it was given because invasion landings had actually taken place. The account published in *Hansard* in November 1946 states:

> *The code word 'Cromwell' signifying 'invasion imminent' was therefore issued by General Headquarters Home Forces that evening (8 p.m., 7th September) to the Eastern and Southern Commands implying 'action stations' for the forward (coastal) divisions. It was also issued to all formations in the London area and to the 4th and 7th Corps in General Headquarters Reserve, implying a state of readiness at short notice. The code word was repeated for information to all other Commands in the United Kingdom.[57]*

Most military officials who received the message immediately put their troops onto a war footing, Auxiliary Units made ready to go operational and a number of Home Guard commanders called out their men by ringing church bells which, in turn, raised alarm that landings were being made by enemy parachutists. In such circumstances senses and fears are heightened and the effect of cloud and shadow on the sea and innocent fishing boats generated a number of false alarms of German E-boats being 'spotted' approaching the coast.[58]

In Eastern and Southern Commands roads were instantly locked down, defences manned and primed, explosives were rigged ready to destroy bridges and roads were mined. Telephone operators refused to accept non-official calls and in some areas the church bells were rung. Before the immediate action orders could be rescinded or clarified a number of people suffered injuries, a few bridges were demolished by Royal Engineers and near Mablethorpe, Lincolnshire, Major Henry Cleaveland Phillips and his driver Private Arthur Scovell of the 2nd Battalion, The Hampshire Regiment, serving in the 1st (Guards) Brigade, suffered fatal injuries when their car was blown up after running over mines that had been laid on the road by local troops after they received the 'invasion imminent' warning.

On 7 September men of the 8th Battalion, Durham Light Infantry had recently returned after a period in reserve to take over defences on the beautiful piece of coastline from Burton Bradstock to Lyme Regis with battalion HQ at Morecambe Lake. The battalion history records:

> *…in the most glorious weather the companies settled down to improving defences, lay mines and erect wire…that night code word Cromwell was received from Brigade Headquarters: this meant 'stand to in battle positions'. Invasion was imminent and troops along the whole length of the south and*

east coasts moved to their action stations. For eleven days the battalion 'stood to'. It was a nerve-racking period and the news on 15 September that the weather was becoming unsuitable for enemy landings was welcomed by those who knew and understood the weakness of the British defences. Hitler had missed his chance.[59]

Over the days and weeks after the 'Cromwell' codeword had been issued a story began to circulate of how an invasion attempt had actually been made by German seaborne forces on that night. Some stories claimed there had been some accident as the Germans set off, another told of how the invasion force had been 'cut up' while at sea by the Royal Navy and bombed and machine gunned by the RAF.[60] The story rapidly spread as a rumour 'from the best authority' which claimed the Channel had been left 'white with bodies'[61] of German dead. Other stories circulated of the beaches on the south and east coast which were claimed to be littered with the bodies of thousands of dead Germans. In one tale the beach at Southend had been so inundated, the corpses were being cleared away with the help of corporation refuse carts.[62]

The rumour soon evolved to claim that the bodies were all badly burned because invasion forces had been foiled by a secret coastal defence whereby the sea was flooded with petrol, set on fire and burned the invaders as they approached the shore. A Petroleum Warfare Department had been established shortly after the Dunkirk evacuation in response to the invasion threat, and there had been experiments with a flame barrage at sea. The idea was sound and the effect formidable, but it had proved harder than anticipated to get the oil to ignite, however, a notable success was achieved on the northern shores of the Solent near Tichfield and this was all the British propaganda organisations needed. Ten tanker wagons pumped tons of oil onto the sea and it was successfully ignited then:

…within a few seconds of the pumps being started a wall of flame of such intensity raged up from the sea surface that it was impossible to remain on the edge of the cliff, and the sea itself began to boil.[63]

The successful demonstration could not have come at a more opportune moment. Intelligence sources were suggesting the invasion of Britain by German forces was planned for early September and the demonstration of the barrage with film or photographs could be deliberately planted on German intelligence and, through channels calculated to leak stories of burning sea defences, out to the invasion forces too. Leaflets were also dropped by the RAF on German troops in the ports where the invasion barges were massing purporting to be sheets of useful phrases for German invasion forces in

Demonstration of the flame barrage designed to burn enemy invasion forces at sea before they landed, Studland Bay 1941.

German, French and Dutch such as: *'What is that strong smell of petroleum?'* *'What is setting the sea on fire?'* and *'Does not the Captain burn beautifully?'*

The story of the burning sea and flame barrage gained credence and was spoken of for years after the war among members of German forces who had been training for Operation Sea Lion (the German invasion of Britain) as the most feared anti-invasion weapon they would face if a landing was attempted. Many would shake their heads and say frankly they believed: 'We would be burnt to cinders before we hit the beach.'

A night patrol of F Company, 10th Battalion, Devonshire Home Guard found bodies of their own on the beach at Torbay; it is best told in the words of their battalion history:

A shadowy form was silhouetted against the breaking surf. The challenge 'Halt' rang out and the man stopped. Unable to produce an identity card, he was evidently on a secret mission. His conversation was vague and unhelpful, his only coherent information that he wanted to see 'the body in the bag' which was in the water. Here was a serious matter requiring urgent investigation so we escorted the prisoner to the phone box and detained him there while the police were summoned. The police too, took a serious view of the situation. They questioned the prisoner and decided they had better see 'the body in the bag' and not to be outdone, the night patrol went along.

Sure enough, there in the surf at the water's edge, lay a bag of sorts resembling a shroud. Filled with a sense of our own importance we dragged the object to the sand and in the eerie darkness we braced ourselves for the unpleasant task ahead and cut the bag open.

There we stood gaping, peering closely…not only did we find one body but three. They were carcases of mutton washed up from a wreck. The night guard heaved a sigh and continued their patrols.[64]

Chapter 5

The Coast Carries On

Where the enemy lands, or tries to land,
there will be most violent fighting…
For all of you then the order and duty will be:
STAND FIRM

Winston Churchill, 1941

In retrospect, all these years after the end of the Second World War, some historians can sagely look back on the window of opportunity for invasion Hitler had in September 1940 and take the view the threat of invasion was over. In the post war years Hitler's directives can now be clearly seen postponing Operation Sealion on 17 September 1940 followed by orders

Well uniformed, well equipped and well trained at last! Portsmouth West Home Guard that had responsibility for the Naval Dockyard pictured c1942.

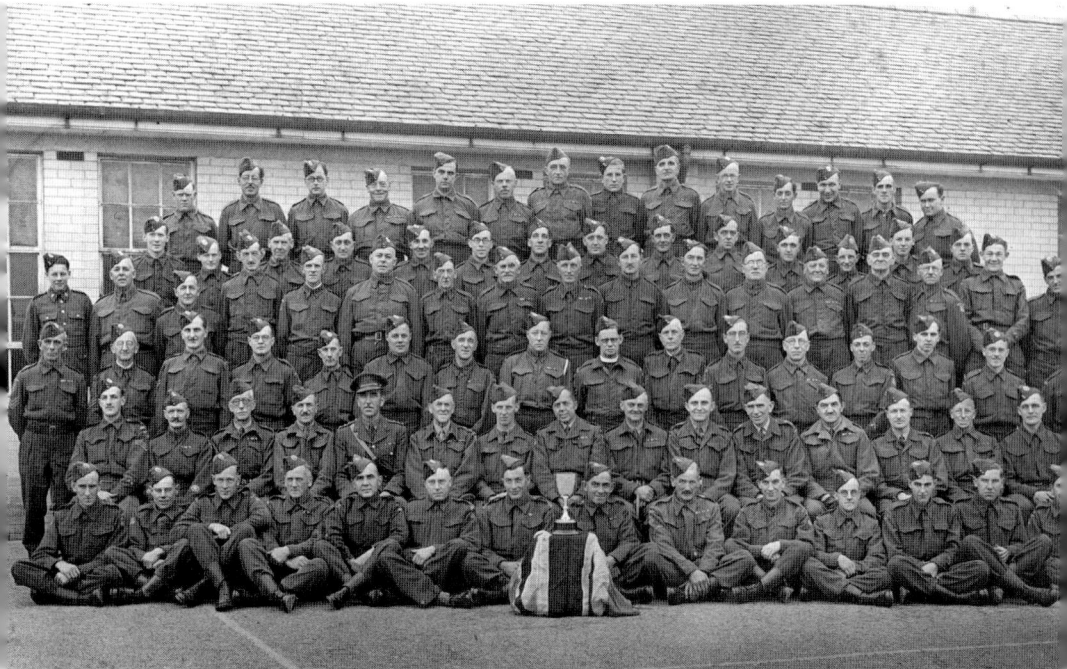

issued on 19 September for the strategic concentration of shipping to cease and existing concentrations of invasion barges to be dispersed. In October Hitler postponed Sealion pending a review in the spring of 1941, but after he began to release troops from invasion training in December 1940 the likelihood of an invasion taking place diminished greatly and the Führer switched his focus on his new campaign against Russia.

The problem was the people of Britain and British intelligence services did not know all this at the time. An appreciation of the intelligence as it stood in early October 1940 gathered by MI14 (the department of the Directorate of Military Intelligence specialising in intelligence about Germany) was recorded in the diary of Guy Liddell, head of MI5 B Division that had responsibility for home security. The MI14 findings were explicit:

> There are no indications that Germany has abandoned the intention of invading the UK. Furthermore, we believe that Germany will maintain forces on the coast of France and the Low Countries which will act as a constant threat to the security of the UK.[1]

Indeed, there still seemed to be active efforts by the Germans preparing for invasion. Intercepted messages showed the funnels of shipwrecks were being used for the installation of wireless sets from which information could be transmitted about allied shipping and could be used 'for directing an invading party'.[2]

It was clear the political and military authorities in Britain did not wish people to become complacent and there were still concerns about our state of readiness to repel an invasion. Sir John Dill, Chief of the Imperial General Staff was reported widely in February 1941, warning:

> Hitler might be forced by strategic, economic and political stress in Europe to try to invade these islands in the near future...[3]

Prime Minister Winston Churchill also made a radio broadcast on 9 February 1941 that was reproduced in detail in many newspapers over the following days in which he recognised Dill's concerns, adding:

> We must all be prepared to meet gas attacks, parachute attacks and glider attacks with constancy, forethought and practised skill.

Churchill also offered the reassurance 'Naturally, we are working night and day to have everything ready.' He expressed his confidence in General Brooke and his commanders and spoke of how the country's armed forces were far stronger and better equipped than the previous year, concluding:

But most of all I put my faith in the simple and effective resolve to conquer or die which will animate nearly four million Britons with serviceable weapons in their hands.'[4]

Over the latter months of 1940 and into 1941 the divisions of the BEF, so battered and depleted during the Battle of France and the Dunkirk evacuation, were rebuilt and, along with troops who had escaped from occupied countries such as Poland and Norway and contingents of troops from British Dominions and across the Empire such as Canada, Australia and India, troop numbers in Britain were greatly boosted. Brooke's new scheme of anti-tank 'islands', defended areas and mobile troops took shape. Work even continued on a few of the regional stop lines. The coastal defences were also enhanced (but not the aesthetics of the beaches) with the erection of hundreds of miles of Admiralty scaffolding, sometimes with mines attached, which would become partially or fully submerged at high water with the intention of tearing the bottoms out of enemy landing barges if a seaborne invasion was attempted.

There were both eyes and ears that maintained a constant watch on the enemy. The Chain Home Radio Direction Finding (CH RDF) stations monitored for enemy aircraft approaching over the sea and the members of the Observer Corps watched on the skies over the coast and across the land. A far more secret branch of the services had also come on apace since the dark days of Dunkirk and was providing a significant element of our intelligence gathering. The wireless interception branch known as the Y Service (the Y is a phonetic version of the abbreviation Wi for wireless) listened in to enemy wireless communications from over forty stations dotted around the coast. The service was also assisted by ham radio enthusiasts and short-wave listeners who had offered their services for the Voluntary Intercept Service. The Y Service posts were sometimes situated in requisitioned private dwellings, others were purpose built but never located far from the cliffs.

The Y stations were operated by specialist units of the Royal Navy, Army and RAF staffed by between twelve to twenty personnel. Many of the operators were from the women's services such as the Women's Royal Naval Service, ATS or WAAF. All of them would have been highly skilled young women providing continuous cover working day and night shifts on radios capable of listening to enemy shipping or low flying aircraft radio signals which would be diligently transcribed by hand by the operators. If the messages were in plain German they would be sent to filtering centres and then forwarded to the Government Code and Cipher School at Bletchley Park (Station X). If the message had been encrypted, they would be sent by motorcycle courier or teleprinter to Station X to be deciphered. Pieced together, the information provided by the intercepts provided a priceless insight into what the enemy was doing. Land based direction finding (D/F) stations concentrated on the location of enemy vessels at sea played a vital role detecting the movements of U-boats during the Battle of the Atlantic.

The Civilian Population

For coastal residents it was a time of yet more upheaval and concern. In 1940 over 700 holiday destinations were in the 'defence zone' and closed to visitors. Thousands had been evacuated or chose to find alternative accommodation to their seaside homes and with tourism decimated, businesses just boarded up their frontages 'for the duration'. Evacuation was not compulsory and some families decided to 'stay put' but statistics compiled by the Ministry of Information, show many towns on the south east coast saw a reduction of 20 per cent, Folkestone was recorded as 50 per cent and Ramsgate, Margate and Broadstairs reduced to just 40 per cent of the pre-war population still resident in the town in June 1940.[5]

In Folkestone it was not only shops that closed, the Folkestone *Express* and *Hythe Reporter* newspapers ceased publication, but still there was concern from the regional commissioner that more people should take the chance to leave the town. Police notices and posters urged departure and free railway vouchers were offered to those who would evacuate voluntarily. But not all went smoothly and when a second message was broadcast from loudspeaker vans it was misheard and led to some alarm and indignation among local people.[6]

J.B. Priestley, whose rich and warm voice and prose had done so much to elevate morale and turn the disaster of Dunkirk into a quintessentially British and miraculous rescue, visited Margate during what should have been the height of the holiday season in 1940:

Everything was there: bathing pools, bandstands, gardens blazing with flowers, theatres and the like and miles of firm golden sands spread out under the July sun. But no people – not a soul. Of all the hundreds of thousands of holiday makers, of entertainers and boatmen – not one. And no sound – not the very ghost of an echo of all that cheerful hullabaloo – children shouting and laughing, bands playing, concert parties singing, men selling ice cream, whelks and peppermint rock, which I'd remembered hearing along this shore. No, not even an echo. It was as if an evil magician had whisked everybody away...[7]

Many of those who had evacuated in 1940 drifted back home over weeks and months so, with the renewed threat of invasion in 1941, there were new

DANGER of INVASION

Last year all who could be spared from this town were asked to leave, not only for their own safety, but so as to ease the work of the Armed Forces in repelling an invasion.

The danger of invasion has increased and the Government requests all who can be spared, and have somewhere to go. to leave without delay.

This applies particularly to :—
SCHOOL CHILDREN
MOTHERS WITH YOUNG CHILDREN
AGED AND INFIRM PERSONS
PERSONS LIVING ON PENSIONS
PERSONS WITHOUT OCCUPATION
OR IN RETIREMENT

If you are one of these, you should arrange to go to some other part of the country. You should not go to the coastal area of East Anglia, Kent or Sussex.

School children can be registered to join school parties in the reception areas, and billets will be found for them.

If you are in need of help you can have your railway fare paid and a billeting allowance paid to any relative or friend with whom you stay.

If you are going. go quickly.

Take your
NATIONAL REGISTRATION IDENTITY CARD
RATION BOOK
GAS MASK

ALSO any bank book, pensions payment order book, insurance cards, unemployment book, military registration documents, passport, insurance policys, securities and any ready money.

If your house will be left unoccupied, turn off gas, electricity and water supplies and make provision for animals and birds. Lock your house securely. Blinds should be left up, and if there is a telephone line, ask the telephone exchange to disconnect it.

Apply at the Local Council Offices for further information.

Private Car and Motor Cycle owners who have not licensed their vehicles and have no petrol coupons may be allowed to use their cars unlicensed for one journey only and may apply to the Police for petrol coupons to enable them to secure sufficient petrol to journey to their destination.

ESSENTIAL WORKERS MUST STAY
particularly the following classes :—
Members of the Home Guard
Observer Corps
Coastguards, Coast Watchers and Lifeboat Crews
Police and Special Constabulary
Fire Brigade and Auxiliary Fire Service
A.R.P. and Casualty Services
Members of Local Authorities and their officials and employees
Workers on the land
Persons engaged on war work, and other essential services
Persons employed by contractors on defence work
Employees of water, sewerage, gas & electricity undertakings
Persons engaged in the supply and distribution of food
Workers on export trades
Doctors, Nurses and Chemists
Ministers of Religion
Government Employees
Employees of banks
Employees of transport undertakings,
    namely railways, docks, canals, ferries,
    and road transport (both passenger and goods).

When invasion is upon us it may be necessary to evacuate the remaining population of this and certain other towns. Evacuation would then be compulsory at short notice, in crowded trains, with scanty luggage, to destinations chosen by the Government. If you are not among the essential workers mentioned above, it is better to go now while the going is good.

Danger of Invasion *poster displayed in coastal areas considered particularly vulnerable to invasion, urging all people not engaged in essential war work with places to stay to leave as soon as possible 1941.*

132

Issued by the Ministry of Information in co-operation with the War Office

and the Ministry of Home Security

Beating the INVADER

A MESSAGE FROM THE PRIME MINISTER

IF invasion comes, everyone—young or old, men and women—will be eager to play their part worthily. By far the greater part of the country will not be immediately involved. Even along our coasts, the greater part will remain unaffected. But where the enemy lands, or tries to land, there will be most violent fighting. Not only will there be the battles when the enemy tries to come ashore, but afterwards there will fall upon his lodgments very heavy British counter-attacks, and all the time the lodgments will be under the heaviest attack by British bombers. The fewer civilians or non-combatants in these areas, the better—apart from essential workers who must remain. So if you are advised by the authorities to leave the place where you live, it is your duty to go elsewhere when you are told to leave. When the attack begins, it will be too late to go ; and, unless you receive definite instructions to move, your duty then will be to stay where you are. You will have to get into the safest place you can find, and stay there until the battle is over. For all of you then the order and the duty will be : " STAND FIRM ".

This also applies to people inland if any considerable number of parachutists or air-borne troops are landed in their neighbourhood. Above all, they must not cumber the roads. Like their fellow-countrymen on the coasts, they must " STAND FIRM ". The Home Guard, supported by strong mobile columns wherever the enemy's numbers require it, will immediately come to grips with the invaders, and there is little doubt will soon destroy them.

Throughout the rest of the country where there is no fighting going on and no close cannon fire or rifle fire can be heard, everyone will govern his conduct by the second great order and duty, namely, " CARRY ON ". It may easily be some weeks before the invader has been totally destroyed, that is to say, killed or captured to the last man who has landed on our shores. Meanwhile, all work must be continued to the utmost, and no time lost.

The following notes have been prepared to tell everyone in rather more detail what to do, and they should be carefully studied. Each man and woman should think out a clear plan of personal action in accordance with the general scheme

Winston S. Churchill

STAND FIRM

I. What do I do if fighting breaks out in my neighbourhood?

Keep indoors or in your shelter until the battle is over. If you can have a trench ready in your garden or field, so much the better. You may want to use it for protection if your house is damaged. But if you are at work, or if you have special orders, carry on as long as possible and only take cover when danger approaches. If you are on your way to work, finish your journey if you can.

If you see an enemy tank, or a few enemy soldiers, do not assume that the enemy are in control of the area. What you have seen may be a party sent on in advance, or stragglers from the main body who can easily be rounded up

The Beating the Invader *leaflet issued to every household in May 1941, this version includes the addenda for coastal areas printed in red, top left.*

rounds of evacuations of children and adults employed in non-essential work from coastal areas.

The Ministry of Home Security announced from midnight on 23 March a ban on visits to coastal areas for holiday, recreation or pleasure was to be extended to include the coastal belt from Brighton up to and including

133

The Battle of the Atlantic is being lost!

The reasons why:

1. German U-boats, German bombers and the German fleet sink and seriously damage between them every month a total of 700 000 to 1 million tons of British and allied shipping.

2. All attempts at finding a satisfactory means of defence against the German U-boats or the German bombers have failed disastrously.

3. Even President Roosevelt has openly stated that for every five ships sunk by Germany, Britain and America between them can only build two new ones. All attempts to launch a larger shipbuilding programme in America have failed.

4. Britain is no longer in a position to secure her avenues of supply. The population of Britain has to do with about half the ration that the population of Germany gets. Britain, herself, can only support 40 % of her population from her own resources in spite of the attempts made to increase the amount of land under cultivation. If the war is continued until 1942, 60 % of the population of Britain will starve!

All this means that starvation in Britain is not to be staved off. At the most it can be postponed, but whether starvation comes this year or at the beginning of next doesn't make a ha'porth of difference. Britain must starve because she is being cut off from her supplies.

Britain's losing the Battle of the Atlantic means

Britain's losing the war!

The German propaganda leaflet The Battle of the Atlantic is Being Lost *dropped by German aircraft on Britain, 1941.*

Littlehampton, extending inland as far as the northern boundaries of Chanctonbury and Chailey rural districts and including Arundel and Burgess Hill. No permits for access would be issued.[8] A new *Beating the Invader* leaflet was also delivered to every household in May 1941. The text, overseen personally by Churchill, carried far more positive messages than the *If the Invader Comes* of 1940. Gone was the earlier 'stay where you are' which was replaced with the more assertive 'Stand Firm'. The rest the rest of the country were advised to 'Carry on'. The public facing invasion forces were not just told to sit there and await the arrival of armed forces either, the new leaflet concluded by posing the question 'Should I defend myself against the enemy?' with the answer:

> *If small parties are going about threatening persons and property in an area not under enemy control and come your way, you have the right of every man and woman to do what you can to protect yourself, your family and your home.*[9]

Many coastal residents were the first people to receive these notices; their versions also had an addendum printed in red which rather ominously advised under the heading of IMPORTANT NOTICE:

> *This leaflet is being distributed throughout the country. If invasion comes it applies in this town as elsewhere, but before invasion comes those who are not engaged on useful work should leave this town.*[10]

The message was repeated with guidance as to exactly what groups of workers should stay and who should leave on posters erected on prominent display in the coastal towns affected.

Air raids were still a regular occurrence; of over forty night raids against targets other than London in 1941, only a handful were not directed against ports.[11] Newspapers were often prevented by government censorship from being specific about exactly where was being bombed, but people on the coast would see and hear the raiders in the sky and the glow of the fires. Rumour, although officially discouraged, was rife and because the newspapers could not report accurately the stories of what had actually been bombed, the amount of destruction and numbers of dead often became over exaggerated, sometimes to such ludicrous proportions that they beggared belief. Coastal communities where there was both a Royal Navy and Merchant Navy presence were under no illusions. Things were hellishly tough at sea and U-boats continued to be a deadly menace in home waters.

In the hope of getting some uncensored information about the air raids, and maybe even a tip-off of a raid to come, many people tuned in to German propaganda radio stations such as the New British Broadcasting Service for information. Purporting to be broadcasting the real news from Britain, the station was stymied by the use of broadcasters with ridiculous upper class accents; including William Joyce, the broadcaster dubbed 'Lord Haw Haw'.

The problem was the station mixed in facts, guess work, reported bomb damage and listed prisoners of war. It often sounded very convincing but if you actually lived in the places covered by the reportage you would know just how inaccurate it was, but for those who did not know better there was some truth in it and it was bad for morale. The dropping of leaflets by German aircraft stating 'The Battle of the Atlantic is Being Lost' and pointing out our lines of supply were cut, the country will starve and Britain is losing the war, seemed to hit people harder than the leaflets a year earlier. Cumulatively the atmosphere among many British people was that they were willing and able to fight on, once again Britain was vulnerable to invasion…but this time we will be organised!

Despite having received the latest national directives on leaflets, posters, newspapers and magazines, there were still people who did not know exactly what to do if invasion forces threatened their specific area. A raft of measures had been cobbled together in 1940, now the dust of the original invasion scare had settled some of the areas that would have faced the vanguard of attack decided to get more organised and, in the finest British tradition, committees were formed. The first invasion committees were created in Norfolk in May and June 1941. This well thought out idea met the approval of Regional Commissioner Will Spens, Suffolk followed suit and their example was soon followed by parishes across the country.[12]

The scheme was soon adopted by all regional commissioners who would instigate the creation of invasion committees through letters sent out to urban and rural district councils via the clerk of the county council. A typical committee would consist of the local vicar, the schoolmaster, chief air raid warden, principal tradesmen and a member of the Women's Voluntary Service. Other suitable persons could also be invited, but the idea was that the committee consisted of the key people from the local area in the right positions to represent the majority of the population and that decision making should not become a long drawn-out process.

The purpose of the invasion committee was to draw up a plan, as complete in detail as possible, of what was to be done in their local area if it was threatened by invasion. This would not mean actually fighting the invader, that of course remained the domain of the military forces and Home Guard, nor would they be responsible for air raid precautions or dealing with air raid casualties. The purpose of the invasion committee, working with the military, Home Guard and ARP, was to discuss and agree a plan of action and ensure their instructions to the civilian population were carried out where possible. They were to make every effort to ensure that 'Everyone should know what to do and how to do it if the church bells ring.'[13]

Home Guard armed with 'Molotov Cocktails' training in street fighting in Folkestone, March 1941.

The scheme continued over the next twelve months as invasion committees established themselves and were allocated specific officers from their local police, fire service and fire watchers for liaison, some of whom became members of the invasion committees too. The committees also appointed their own parish organisers with specific duties. Suitable buildings to become rest centres, emergency first aid posts, billets and mortuaries would all be arranged. A volunteer labour force with tools and suitable materials for trench construction and emergency repairs would be created, usually by making an agreement with local builders. Emergency transport, both motorised and horse drawn, would also be arranged, and plans made for emergency water supplies and sanitation. Volunteer food officers would be appointed to manage emergency rations, arrange their storage and suitable distribution centres.

Once a local invasion emergency plan had been agreed many places issued their own 'Stand Firm' anti-invasion instructions to local residents and households would receive a leaflet stating who their local food officer was, where food stocks were to be distributed from and what would be available to them. The standard stock consisted of biscuits, tinned meat, tinned stew, tinned milk, sugar, tea and margarine, which would be allocated to each person in equal amounts advised by the Ministry of Food.

New national guidelines were also published to help standardise anti-invasion procedures such as *Advising the Public in the Event of Invasion (Notes for the Guidance of Air Raid Wardens)* published in August 1941. Another push to establish invasion committees in as many parishes as possible came early in 1942 led by Sir John Anderson (Lord President of the Council) in an address to the House of Commons in which he reminded the country that it was the duty of every citizen to 'offer united opposition to the invader'. Sir John continued:

> *Invasion committees are being set up in all areas where such measures were necessary. The duty of the committees was to survey their local problems and consider their needs if fighting should reach their districts and the best way civil and military authorities could help each other…*
>
> *There are countless ways in which the help of civilians will be needed, in cooking and distributing food, filling craters and shell holes to enable military vehicles to pass, digging trenches, providing billets for troops moving in, neighbours bombed or shelled out. In a village or small town the invasion committee will be able to allot specific jobs to particular individuals and most of the able bodied inhabitants will know in advance what their role would be.*[14]

To ensure the composition, duties and parameters of authority of invasion committees were made clear and standardised in England and Wales the *Consolidated Instructions to Invasion Committees* booklet was compiled by the Ministry of Home Security for issue as a 'confidential' publication by regional commissioners in July 1942. Most invasion committees continued to meet until the later months of 1944 and stood down at the same time as the Home Guard.

Chapter 6

Fight on the Beaches

The beaches will be a bloody shambles.

Staff Officer, Western Command

The battalions that had been so badly depleted at Dunkirk were rebuilt and re-armed through the second half of 1940, even if not with supplies of the latest weaponry. The stocks of the P.14 rifles that had been released for the Home Guard also provided rifles for many battalions of soldiers in training. Infantry battalion transport was still a running joke well into 1941; there were still battalions mounted on bicycles for coastal patrols but there were more lorries, albeit old stock originally made for civilian commercial markets or even requisitioned from hauliers or builders. Painted army green or brown, or even in camouflage livery, they didn't look too bad and a canvas and frame over the back kept the soldiers dry. The miles regularly marched in all weathers were greatly reduced and ultimately our coastal forces and

Soldiers of 7th Battalion, The Suffolk Regiment tackling barbed wire obstacles during beach training at Sandbanks near Poole, Dorset, March 1941.

mobile reserves became far better equipped for rapid deployment. These lorries served our coastal forces well.

Famously, Churchill had declared, 'We shall fight on the beaches' and as the new year progressed soldiers around the entire coast of Britain and Northern Ireland spent more time in battle drills, beach obstacle and cliff assault exercises. The new beach exercises also showed up some deficiencies in our thankfully untested defences, especially those on the south-west and west coast where the threat of invasion had not been felt quite so acutely. At a combined services conference after a large anti-invasion exercise in the south-west, the senior Royal Navy and Royal Air Force officers expressed their opinion they could not commit to a stronger presence in the area because they were needed elsewhere. The army commander remained undaunted and said, 'Well, it means that we will have to stop the invasion ourselves,' to which one of the Army staff officers added, 'But you can take it from me that the beaches will be a bloody shambles.'[1]

There may have been a few grumbles but this new scheme of training for attack rather than defence imbued troops with the skills to take the fight back to the enemy in new theatres of war. The later months of 1940 and the year 1941 were recalled by many veterans on coastal defences as a period of numerous official visits from the likes of their brigade and divisional commanders, usually just before a visit by senior members of the general staff which, in turn, would mean in the not too distant future there would be an official visit by a dignitary, sometimes a prominent politician in a senior cabinet position, foreign dignitaries and royalty from Allied countries. There could even be a visit from Churchill himself or members of the British royal family.

As the months of re-equipment, training and official visits passed troops were invigorated with a new feeling of purpose and adventure, especially when the units were issued with khaki uniforms and pith helmets, then imaginations ran wild over where they were going to be deployed. There was also plenty of laughter when they saw each other in shorts and pith helmets for the first time. Within the next twelve months most of the rebuilt divisions were deployed abroad again to active service in the desert or the far east.

The coastal defences were changing too. Back in 1940 the anti-aircraft firepower along Britain's coast (and around several inland cities) had been enhanced by the introduction of rocket batteries. The rockets, still listed as secret and shrouded in some mystique, became known as 'Z Batteries', named after the Zeda projector from which the rockets were launched. As 1941 progressed thousands of Royal Artillery gunners were being deployed abroad and members of the Home Guard were taking over the manning of the coastal batteries, so in September 1941 a trial was set up for Home Guard

General Alan Brooke inspecting 508 Regiment, Royal Artillery at Tynemouth Priory, Northumberland during his tour of defences in the north east, November 1940.

Home Guard taking up action stations and loading Anti-Aircraft Zeda rocket projectors at a 'Z' Battery on Merseyside, July 1942.

Launching the rockets, Merseyside, July 1942.

personnel to man the Z Batteries in Liverpool. The trial proved successful and members of the Home Guard were soon training to man Z Batteries all over the country. The single barrel projector was the main weapon, with sixty-four of these grouped in one location, each site required 178 HG for each nightly duty. In a week with eight shifts just over 1,400 men were required for every rocket site manned by members of the Home Guard.

The year 1941 also saw the design and commencement of construction of the last major fixed defences for the coast. The problem that confronted the War Office were rivers. Be it day or night every major city in Great Britain was on a river and if all else failed pilots and navigators knew if they followed a river they would reach a target worth attacking; the Thames and London was a particular case in point. It was also imperative to stop enemy aircraft from laying mines in rivers that were important shipping channels.

There were anti-aircraft guns and batteries along the coast, on the banks of major rivers and across the country and also nearly 3,000 barrage balloons, some of which were flown from balloon barrage vessels converted for the purpose from commandeered drifters, barges or trawlers crewed by Royal Navy personnel. The flying and maintenance of the balloon was the responsibility of a small detachment of RAF personnel (usually one sergeant and eight airmen) who would also be on board, but everyone would work very

142

A barrage balloon tethered to balloon barge **Norman** Wade *on the Humber at the No 17 Balloon Centre, Sutton on Hull, January 1943.*

much as a team. These vessels were deployed to harbours and the wide waters of river estuaries, but there was only limited firepower such as machine guns on the smaller vessels to engage enemy aircraft.

The Admiralty addressed this by approaching the noted civil engineer Guy A. Maunsell, who had gained his reputation through his innovative work in hydro–electric construction and the Rosyth Naval base. Maunsell had worked on the design and construction of concrete ships and 'mystery' towers with the Ministry of Transport during the First World War. He was appointed the first chief engineer of the Ministry of Transport before returning to civilian engineering during the 1920s and 30s when he carried out a number of notable projects with bridges. These included the construction of the Storstrøm Bridge in Denmark, in its day the longest bridge in Europe.[2] Maunsell was the ideal man to be given the challenge of designing off-shore 'forts' to take the fight back to airborne enemy intruders.

Maunsell began with naval forts, the first, Fort (U1) was to provide protection for the protection of the ports of Felixstowe and Harwich. Construction began in October 1941 at Red Lion Wharf on the border between Northfleet and Gravesend on the Thames. The basic structure was towed out to its site at Rough Sands under the personal supervision of Maunsell and was sunk into

143

One of the Maunsell Naval Forts in the Thames Estuary c1943.

position on 11 February 1942.[3] Other forts followed soon after at Sunk Head (U2), Tongue Sands (U3) and Knock John (U4). Each fort was supported by two 60ft tall, 24ft diameter concrete towers built on a reinforced concrete pontoon base. These towers were divided into seven floors, four floors for crew quarters and the rest for a dining area and storage for ammunition, freshwater tanks and generators. Once in place the towers were capped off and linked by a steel platform deck upon which an upper deck and central tower would be added. Manned by Royal Navy personnel and Royal Marines, these naval forts were equipped with anti-aircraft guns, searchlights and radar equipment.

Maunsell's naval forts on the Thames estuary were heralded a great success and he was asked by the War Office to create a similar solution for offshore anti-aircraft defences to be manned by Army personnel. He created a brand new design for these forts based as near as possible on the standard layout of anti-aircraft batteries on land. Each completed fort would consist of seven 90ft high fortress towers with steel platforms connected by walkways. Four of the towers, each with a 3.75-inch anti-aircraft gun on top, would be sited forward of the central control tower (which had a Bofors 40mm gun on top). The seventh tower would be sited to one side of the gun towers and would be for a searchlight.

Three of these Maunsell army forts: Nore (U5), Red Sands (U6) and Shivering Sands (U7), also built at Gravesend, were sited in the Thames

Maunsell Army Forts in the Thames Estuary photographed from an approaching supply vessel, November 1943.

estuary. A further three Army forts – Queens, Formby and Burbo AA Towers were constructed at Bromborough Dock on the Mersey and installed in Liverpool Bay. Proposals were also in the pipeline for further forts to be constructed for the Humber, Portsmouth, Rosyth, Belfast and Londonderry but these did not materialise.

So, you may ask, how effective were these Maunsell forts that looked like the product of the imagination of H.G. Wells? The forts in Liverpool Bay would never see action, but those on the Thames Estuary could claim twenty-two aircraft and approximately thirty flying bombs brought down by their guns. Tongue Sands Fort (U3) could also claim an E-boat.

Adopt, Adapt, Invent

Holiday camps had been among the first to be taken over for wartime purposes in coastal resorts. Many of them had their holiday trade decimated because they had become part of a coastal strip designated a defence zone where hotels, guest houses and even private houses were taken over to become entirely or in part military billets. Some of the dance halls, places of entertainment and pleasure gardens were also converted for military training purposes.

No.10 (Signals) Recruits Centre receiving morse training in the Olympia Exhibition Hall at the Winter Gardens, Blackpool c1942.

The west coast, notably Blackpool, was considered the least likely for invasion, and drew theatrical impresarios and acts attempting to avoid the bombing in London. The accommodation offered by its thousands of guest houses led the RAF to select Blackpool for one of its initial training wings comprising the No.3 School of General Reconnaissance at RAF Squires Gate, which had a tactical floor of realistic model boats and sea marks to help air crew learn to identify vessels at sea. There was also the No.5 School of Technical Training for Air Mechanics with barracks at Weeton and Kirkham.

The Olympia Exhibition Hall at the Winter Gardens became the No.10 (Signals) Recruits Centre training school where row upon row of young men sat at long mess hall tables, headphones on, key in hand and message pad at the ready to learn Morse code. The Polish training school was established at the Lansdowne Hotel in 1942 and the golden sands played host to large groups of recruits being put through early morning physical training sessions. During the war Blackpool became the RAF's largest training area where men from all over the UK and allied countries all over the world came to learn the skills to serve as aircrew in the RAF.

Blackpool was also host to units from the American Army Air Force and thousands of gunners from the Royal Artillery. The landladies of the town

RAF aircrew learning how to identify vessels at sea using models on the Tactical Floor in No 3 School of General Reconnaissance, Squires Gate, Blackpool, April 1944.

offered over 5,000 billets that housed over 853,768 members of the forces over the war years; over 700,000 of them were members of the Royal Air Force.[4]

Fearing bombing or even an enemy commando raid to snatch scientists or technical information from sites on the east coast, the Air Ministry's top secret radar research station at Bawdsey Manor on the Suffolk coast was 'evacuated' to University College Dundee in September 1939. Likewise, the Shoeburyness Small Arms Experimental Estate in Essex went to Pendine Sands in South Wales and the Coast Artillery School moved to Great Orme, Llandudno. The Royal Artillery Experimental Station at Shoeburyness, however, carried on in situ providing a major centre for the testing of new weaponry, notably the development and monitoring of the performance of anti-aircraft shells. During the course of the war over one and a quarter million rounds were fired at the site.

In 1941 Birnbeck Pier on the Bristol Channel at Weston-super-Mare, Somerset – where once holidaymakers strolled along its boards and embarked on the steamer for day trips to Cardiff, Clovelly, Bristol or Lundy

Some of the thousands of RAF personnel in training in Blackpool photographed in front of some of the guest houses where they were billeted c1942.

Island – became the Royal Navy shore establishment HMS *Birnbeck*. This was no ordinary base for it was here the Royal Navy's deliberately vaguely named Directorate of Miscellaneous Weapon Development (nicknamed the Wheezers and Dodgers), a clandestine team of military and civilian scientists would be based for the rest of the war. DMWD saw the potential of some of the buildings on the pier to become ideal workshops and developed a number of weapons and launchers based around rockets.

Birnbeck Pier, Weston Super Mare became HMS Birnbeck the shore base of the Naval Directorate of Miscellaneous Weapons Development in 1941.

As in all experimental areas they had their failures, one being the Panjandrum. Working on the principle of Catherine-wheel fireworks, this consisted of two 10ft high wheels that were propelled along by nine rockets installed around the inner hub of the wheel. Once set in motion it was intended to be propelled by the rockets up a beach then, once defences such as wire entanglements were contacted and hopefully tangled over it, the 4,000lbs of explosive the assault wheel was carrying would detonate and blow a gap in that area of the defences. That was the idea at least, but once built tests of the weapon were not promising and its final outing on the beach at Westward Ho! saw it spin out of control over the beaches where it was released and then wobble back to the sea area where it started from in the first place.

DMWD also had notable successes like the rocket landing craft they developed that was famous for firing salvo after salvo onto the Normandy beaches shattering the morale of German coastal units and preparing the way for the D-Day landings on 6 June 1944. In its day the rocket landing craft was described as the most formidable weapon in all the long history of shore bombardment.[5]

In December 1942 the first air drop trials of Barnes Wallis's 'bouncing bomb' were carried out on the waters of the Fleet Lagoon near Langton Herring, part of the Chesil Beach bombing range in Dorset. These early trials used modified Vickers Wellingtons, but it soon became clear the bigger Avro Lancasters would be more capable of carrying the bombs and specially modified versions of the Lanc were first used in the trials of the bomb off Reculver in Kent. Here the twin towers of St Mary's church made an excellent marker for the point of release during these trial bombing runs. The bombs were not always successful, but the principle was there, and it was through these trials that the drop height was reduced from 150ft to 60ft and the bombs were modified to stop them fracturing as they hit the water. At the third trial at Reculver on 29 April 1943 the bomb did not fracture and really skipped over the water for the first time and Barnes Wallis jumped for joy waving his hat in the air on the dunes. In the final tests conducted 5 miles off Broadstairs on 13 May 1943, the bomb bounced seven times then sank and detonated.

Three nights later on the night of 16 May 1943 the Dams Raid took place. The bouncing bombs dropped by the Lancasters of 617 Squadron under Wing Commander Guy Gibson blew the Möhne and Eder dams, sending 300 million tons of water into the western Ruhr valleys, and 617 Squadron would be known for evermore as 'The Dambusters'.

Seaside features were also repurposed at resorts around the country. Tall structures in fairgrounds and the upper stories of hotels, cinemas and private seaside residences became useful vantage points for artillery observers and

A defence post at the Regent Cinema, Sheringham, Norfolk.

Model Boat Pond at Gorleston-on-Sea in Norfolk converted to a military vehicle waterproofing test tank, for 'Water Splash' courses, pictured in May 1944.

a host of buildings and seaward-facing shops and kiosks were sandbagged to become defensive positions. Even the model boat pond at Gorleston was converted to become a drive-through water feature to test the waterproofing of armoured fighting vehicles in 1944 as the forces in Britain geared up for the D-Day landings.

More remote areas of the coast away from inquisitive eyes were ideal for the Ministry of Home Security Research and Experiments Department to conduct their trials. For example, a secret site at Brancaster Beach on the North Norfolk coast was used to test the temperatures pillboxes could withstand if subjected to fire. The area also had puddle clay that was ideal for testing the calibre of bombs and other missiles by exploding them in or on the clay and measuring the diameter and depth of the craters caused by the explosion.[6]

One of the most unusual weapons of the war was also developed on the coast at Harwich under the codename of Operation Outward. During the early stages of the war an organisation was set up under Lieutenant Colonel J. O'Hea for releasing fire balloons from French territories with a view to harassing the Germans. These balloons were of the hot air type and it was the intention that they should be controlled by Direction Finding apparatus and made to release their bombs, be they HE or incendiaries, over a reasonably well-defined area. With the fall of France the fire balloon party had to return to England and the project was not pursued because there were elements in the War Office of the opinion such attacks were in fact dirty tricks and 'should not be originated from a cricketing country'.[7]

In September 1940 a number of barrage balloons from British sites were torn from their moorings by gale force winds and carried across the North Sea to Sweden, Denmark and Finland. Reports were soon received of the confusion and alarm the balloons had raised and the damage to power lines that had been caused by both balloons and the wire cable ropes trailing beneath them. Churchill heard about this and directed that the use of free-flying balloons as an offensive weapon against Germany should be investigated. Captain Gerald Banister, the Director of Boom Defence, fostered the idea and prepared a report. Bannister argued the case for the use of the large surplus stock of thousands of meteorological weather balloons that could be filled with hydrogen being released from the coast of East Anglia where the wind currents would be ideal to blow balloons carrying 6lb 'incendiary freights' across to Germany and start fires, adding:

> It could be devastatingly effective and deny sleep over unlimited period to millions of the inhabitants of the Reich. It may lay waste to crops, heaths and forests over immense areas.[8]

Officers and Ratings of the The Women's Royal Naval Service officially engaged in 'Boom Defence' but actually working on Operation Outward, 1942.

Balloons could also carry trailing wires to interfere with the Reich's power supplies or telecommunications by damaging overhead wires. A launch base was established at HMS *Beehive* in Harwich staffed by 6 Royal Navy and Royal Marine officers, 80 Royal Marines, 7 Women's Royal Naval Service officers and 140 Wrens who worked under the cover of being engaged in 'Boom Defence'. The first offensive balloon releases took place on ground at the Felixstowe Ferry Golf Club in March 1942. The balloons were indeed carried on the wind to Germany and there were even reports of forest fires from near Berlin. The problem was it was often difficult to prove if the fire had actually been started by an incendiary carried by a balloon or by other means, but they seemed to be getting results and a second launch site was set up at Oldstairs Bay near Dover in July 1942. By August 1942 10,000 balloons were being released every day until the operation was curtailed because of the danger the balloons presented to the airspace required for allied aircraft activities in support of the D–Day landings. The last offensive balloons of Operation Outward were launched in September 1944.[9]

Commandos!

As Britain faced up to the danger of invasion Churchill never wanted to just defend the country, he wanted to fight back. In a minute to Major General Hastings 'Pug' Ismay, his principal link to the chiefs of staffs, on 6 June 1940 Churchill set the matter in motion:

> *Enterprises must be prepared, with specially-trained troops of the hunter class, who can develop a reign of terror down these coasts, first of all on the 'butcher and bolt' policy…*[10]

Chief of the Imperial General Staff, General Sir John Dill turned to his military assistant Lieutenant Colonel Dudley Clarke to prepare a paper on just such a force. Clarke, who proved to be a leading light in special operations throughout the war, drew his inspiration from the Boer 'commando' units that worked along similar lines during the South African War 1899–1902.[11] The scheme was approved and resulted in the creation of a four battalion Special Service Brigade, which rapidly evolved into what became known as Commando units. If these new units were going to conduct raids on the enemy coast they would need to train on similar terrain and so the first training of the Commandos began on the south coast of Britain.

Brigadier John Durnford-Slater, (then a lieutenant colonel) had been appointed to raise one of the first of these units (No.3 Commando) and recalled how they became part of the local community where they were based:

Instead of putting troops into barracks the Commando system was to give each man a subsistence allowance of 6s 8d a day; the man was then required to find his own accommodation and food. This was in every way a splendid arrangement, it increased a man's self-reliance and self-respect, developed his initiative and made him available for training at any time day or night. Nobody had to be left in barracks for administrative duties and every officer and man was able to concentrate entirely on training; the old barrack room boredom and bad language were eliminated. Furthermore, wherever we went we were always welcomed by our landladies, who took a pride in the unit and did everything to help the men they were billeting. I merely allotted an area of Plymouth to each troop and left the officers and men to find their own accommodation.[12]

By the autumn of 1940 over 2,000 men had volunteered and twelve Commando units had been created, each containing approximately 450 men. With such large numbers involved, instead of independent companies each being responsible for their own training, it really needed to be centralised. An area with enough space for accommodation and challenging terrain for the high level of training and fitness was required so the bulk of the Commando units were concentrated in the West of Scotland at what would become known as No.1 Combined Training Centre, Inveraray, on the shore of Loch Fyne from October 1940. There was also the Special Training Centre for officers and NCOs at Lochailfort which had been established earlier in the year.

The training was tough and relentless, a chance for men to tackle rugged mountains, become resilient in adverse weather conditions and it built incredibly strong Commando units. John Durnford-Slater recalled:

Army Commandos in a landing craft prepare to hit the beach during training in Scotland, February 1942.

> *I thought we had found our weaknesses at Plymouth but this tough life at Inverary sorted out still more who could not take it. It really was a hard life, there was nothing to do but work. We would start on the landing craft at 8am and follow on with drill, marching, shooting and long schemes on the hills. We also went in for obstacle courses and close combat, which included wrestling and work with knives and pistols taught by two ex-Shanghai policemen.*[13]

They were also trained in how to enter buildings and in the use of grenades, explosives and a variety of weapons including the Thompson sub-machine gun. Even after dark their work was not done, the men had to become proficient in working at night so three nights a week they were engaged in night exercises.

In December 1941 a dedicated Commando Training Depot was established at Achnacarry Castle. No.1 CTC Inverary continued as a combined services

154

Lord Louis Mountbatten (on right) watching troops make a practice landing from a dummy landing craft on the beach at the Combined Operations centre at Dundonald Camp, 1942.

assault brigade training centre and over forty associated specialist training centres were established in the area for specific elements of combined operations. In February 1942 the first two Royal Marine Commando units were raised and assembled at Deal where they were given their initial training, testing and assessment. Those who passed would be sent to Achnacarry which was now the centre for all Commando training.

Between 1940 and 1944 a total of fifty-seven Commando raids were launched from the shores of Britain against Nazi occupied France, the Channel Islands, Norway, Belgium and The Netherlands. Usually, these operations would consist of small parties of between two and ten men; the largest by far was a combined forces operation including No.3 and No.4 Commando with a majority force of Canadian infantry from the 2nd Canadian Infantry Division. Codenamed Operation Jubilee, it was better known to the public as the Dieppe Raid, which took place on 19 August 1942. Described as a 'reconnaissance by force' by its planners, the idea was to test the concepts and equipment that would be required for a full-scale amphibious assault to gain a toe hold back in occupied France that could pave the way for the liberation of north western Europe.

Over 6,000 men set off in landing craft from the south coast ports and harbours of Portsmouth, Southampton, Cowes, Newhaven and Shoreham.

Combined Operations practice landings during Exercise Walter on the Isle of Wight, May 1942.

Aircraft were spotted flying high over the Channel in support and by mid-morning reports were being filed of 'the distant roll of guns from France' being heard in Folkestone.[14] The lessons learned from the raid proved valuable to allied planners and the Germans were led to believe, to a certain extent, if the allied forces were to return they would do so in the same area and diverted resources there accordingly. Tragically though, the cost of the raid was heavy in the loss of life and equipment. Out of the Canadian contingent of nearly 5,000 some 3,367 were killed, wounded or taken prisoner; of the 1,000 British Commandos 247 were lost.

The troops who made it back to the south coast were seen by local people in their battle stained, tattered and bloody state. Newspapers spoke of the many wounded being carried across the harbours and loaded onto waiting hospital trains and the Canadian motor ambulance convoys. The quayside dance hall had been rapidly converted to become a casualty clearing station with hundreds of gallons of tea being dispensed to returned troops.[15]

The return of the British Commandos to Newhaven remained a vivid memory for many locals who saw it from first light on what turned out to be the

Lieutenant Colonel The Lord Lovat, Commanding Officer, No.4 Commando at Newhaven after returning from the raid on Dieppe, 19 August 1942

Unteroffizier Leo Marsiniak, captured at the gun battery at Varengeville, Dieppe by No.4 Commando being escorted at Newhaven 19 August 1942.

hot, sunny day of 20 August. They saw Commandos clustered on the quayside sharing a cigarette after clambering off their boats, many would recall the men still had a smell of cordite and oily smoke about them. The bedraggled German prisoners they had snatched from the beach and defences of Dieppe also caused quite a stir.

* * *

As Britain's armed forces trained for active service abroad numerous areas of land were taken over as army camps where new brigades and divisions could concentrate as they were formed and areas of land were requisitioned as training areas. Along the coast a number of communities would be affected and even ended up being permanently dispersed with their villages, hamlets, and seaside homes being taken over, or even destroyed, for military purposes.

Soldiers training at the 45th Division Battle School at Frinton-on-Sea, Essex, October 1942.

The destruction began back in 1940 when a number of disused or down-at-heel hotels, windmills and distinctive buildings along the coast, considered conspicuous landmarks that could be used as navigation aids for seaborne or airborne enemy forces, were demolished.

In July 1940 in East Sussex those who resided near the beach at Camber, Winchelsea, Rye and Pett Level – with the exception of a few farmers – were given just forty-eight hours to evacuate their homes to enable beach defences to be installed and local marshes allowed to flood as an anti-invasion measure. Bungalow Town at Shoreham-by-Sea in West Sussex was not only evacuated at short notice, but the majority of the buildings were demolished soon after, leaving only the Church of the Good Shepherd as a reminder of the community that was once there.

These drastic actions were far from popular, even among the most war-effort minded of the residents would bemoan the fact they had been determined to dig their heels in the face of Hitler's invasion 'only to be ousted by our own side'. The removal of communities was also criticised for the lack of help residents received with finding new places to live, a matter highlighted by the secret daily report on morale received by the Ministry of Information on 10 September 1940 which reported:

Residents of Shoreham Beach Bungalow Town were recently ordered to leave by military authorities, and it seems that distress has been caused as many of the bungalows were built as an investment by elderly people, and it is reported that no provision has been made to look after them.[16]

The areas used by the military for training presented a recurring problem from children wandering onto those sites, despite there being warning signs and wire. Some were killed or badly injured after finding and playing with discarded ordnance such as hand grenades, unexploded shells and rounds of live ammunition. Areas of beach along the coast that were mined also proved lethal to local people, both adults and children who wandered into them. Not all soldiers avoided the mines either, Major General Clifford Malden, GOC 47 Division was killed after he accidentally trod on a beach mine on Shoreham Beach when he was inspecting coastal defences on 25 March 1941. In one of the most tragic incidents seven soldiers of the 5th Battalion, Royal Berkshire Regiment were killed when they wandered into the minefield on Thorpeness beach on 14 October 1942.

In a number of areas the beaches were completely locked down and no members of the public were to be admitted or only a very limited area was left open for local civilians with passes from the appropriate military commander granting them access for their work as fishermen, or for those who undertook regular sea bathing for reasons of health and fitness. In 1942 members of the public were also banned from vast stretches of downland between Brighton and Eastbourne as that too was given over to become a military training area. Farmers had to give up their land and the 100 residents of Stanmer, a tiny hamlet between Lewes and Brighton which consisted of just twenty cottages, a shop and church all had to evacuate and find new homes.

Buoyed up after significant victories in the desert, development of military technology for forces on land, sea and in the air and the production of munitions to support it, Allied leaders and military commanders felt confident they could come together to formulate a plan for the invasion of France and the liberation of north western Europe. The meeting, held in Canada between 17–24 August 1943, became known as the Quebec Conference and the plan that was drafted as a result was codenamed Operation Overlord which would commence with the D-Day landings set for a provisional date of 1 May 1944. Training was to begin in earnest in the spring and the British coast was to be the main training area for the seaborne assault.

A young girl about to be evacuated with her family from their home in Slapton Sands when the South Hams were cleared of civilians to become a military training area in December 1943.

The idyllic Worbarrow Bay, Dorset, requisitioned along with the village of Tyneham and 7,500 acres of heath and downland for military training purposes in 1943.

A new raft of restrictions for residents and the lock-down of coastal areas in preparation for them becoming training areas began soon afterwards. For most it was much the same experience they had become used to since the coast defence areas were defined in 1940. The new exercises preparing soldiers for Operation Overlord would use more live ammunition than ever before and would be conducted on unprecedented scales and some areas would need to be completely evacuated of their civilian population.

Two areas were drastically affected. The residents of the coastal villages of Slapton, Torcross, Strete, Blackawton, East Allington, Sherford, Stokenham and Chillington in the South Hams district of the south coast of Devon received notifications on 12 November 1943 they had to evacuate their homes little more than a month later on 20 December. Public notices from the Ministry of Home Security emphasised:

> *They* [local residents] *will not, except for special reasons, be disturbed in their possession until December 21st, but from that date the Admiralty may at any time, and without prior notice, enforce their right to immediate possession. People should leave by 20 December. On December 21st the supply of electricity in the area will cease. The present measures for supplying food will not be continued, but will be replaced by arrangements of a purely emergency character. The police stations will be closing during the present week.*

On 16 November 1943 a similar letter was received by the inhabitants of the village of Tyneham and the residents over the surrounding 7,500 acres of heath and downland in the adjoining parishes of East Lulworth, East Stoke, East Holme, Steeple and Worbarrow Bay in Dorset. They were left with even less time, having to leave their properties by 19 December.

The tone of both pre-printed letters sent to the local residents were similar, for those in the East Holme area stated:

> *In order to give our troops the fullest opportunity to perfect their training in the use of modern weapons of war, the army must have an area of land particularly suited to their special needs and in which they can use live shells. For this reason you will realise the chosen area must be cleared of all civilians.*
>
> *The most careful search has been made to find an area suitable for the Army's purpose and which, at the same time, will involve the smallest number of persons and property…It is regretted that in the National Interest it is necessary to move you from your homes, and everything possible will be done to help you, both by payment of compensation and by finding other accommodation for you if you are unable to do so yourself.*
>
> *The date on which the military will take over this area is the 19th December next, and all civilians must be out of the area by that date…*
>
> *The Government appreciate that this is no small sacrifice which you are asked to make, but they are sure that you will give this further help towards winning the war with a good heart.*[17]

Despite the official line implying there had been some consultation with local councils, nothing of the sort had actually taken place. Information centres were provided for both areas, compensation was offered, transport was provided and most were relocated peacefully to towns and villages a short distance away. Terms like evacuated and relocated were used by authorities on notices and correspondence throughout the process, but most of the local people, especially those in the Tyneham area, saw it as an eviction. Some waited until the very last moment to go, others like Ralph Bond, a local magistrate and commander of the Tyneham Home Guard platoon were evicted. Ralph, along with the servants from his Elizabethan mansion, some local farm labourers and the last fishermen of Worbarrow Bay all suffered the same fate.

The bitter pill was sweetened for residents of both communities because they were promised that after the war they would be able to return to their homes. The people of the East Hams villages in Dorset were indeed able to return to their homes, albeit many were battered around with doors smashed inside and gardens high with weeds. It would also be years before their beach was cleared of all the explosive ordnance from the exercises that took place there, but they did receive compensation and the communities were rebuilt.

The people of Tyneham and its surrounding area were not to be so fortunate, the land was compulsorily purchased by the army in 1948 and, despite a bitter dispute between former residents and the Ministry of Defence lasting for decades afterwards, no one was allowed to return to their homes. Today the whole area remains part of the MOD Lulworth Ranges and is only accessible when the ranges are open to the public.

To all intents and purposes the village of Tyneham became a 'ghost village' in 1943. A poignant note was left on the church door by one of the last to leave:

> *Please treat the church and houses with care; we have given up our homes where many of us lived for generations to help win the war to keep men free. We shall return one day and thank you for treating the village kindly.*

Chapter 7

Strangers on the Shore

Three people arrived in a rubber boat in the early hours of this morning on the east coast of Scotland…

Guy Liddell, MI5

German prisoners of war, captured after the sinking of Kriegsmarine vessels – often several hundred crew could arrive at the same time – aircrew from Luftwaffe aircraft brought down in the waters off our coast, or soldiers brought to Britain after capture 'in the field' were frequently seen arriving at ports and harbours around Britain throughout the war. They

Blindfolded U-boat prisoners disembarking at Greenock before being removed to their prisoner of war camp, 11 October 1943.

usually didn't hang around for long, the ship would have signalled ahead to alert military authorities to arrange reception of the prisoners and for large numbers of PoWs British and allied troops armed with rifles with fixed bayonets would be positioned from the gang plank and spaced along a prepared route to the lorries that would be waiting to whisk them away to prisoner of war camps. For a small number of aircrew a car and armed military police escort usually sufficed. The pace was kept swift and most people would only catch the briefest glimpse of the prisoners as they passed through the docks.

Prisoners would often arrive with their eyes bound with field dressings and bandages that led, on occasion, to rumours of them appearing to have been blinded. The reason for the eyes being bandaged was to hinder any escape attempts, a blindfolded man tends to be far more docile and will tend to go exactly where he is guided to go. Authorities also did not want the prisoners getting sight of defences nor landmarks that could help them determine exactly where they were in Britain or help them find their way to docks or harbours just in case they did try to make a successful escape.

The first four German spies known for certain to have arrived on Britain's shores during the Second World War landed either side of the Dungeness peninsula on 3 September 1940. More would soon follow under what became known as Operation Lena. Abwehr head Admiral Wilhelm Canaris had entrusted the operation to Colonel Erwin von Lahousen, Head of Abwehr II in June 1940. In turn Lahousen chose Ast Hamburg, under the overall command of Korvettenkapitän Herbert Wichmann to see the operation through, with Section I-L (Air Intelligence, the 'L' was for Luft) under Hauptmann Nikolaus Ritter to oversee agents parachuted into Britain and section I-M ('M' for Marine) for boat landing agents under veteran Abwehr officer Hilmar Dierks.

Lena agents were to be recruited from occupied countries, trained and sent to Britain to gather information about military defences, emplacements, troop concentrations, minefields in specific coastal areas to provide invasion planners with the latest information about areas where invasion forces were being planned. Agents were also ordered to discern what they could of the morale of the British people and to get amongst the population at the moment of invasion. Findings were to be regularly transmitted back via radios using agreed codes and during specific windows of time. There were also to be Abwehr groups landed with the specific remit of sabotage of communications and military installations to hinder the efforts of the anti-invasion forces in Britain.[1]

Agents delivered via seaborne landings in the south of Britain were the part of the operation known as *Hummer Süd* (Lobster South) for landings and *Hummer Nord* (Lobster North) was for landings in the north.

All four spies landed on the south coast on 3 September 1940 had been caught within forty-eight hours of arrival; the landings in the north were

Portgordon looking west, with the station building in the left foreground, where a suspicious couple arrived with their shoes and lower garments wet with sea water on 30 September 1940.

hoped to have better results. The first three agents of Hummer Nord I, were two men, Karl Drücke who was supplied with false documents and a cover story under the name of Francois de Deeker, a French refugee from Belgium, and Robert Petter who was given papers in the name of Werner Heinrich Wälti, a Swiss subject living in London. The third person was Vera Schalburg (probably known at the time as Vera von Wedel) the first and only known woman spy to land in Britain during the war, who had been given the cover identity of Vera Eriksen, a Dane living in London. Flown in an X. Fliegerkorps He 115 seaplane from Stavanger, Norway, the three were set down on the waters of Moray Firth off the coast between Buckie and Portgordon in what was then known as Banffshire, in the eastern Highlands of Scotland around dawn on 30 September 1940. They paddled ashore in their 4ft x 10ft rubber dinghy, the two male agents rowing for three and a half hours before they came to the shallows at the mouth of the Burn of Gollachy near Portgordon.[2]

Once they were ashore the three agents decided they would increase their chances of success if they split up. Vera and Drücke headed for Portgordon and Petter headed to Buckie. Strangers suddenly appearing in the quiet Scottish villages soon drew attention, especially if like these three they spoke with foreign accents and had lower garments soaked with sea water. Alert station staff at Portgordon summoned the police and Vera and Drücke were soon in custody. Petter had also aroused suspicion when he arrived at

166

Buckie station, but he managed to catch his train and got as far as Waverley Station, Edinburgh where he too was arrested.[3] Along with the radios and Mauser automatic pistols recovered from the agents, there was also a haul of maps covering much of the east coast and eastern counties found in Petter's suitcase. Drücke and Petter would stand trial and were executed as spies in 1941. Vera co-operated with British intelligence services, did not stand trial and remained in custody for the rest of the war.

On 24 October 1940, less than a month after the landing of Vera, Drücke and Petter, another three agents landed south of the Moray Firth about 15 miles north east of Inverness on 25 October 1940. Legwald Lund, Otto 'Max' Joost and Gunnar Edvardsen had been given a sabotage mission which was supposed to consist of bicycling across Scotland cutting telephone lines in an attempt to create alarm and to perform acts of sabotage wherever and whenever opportunities presented themselves.

The group were dropped off by flying boat and rowed ashore in their dinghy landing at Culbin Sands near Findhorn, Morayshire. Every group of agents had been issued bicycles and every time they were lost or ditched over the side of the dinghies before they made landfall. The sabotage group decided they would walk toward the nearest town of Nairn where, as they approached, they were stopped and arrested by a local police inspector. The group apparently had not been supplied with a radio transmitter so had no way of communicating success, failure, difficulties or observations with their base. In fact, the only equipment they seemed to have been issued with to carry out their task were two bicycles, a revolver, a torch, insulated pliers and each man had £100 in notes.[4]

The final group, consisted of just two agents, Norwegians Tor Glad and John Neal Moe (born in London) who were landed by sea plane south of the Moray Firth on 7 April 1941. Just like their predecessors they rowed ashore in a rubber boat, in this case landing at Pennan, Banffshire. Their primary mission was to sabotage food dumps and military clothing stores. Secondly, they were to radio back reports of what they could glean about air raid damage, troop movements, airfields and morale in the Aberdeen and Edinburgh areas.

Neither wanted any part of the operation and they immediately made their way to a cottage near the beach and asked where they should go to give themselves up to local police. Having obtained directions from the cottager they set off, got lost and had to ask for more directions from a man working in a field. The police superintendent of Banff had already been alerted, set off looking for the pair and encountered them just outside the town. Moe and Glad also became double agents for the rest of the war working under the code names of Mutt and Jeff.[5]

Six agents were also dropped by parachute on inland locations in the eastern counties and south east over the months between September 1940 to May 1941.[6] British intelligence was confident it had been on top of the Lena spy landings in Britain thanks to Arthur Graham Owens. In the years before the war Owens had worked as an electrical contractor in British and German shipyards and had dabbled in some espionage for SIS (Secret Intelligence Service) providing them with information about German shipyards where he had worked, until he was found also to be reporting to the Abwehr without the knowledge of his British handlers. On the outbreak of war he saved his skin by striking a deal with MI5 to turn double agent. He was accepted and given the codename SNOW.[7]

During the war there were concerns the Lena agents that had been caught had been apprehended too easily. Once they were interrogated it soon became clear they had only been given limited training and a number of senior members of MI5 expressed concerns that the agents they had apprehended to date had been sacrificial personnel deployed as distractions while more covert arrivals of other agents were taking place elsewhere. This view was confirmed in a number of minds after Jan Willem Ter Braak, a previously undetected agent, was only discovered after he committed suicide and his body was discovered in a public air raid shelter on Christ's Pieces, Cambridge on 1 April 1941.[8] There is a good chance he was not unique.

Several possible candidates emerged during the interrogation of captured German agents Waldberg, Meier, Drüke, Schalburg and Wälti. All had independently mentioned one of their instructors, Oberleutnant Werner Uhlm, who was originally of Ast Wiesbaden and later Ast Hamburg, and who was lauded for having made a successful clandestine reconnaissance mission to England in 1940. It was claimed he had been parachuted into Norfolk where he reconnoitred some of the defences along the coast and the Wash, and then made his exit by boat off the coast of Cromer where he was picked up by a sea plane.[9]

There was also the athletically-built German Army NCO Peter Schneider who was present at a lecture given to a number of the agents now in British hands. They shared the understanding that Schneider was destined to come to the south coast of England 'clandestinely by boat, with another German NCO. He was a member of a special assault company and trained in pontoons and mines work.'[10] Others that were mentioned in interrogations were Oberleutnant Paul Koch, who was 'destined to be dropped by parachute in Norfolk or Suffolk'. Captured Lena agent José Waldberg also mentioned German soldiers Walter Pfeiffer and Paul Schneider (cousin of Peter Schneider) who he believed were both destined to spy in the UK.[11]

A ship's lifeboat washed up on Cromer beach, March 1940. Was it a genuine loss from a shipwreck or a means by which German spies had come ashore?

During the Battle of Britain and over the subsequent war years the coastal areas of the country became accustomed to seeing rubber dinghies washed up or drifting offshore which had been used by British or German aircrews whose aircraft had been brought down in the sea. It was known that if the aircrew were rescued the boat would simply be left at sea.

Throughout the U-boat campaign in British coastal waters, and especially in the wake of the Dunkirk evacuation, the lifeboats of vessels that had been sunk would also be washed up on our shores, found adrift by fishermen and in numerous incidents the coastguard and lifeboat crews were alerted to the presence of the boat just in case there were crew in need of help aboard.[12] If the boat was found empty of personnel, ascertaining where it had come from or whether it had been used for the comings or goings of enemy agents was difficult to discern. On 14 August 1940 parachutes, harness and equipment had been dropped over parts of Yorkshire, Derbyshire and south-west Scotland, presumably in an attempt to create a scare that a landing of parachute troops had taken place. The aim may have been to cause a 'flap' among local military and Home Guard units,[13] but there was also the possibility that such empty boats were being sent as yet more scares in the 'jitter war'.

A typical example was recorded in the MI5 B Division Intelligence Summary of 30 January 1941. A rubber boat containing paddles, an inflating pump, uniform side hats, a blue tunic, letters, a Christmas card and an identity disc bearing the name of Karl Schmidt were discovered after being washed ashore on beach near Shorncliffe on the afternoon of 21 January 1941. At 9pm that night an unidentified person was spotted and challenged by a sentry, a shot was fired and he or she disappeared into the darkness. The following night another individual was challenged by a sentry at a nearby location, more shots were fired but the intruder eluded capture. Regional Security Liaison Officer, Major Cyril Grassby wrote up his findings:

The rubber boat was found unoccupied at 4pm when it was first seen but this does not necessarily mean that no-one came in it. It may be that the person landed further along the coast and pushed the boat out to sea. This would have been an easier and more effective method of getting rid of all papers of identification than by tearing them up and strewing them along the beach. Furthermore, the reports of two sentries on two different dates of the appearance of a stranger who was fired at strengthens the supposition that someone might have been in the locality. Both soldiers could not have suffered from hallucination...[14]

The problem was the local military (XII Corps) headquarters had not been informed of the boat until 23 January, it was also some time before the Kent police were informed and consequently a search of the area for traces of the person or persons who arrived by the boat was not conducted while the discovery was still fresh. Subsequently a yellow life preserver with eight air pockets was washed ashore at Sandgate. There was no further update about the rubber boat or its passengers published in the later intelligence summaries.[15] This is not surprising, with alleged sightings of enemy parachutists still being reported, along with a resurgence of reports of Fifth Columnist activities after 'thousands of enemy aliens' had been released from internment, and the flashing of lights supposedly signalling to the enemy. These all needed to be investigated and the unidentified boats were just one more item added to the already crammed to-do list of the local police, military intelligence officers and MI5's regional security liaison officers in coastal areas.[16]

There were also some very genuine escapes made from the continent as the Nazi heel ground into France. The first to hit the headlines was debonair young French aviator Maurice Halna du Fretay (born

The debonair young French pilot Maurice Halna Du Fretay

170

The Zlin 2 kit aircraft Maurice Du Fretay rebuilt with the help of friends to fly to Britain from occupied France to join the Free French Air Force on 15 November 1940.

1920) who had been a keen flyer from the earliest age at which he could gain his pilot's licence and had already flown across the Channel as a pleasure trip in the late 1930s. When the winds of war blew, he tried to enlist in the French air force as a pilot, but he was turned down and told they were not recruiting pilots at that time. When German forces marched into France, rather than have his aircraft seized he dismantled his two-seater Czech 45 CV Zlin XII monoplane and hid it around his family property's barns and outbuildings.

After the fall of France Maurice was determined to join the Free French Air Force in England, so with the help of friends he rebuilt his aircraft, acquired fuel and, joined by French Foreign Legion officer Major Paul Devred, the pair took their lives into their own hands in the untested rebuilt plane and took off from an airfield in Brittany making for Britain on 15 November 1940. An hour and a half later they landed on a field in the south-west Dorset village of Stinsford. Maurice du Fretay was hailed a hero of France and was personally decorated by General de Gaulle with the Cross of the Liberation in February 1941; he also received The British Empire Medal. Maurice was accepted into the Free French Air Force and was soon flying in action with the Royal Air Force.[17]

In an episode reminiscent of Second Lieutenant Timothy Stoyin Lucas's escape from Dunkirk, two pairs of brothers, Pierre and Jean Paul Lavoix; Guy and Christian Richard and their friend, Reynold Lefebvre, all aged between 16 and 19, from Fort Mahon Plage, Somme in northern France obtained canoes, repaired them, made them seaworthy and kept them hidden from

German occupation forces. After twelve months of planning they set off to row across the Channel on 16 September 1941. Thirty hours and 60 miles later they landed at Beachy Head, Eastbourne, East Sussex.

The story goes that shortly after their arrival they heard the order 'Halt' barked out to them. Looking round they saw what they initially thought was a woman armed with a rifle, wearing a short skirt, battledress blouse and a tin hat. Fatigued and disorientated, the boys were clearly confused at what was going on, but were holding a French flag in case of just such an emergency and fortunately the sentry spoke French. As he approached they exchanged a few words and it was rapidly made clear to the boys they were being challenged by a soldier wearing a kilt who was serving in a Scottish Highland regiment which had been deployed to the defences of the south coast.

Handed over to the police, the boys were removed to London where they were interviewed to make sure they were not actually German infiltrators. Their stories checked out and they were presented to General de Gaulle and met and received warm praise from Winston Churchill when they were given an audience with him at 10, Downing Street. All five of the boys went on to join the Free French Forces in Britain.

Seaforth Highlanders on guard duty on chalk clifftops near Dover, 1940.

Others would follow by both sea and air but not every group crossing the Channel was so welcome. Considering all the harbours and ports around Britain's coast, imagine trying to police the comings and goings of allied shipping, be they large merchant vessels or fishing boats. Some would be found to contain people fleeing from Nazi occupied countries in Europe but the Abwehr were cunning and mixed in their agents with the refugees, in some instances entire crews were found to be made up of those in the pay of Nazi intelligence services.

The first major example of this new method of entry to be detected was the cutter *La Part Bien* that put into Plymouth on 23 September 1940. Captain Hugo Jonassen and two crew members Edward de Lee and Gerard Libot claimed they were proceeding from Brest to Le Touquet but had got so drunk they decided to dock in England. Held pending investigation it soon transpired all three crew had been recruited in Antwerp for espionage work.

In a similar incident the fishing smack *Josephine* under Dutch captain Cornelius Ebertsen landed at Milford Haven on 12 November 1940. When asked their business at the port by a naval patrol, Ebertsen claimed he was en route from Brest bound for Dublin when one of his passengers, Nicolas Pasoz-Diaz had an abscess that had become inflamed and required urgent medical treatment. The boat crew and passengers were landed as refugees, but were sent for further interrogation during which it was soon revealed the vessel had four crew and three passengers, Cubans named Silvio Ruiz Robles, Pedro Hechevarria and Pasos-Diaz. The crew revealed the three passengers had been recruited by the Abwehr as saboteurs and were to have been landed in the Bristol Channel to carry out acts of sabotage around the Bristol area.

Reciprocally the Cuban passengers claimed the captain and two of the crew (Arie van Dam and Peter Krag) were German or in the pay of the Abwehr. A search of the boat revealed a hidden Browning automatic pistol and materials for sabotage, including explosives hidden in tin cans labelled 'Green Peas'. Removed to and interrogated at Camp 020 (Latchmere House), the entire crew were imprisoned and deported after the end of the war, with the exception of Pasoz-Diaz who died while in Liverpool prison in April 1942.[18]

The information from the boat crews and other intelligence sources from MI5 and MI6 were compiled to reveal the method and scale of the operation:

French fishing vessels of various types are used by the German intelligence in attempts to land agents in Britain and Ireland for espionage or sabotage. It is also strongly suspected that these vessels are used for reconnaissance work after they have been fitted with wireless transmitters...The control and organisation of these activities is primarily the work of the German intelligence Station at Brest... At Brest the vessels are selected and purchased and the crews and agents trained. Most of the vessels are then sent round the coast to Le Touquet where there is a subsidiary German Intelligence Centre which undertakes the despatch of the vessels for England…

It is considered possible that activities of this sort may be based on other ports between La Rochelle and Boulogne besides Brest and Le Touquet and may also be based in the Low Countries for operating against our East Coast…

Waters off the east coast of Ireland, the Scillies and Lands End are normally fished by French fishing fleets, the opportunities for rendezvous in those waters and communication between German agents sent from France and the vessels from English ports is obvious. It is therefore of paramount importance that the fishing crews based on ports between Brixham and Fleetwood should be supervised to ensure that they do not take out information which could be of value to the enemy or bring back questionnaires, instructions, wireless apparatus etc or avail themselves of these opportunities for 'communicating' with crews of French craft.

It is known at present there is a considerable accumulation of boats of the type described above at Le Touquet, probably not less than a dozen and it is conjectured that these may be held in reserve to effect a large scale landing of spies on the south coast of England when the opportune moment arrives.[19]

From early 1941 MI5 had to admit they were now facing more difficult challenges posed by the spies arriving in boats, particularly in the Scottish harbours on Shetland and Wick[20] from Norway:

This class is, perhaps, the most difficult of all the German agents to detect, since there is a flood of genuine refugees from Norway reaching this country and there is good evidence that the Germans have penetrated some of the escape organisations. It appears that the Germans are willing to let bona fide refugees escape to act as unconscious cover for a single agent inserted among them and the task of detecting the agent among the genuine refugees is extremely difficult since they do not come with any of the suspicious gear of equipment which has assisted in the detection of other types of agents.

It seems the one object of this type of agent is to establish himself among the Norwegians fishing in this country and so exploit the opportunities which fishing would offer to act as couriers between here and the Germans in Norway. It is also considered possible that the Germans may intend that a number of agents should make their way into Free Norwegian Forces here, so as to operate as a 'Trojan Horse' in the event of invasion.[21]

At the time the report was published in 1941 four agents of this type had already been detected and there were several others, although not proven to be agents beyond a shadow of a doubt, who had some evidence against them who were being detained while further investigations were being made.

There are also stories from a number of locations on the east and south coast of German reconnaissance parties making clandestine landings. Some stories even tell of sentries being snatched away and returned to German bases for interrogation. Home Guard messenger John Wilson recalled one night in August 1942 when there was a loud banging on the door of his family home from an army despatch rider who had come to inform his Home Guard father that the invasion alert had been given. As his father sped off to the local headquarters young John set off on his bicycle to 'knock up' the rest of the platoon. As he did so he looked out towards the Stour Estuary and saw 'all hell had been let loose' with the night sky lit by star shells, flares and the muzzle flashes of machine-gun fire. Even the anti-aircraft guns at Manston appeared to be cranked down as low as possible and were firing almost horizontally across Pegwell Bay.

When attempting to find out what had been going on, John's father spoke to one of the sergeants of the Dorset Regiment based on the coastal defences that he had got to know through his work in the Home Guard. All the sergeant would say was 'Well it was their own fault, they were asleep.' So what had happened? Had a German recce party come ashore? John remembered one of the local girls was dating one of the Dorset Regiment soldiers and he did not turn up for their meeting on the night of the invasion alert, nor did she hear from him again until months later when she received a Red Cross postcard from her boyfriend who was then a prisoner of war in Germany.[22]

Historian James Hayward, author of *Myths and Legends of The Second World War* (2003) researched the German recce and raiding party stories back in the 1990s and tracked down a few people with stories relating to such incidents. Among them was Edward Leslie who was responsible for the debriefing of British prisoners of war at a South Wales transit camp in 1945. Mr Leslie distinctly recalled questioning a regular soldier who when asked where, when and in what manner was he was taken prisoner of war was 'highly embarrassed' when he admitted he had been snatched by a German recce party from St Margaret's Bay in Kent in 1940.

Royal Army Service Corps Driver Eddie Sharpin also vividly remembered when he was a prisoner of war held at Stalag VIIIA (Wolfsburg) there was one man who stood out because of his grey hair and aged features; he looked far older than all the other soldiers in the camp. Eddie recalled the soldier's name was Avery or Amery, but everybody knew him as 'Pops'. When asked how he came to be there 'Pops' freely admitted he was actually a Home Guardsman who had been snatched from a beach in Kent by a German raiding party.

A Kent Home Guard detachment patrolling along cliff paths near Dover, March 1941,

Eddie and other prisoners of war did wonder if poor old 'Pops' was actually a stool pigeon placed in the camp by German intelligence to lower morale and to listen in to their conversations, but as Eddie pointed out, 'Pops' even claimed he had played football at Craven Cottage, the home of Fulham Football Club, but what happened to him in the end? All Eddie could say was: 'Pops was sent to a notorious labour camp, an iron ore mine at Eisenerz and we didn't hear from him again.'[23]

Hayward also communicated with Jack Driscoll then Hon. Secretary of The National Prisoners of War Association. Mr Driscoll had been held as a prisoner of war at Stalag VIIIB at Lamsdorf in 1943 where he also encountered a man in Home Guard uniform:

It was when I was walking around the compound that I saw this chap with Home Guard on his shoulder [a cloth Home Guard shoulder title], *I stood back in amazement and asked if this was a joke. I was then told of how whilst on duty on the Kent coast a U-boat surfaced and the landing party came ashore and grabbed one of the lookouts.*[24]

The problem is that although those who are telling the stories are quite sincere, they did not witness the abductions personally and they could not be precise about the name of the soldier who was snatched. In fact, not a single soldier or Home Guardsman who was snatched from the British coast by a German raiding party during the Second World War has yet been positively identified.

There are, however, a few tantalising incidents where something appears to have happened. One incident may have occurred at Pevensey Bay, near Eastbourne on the evening of 4 February 1942. This sector of the south coast was held by the Fifth Infantry Brigade, 2nd Canadian Infantry Division. It must be borne in mind that at this time Exercise Beaver II was in progress, but there were not actually supposed to be any seaborne landings at Pevensey that night. It was shortly before 8pm on that dark night when two French Canadian soldiers from the Le Régiment de Maisonneuve were patrolling the beach at Pevensey Bay when their attention was drawn by the sound of feet running on shingle and shadowy figures running towards what appeared to be a rubber dinghy. The soldiers opened fire, but the boat sped off towards a vessel that was flashing a light just off the bay.

The sentries rushed back to report the incident. The Black Watch of Canada were nearby, sure enough their War Diary records the events of the exercise for the day but, significantly, they record a separate incident:

This evening, at 11.55hrs, there took place the first real 'AFLOAT' [code word alerting units an enemy landing vessel was believed to have been sighted in their sector] *The real or suspected danger came from the direction of BRIGHTON; the only thing observed by troops in this area were flares from the West… The excitement was short-lived: nothing happened and 'STAND DOWN' was ordered at 2115hrs.*[25]

The incident is similarly recorded in the War Diary of 552 Coast Regiment, Royal Artillery at Bexhill also recorded at 21.10: 'Possibility of enemy raid. All batteries stand to.' All batteries were stood down at 21.35.

A little less than two months later The Canadian Black Watch War Diary recorded their brigade major had telephoned at 8pm on 2 April to warn them that a raid by seaborne and/or airborne troops was expected on the RAF Pevensey Chain Home Radio Direction Finding station. The codeword

'BUGBEAR' was issued for units to adopt anti-raid positions. On 3 April the Black Watch of Canada War Diary recorded:

The carrier platoon was ordered to stand to and the duty company also. At last it looked as though something might happen. Shortly after midnight the alert went but the all clear sounded some minutes later. And so the night went – no paratroops, no seaborne troops, no enemy and NO SLEEP!

The order to stand down was issued from brigade headquarters at 0726hrs. Pevensey Bay would make a good landing place; the RAF Pevensey Chain Home station would make a logical target for a raid and a German recce party landing on a south coast beach of Britain is just as likely and as possible as a British commando raid on the coast of occupied France, such as Operation Biting where British combined operations successfully conducted a raid to obtain some of the technical equipment from the German coastal radar installation at Bruneval on 27–28 February 1942.

The problem that remains is that despite the passage of time and the release of declassified files there is no solid evidence, despite great efforts by numerous historians to find it, that any German reconnaissance raids took place anywhere on the British coast during the Second World War. However, the rumours persist and there are numerous War Office and Home Office files in the National Archives and country record offices that have yet to be fully examined and files that still have not been released.

As Major General Robert Laycock, Chief of Combined Operations from 1943 candidly commented after presenting his paper *Raids in the Late War and Their Lessons* to the Royal United Services Institution in 1947, when asked by Vice Admiral Cecil Usborne, former Director of Naval Intelligence if there were any examples of German raids which are at all comparable to our own, Laycock replied:

There was one absolutely splendid raid carried out by the Germans from the Channel Islands which was almost one hundred per cent successful. As far as I know it is the only example of that type of raid. I can't think why the Germans did not try more.[26]

Almost certainly, Laycock was referring to the Granville raid from the Channel Islands against the French coast on 8–9 March 1945.[27] A month later, however, a group of soldiers in German uniforms made a landing on a beach on the east coast of Britain. It was on the night of 10 April 1945 when coast guards Reg Earl and Howard Dawes were peering into the darkness across Mundesley beach on the Norfolk coast, as they had for countless hours before. The end of the war was less than a month away and both men were confident they would have a

Major General Sir Robert Laycock, Chief of Combined Operations, talking to Royal Marine Commandos during an inspection shortly before D-Day 1944.

quiet night on duty when they spotted a boat near the shore and very soon they could see figures coming up the beach and unless they were mistaken they were wearing German uniforms. Fortunately, the coast guard were armed with rifles and sten guns during the war and they mustered up a challenge. They need not have worried, most of the fourteen figures were indeed wearing German uniforms but they approached unarmed with their hands up.

Once taken inside, the language barrier and the lack of an interpreter meant that an explanation for their arrival took some time. The refugees were a mix of Georgian soldiers and residents of the tiny Dutch Island of Texel. German forces had occupied the island in 1940 and it became part of Hitler's *Atlantikwall*. A battalion of Georgian infantry the Germans had pressed into military service was also posted to the island. On the night of 5/6 April 1945 there was an uprising among the Georgian troops who attacked the German garrison troops. The fighting was fierce and continued for days, so while this was going on the local men being pressed into military service and some of the Georgian troops saw the opportunity to make their escape aboard the island's lifeboat.

After a perilous journey of over 27 hours during which the petrol had run out and the boat had to drift, fortunately the current carried them to the Norfolk coast where they landed on Mundesley beach. Military authorities arrived and removed the Georgians and islanders to London where they were kept in barracks and interrogated, but all their stories checked out and they were received by Queen Wilhelmina who was in exile in London soon after their release. The link between islanders and the people of Mundesley lasted for many years after the war, regular return visits were made and a local cul-de-sac was named Texel Way in remembrance of the remarkable incident.

Chapter 8

Cross Channel Bombardments

> *This precious stone set in the silver sea,*
> *Which serves it in the office of a wall*
> *Or as a moat defensive to a house,*
> *Against the envy of less happier lands,*
> *This blessed plot, this earth, this realm, this England.*
>
> William Shakespeare

On a clear day the cliffs of the northern French coast can be seen with the naked eye from the cliffs and hills around Dover. When concerns over invasion ramped up in May 1940 the mere 27 miles between Dover and Calais was emphasised by the often repeated comment that 'with a decent pair of binoculars you could tell the time on Calais town hall clock,' a remark often replied to with the words 'Thank God we have a Channel.'

The shape of things to come. A 1939 artist's impression of the range thought possible of a long-range railway gun firing across the North Sea from Walcheren Island in the Scheldt Estuary.

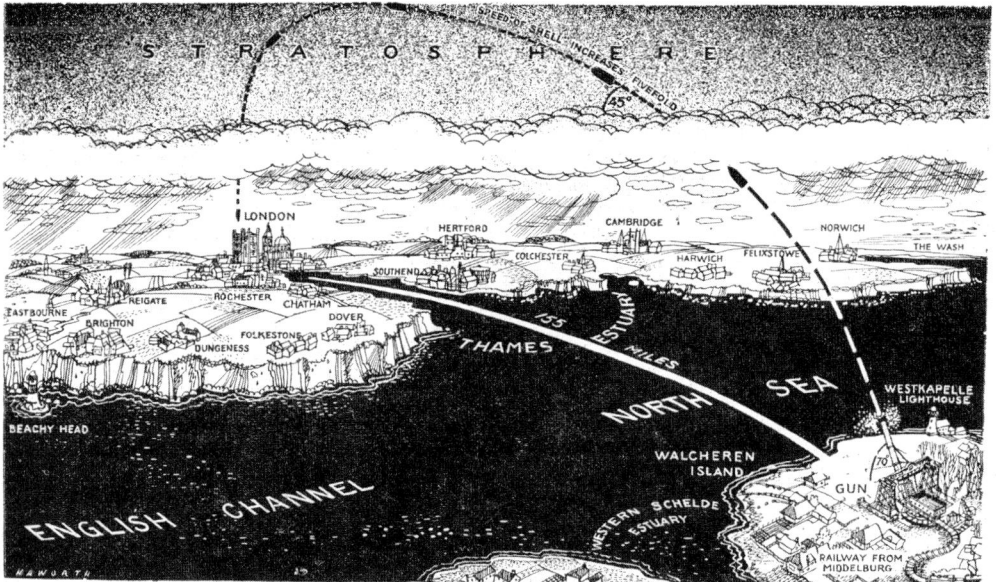

The shores of Britain had been directly threatened on only a few occasions since the last successful invasion by William the Conqueror in 1066. Defences were built and preparations had been made to meet the threat of the Spanish Armada in 1588 and were addressed again during the Napoleonic Wars in the late eighteenth and early nineteenth centuries. Of course, there was a fear of invasion during the First World War. During that conflict flotillas from the Imperial German Navy shelled coastal places such as Great Yarmouth, Whitby, Scarborough, Hartlepool and Lowestoft and we were bombed from the air by aeroplanes and Zeppelins. Since the outbreak of war in 1939 Britain's shipping had been subject to attack from the air and after the fall of France in June 1940 air attacks were frequent occurrences, but Britain had never been shelled by land-based guns fired from a foreign country.

That all changed just minutes after 10am on 12 August 1940. On that day the Luftwaffe began a systematic assault on the forward airfields of Fighter Command at Manston, Hawkinge and Lympne; they also bombed the RDF station on the south coast and one of the three 280mm German K5 railway guns in the Pas de Calais was rolled out from the shelter of its reinforced concrete tunnel and fired its shells to land on the English mainland. The first shell landed on Campbell Terrace, Campbell Road, just a couple of rows of houses behind the sea front at Walmer, Kent. The explosion caused widespread damage to buildings and vehicles near where it exploded, windows were shattered and a number of ceilings collapsed in nearby properties.

Another shell struck the Royal Marines Depot at East Barracks and ricocheted across to where a group of marines were sitting under a colonnade, killing Royal Marine Lieutenant (Quartermaster) William McKinley Brown (60) and injuring several others. Other shells hit the North Barracks, Shingle Alley and shrapnel was found in the roof of the post office in Deal. The casualties stood at one dead and three seriously injured including local man Mr 'Taffy' Hyatt who lost his leg.

Further salvoes followed an hour later and more shells landed on Folkestone and Dover shortly after 11am. Folkestone received a total of four shells, the first tore the frontage off 14 Millfield, the home of Mrs Stone who had just celebrated her 100th birthday until her recent fortunate evacuation. Another shell fell on Cornwallis Avenue causing some damage to houses in the neighbourhood, a third damaged the home of Police Sergeant J. Rowe on Shorncliffe Road, and the fourth landed on open land at Danton Pinch.

Around the same time a further five shells fell on Dover as Raymond Cook recalled:

I was walking along a road above the town at the time and for once there was a stillness overhead and a silence all about me that was uncanny, when at short intervals three or four terrific explosions occurred and about half a mile ahead huge clouds of dust rose into the air.[1]

The shells had fallen near and damaged houses at Edgar Crescent on the town side of the gas works, on Noah's Ark Terrace and on Minnis Lane. The shell which fell on St Radigund's Road killed Mrs Helen Jane Barker (38) and seriously injured Alfred Reid (38) who died after being taken to the casualty hospital on Union Road. Mrs Barker was a Nursing Auxiliary attached to the St John Ambulance Brigade at the Union Road First Aid Post and was on her way to report for duty. Reid was showing her a short cut.

In a tragic twist of fate, the scene was attended by Mrs Barker's husband ARP ambulance driver Bertie Barker who had rushed to the area to help the casualties, it was only upon his arrival there that he discovered one of them was his wife. In addition to the two fatalities in Dover a further twelve people were injured, one house was completely demolished and thirty-one houses were badly damaged.

Given that Britain had never been shelled from across the Channel before the residents of Deal, Folkestone and Dover were divided in their opinions of what had actually caused the explosions. One side were of the opinion they had been caused by bombs dropped by an aircraft flying at such high altitude it had not been spotted, while others believed a long-range gun had been responsible. What exactly had fallen on the coastal towns would soon be debated in both local and national press over the next few days. The hot shards of casing scattered over the areas where the explosions had taken place were soon gathered up by local people, police and members of the military. A number of ex-servicemen from the First World War believed they recognised what they saw but to be certain the fragments were sent to artillery experts for examination. They soon confirmed what the old soldiers' thought it was – shards of high explosive shell casing, moreover such a shell could only have been fired from a long-range gun on the other side of the Channel.

Reporter Frank Illingworth was an auxiliary fireman at Dover and recorded the change of mood among local people:

Suddenly they realised the utter futility of the old conception that because the English flag fluttered from Dover Castle for nine centuries neither the Archangel Gabriel nor Lucifer nor the latter's human counterpart would have the impudence to shoot it down…Few events following the Fall of France brought home with such shattering reality the nearness of the enemy to our portals as the first shelling of Britain.[2]

German propaganda photograph issued in May 1941 showing the White Cliffs of Dover (Swingate Chain Home RDF lattice towers on left) with smoke billowing up from what were claimed to be the fires after a Canterbury steelworks had been bombed.

From that time on Dover, Folkestone, Deal and Ramsgate became the regular targets for shelling and many of their neighbours suffered shells on occasion too. Intermittent bombardment from France became part of each town's wartime life, residents became accustomed to hearing the thud of the artillery pieces disgorging their shells on a regular basis as they engaged in cross Channel duels with our own heavy batteries. The Nazi batteries would send over salvos of anything between two and ten shells in quick succession for such large guns. Observers in Kent would spot flashes from the batteries when they fired a salvo, each shell would take approximately sixty seconds to cross the Channel before hammering into coastal towns on the south coast of Britain.

Initially some areas of the towns were more seriously affected than others as the guns found their range. During the early bombardments on Folkestone a line from the harbour to the golf links, including Tontine Street and Foord, was the place the shells were likely to fall and it became known locally as 'Shell Alley'.[3] As the years of war rolled on shells fell over a wider and more scattered area damaging many houses and business premises in the towns.

Hitler had incorporated long-range guns and coastal batteries in his invasion plans drawn up shortly after the fall of France. The aim of these formidable guns was not only to defend the coast, they were also to be capable of shelling allied shipping in the Channel and even land shells on the English mainland. The first had been *Batterie Siegfried* equipped with a 380mm SK C/34 naval gun at Audinghan, south of Cap Gris Nez. This was soon expanded to a total of four guns housed in huge concrete casemates and renamed *Batteries Todt*. Nearby were the four 280mm guns of *Batterie Grosser Kurfurst* and a further four coastal guns in turrets installed at *Batterie Prinz Heinrich* and *Batterie Oldenburg* at Calais.

Between Calais and Cap Blanc-Nez at Sangatte there were the three huge 406mm 'Adolf Guns' of *Batterie Lindemann* that were installed in casemates of 13ft thick concrete, which fired their first shots on Kent on 22 June 1942. A further three 305mm naval guns were installed at *Batterie Friedrich August* north of Boulogne. A total of eight railway guns would also operate from lines around the Calais area. Arguably the most impressive of all the guns on the occupied Channel Coast was the 8.3-inch Kanone 12 in Eisenbahnlaflette.

The original 14-inch guns emplaced at St Margaret's near Dover, nicknamed 'Winnie' after Prime Minister Winston Churchill. Another 14-inch gun was also emplaced nearby that was dubbed 'Pooh'.

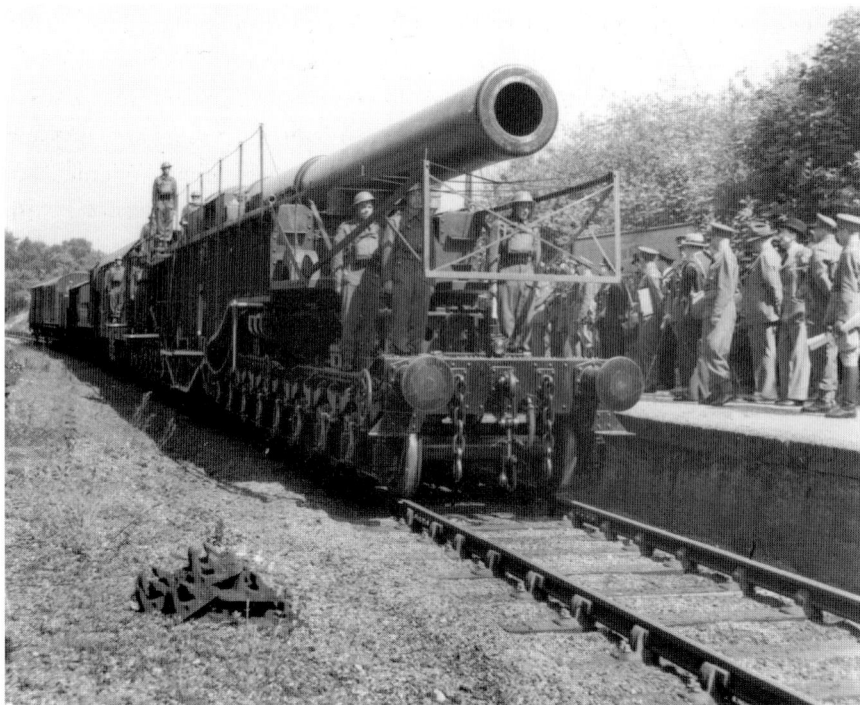

The 18-inch calibre 'Boche Buster' Railway Gun manned by 11 Battery, 2nd Super Heavy Regiment at Bishopsbourne Station on the Elham Valley Line during a visit by Winston Churchill and senior officers, 20 June 1941.

Shrapnel from shells believed to have been fired from this gun was found near Rainham, Kent, some 55 miles from the French coast.

Britain had its own big guns along the coast too. Construction had begun on 10 July for a huge 14-inch gun emplacement a short distance from Dover above St Margaret's Bay. The first to man the gun were twenty-five men of the Royal Marine Siege Regiment. Using an extra powerful charge, it was capable of firing a shell for up to 27 miles and earned the distinction of being the first gun to fire a shell onto mainland France from British soil on 22 August 1940. This gun was named 'Winnie' after the affectionate name given to Prime Minister Winston Churchill by the British public. In February 1941 a 14-inch partner followed nearby. In a coupling with a very different 'Winnie', this gun was named 'Pooh'.

There were also three 13.5-inch railway mounted guns named 'Scene Shifter', 'Peacemaker' and 'Gladiator' deployed to lines of the East Kent light railway at Lydden and Sheperdswell. These impressive artillery pieces rolled out of the cover of a railway tunnel to blaze away and would then retreat back inside to avoid the reply from the German batteries.

186

They were joined in February 1941 by a fourth, run on the Elham Valley Line; a monster of an artillery piece, capable of firing a 6ft 7inch tall, 18-inch shell weighing 1¼ tons, it was dubbed 'Boche Buster'. It looked impressive but its range of 2,300 yards meant it would only be used as an anti-invasion defence. 'Pooh' the artillery piece was also less reliable than 'Winnie', but both 'Winnie' and 'Pooh' and the mighty railway guns were all shown with great pride to visiting dignitaries and their appearance on newsreels and in magazines was superb for morale.

There were also 12-inch guns on specially built sidings at Levington Bridge and Trimley St Martin and a further two at Tollesbury (later removed to Holland-on-Sea) for the defence of the Harwich sector on the east coast. The problem with both British and German super heavy guns was two-fold, they were slow to load and traverse when attempting to engage a moving target and their barrels were worn out and had to be replaced after firing around fifty shells. The big guns and coastal batteries were joined by the 15-inch guns of the Wanstone Battery just inland from the Dover cliffs. This battery maintained a rapid rate of fire on German vessels in the Channel. Among the guns was one named 'Clem' after Labour politician and coalition cabinet member Clement Atlee and another named 'Jane' after the racy *Daily Mail* comic strip character.

The 9.2-inch guns of the South Foreland battery were active from July 1941. They had a range of up to 21 miles and were assisted by the new K-type Radar for tracking and targeting shipping. There were also three 6-inch guns at Fan Bay Battery east of Dover, and the Lydden Spout Battery with its three 13.5-inch guns to the west of Dover.

The stretch of east Kent coast between the North Foreland and Folkestone, which had suffered severely through repeated air raids, acquired the notorious *nom de plume* of 'Hellfire Corner' and after the cross-Channel shelling commenced would also be known as 'Shellfire Corner'.

The coastal guns did not just duel it out firing at each other and at targets on land, they made the Channel a dangerous place for both military and merchant shipping of both sides. Without doubt the prize target for any coastal gun battery would have been an enemy capital ship. The Royal Navy never gave the German coastal batteries the chance of such a coup, but when Hitler was presented with military intelligence suggesting the British were going to invade Norway, he was determined to head off such a task force with a German naval battle group of sixty-six ships including the battleships *Scharnhorst*, *Gneisenau* and the heavy cruiser *Prinz Eugen*. The only way he could get them to intercept in time was to risk sending these ships through the Channel at full speed with as much Luftwaffe air cover as possible and so commenced the infamous 'Channel Dash' of 12 February 1942.

The 15-inch calibre Cross Channel Gun 'Jane' at Wanstone Battery St Margaret's, Dover, manned by 540 Coast Regiment, Royal Artillery, May 1942.

'Jane's' 15-inch calibre Cross-Channel Gun shells at Wanstone Battery St Margaret's, Dover May 1942. Shells of a similar calibre were regularly fired by German batteries on to English south coast towns too.

British military intelligence had received warning of the German plan and prepared a response in Operation Fuller. The grim weather over the Channel that greatly reduced visibility was certainly on the side of the German battleships and they were able to make the majority of their approach undetected. On land only the South Foreland battery with their K-type Radar-guided targeting stood any chance of hitting the ships as they passed and they got off a respectable thirty-three shells. Hopes were high, there appeared to be four hits, the German vessels were also fired on from the air by Fairey Swordfish aircraft carrying torpedoes from 825 Squadron, Fleet Air Arm as well as fighters and bombers of the RAF.

Royal Navy Motor Torpedo Boats and Motor Gun Boats from Dover and Royal Navy destroyers from Harwich also engaged, but incredibly only minor damage was inflicted on the German vessels. The German battle group steamed through and came out the other side and, despite *Gneisenau* and *Scharnhorst* both hitting British mines when they were off the Dutch coast, they both effected emergency repairs and made German docks by the following morning. It had, however, been a costly day for the British forces. The RAF lost 15 bombers, 17 fighters and 15 planes from Coastal Command with a loss of 106 RAF aircrew. There were also 13 aircrew of the Fleet

Children had been evacuated from Dover, but many had been brought back by their parents and at the time this photograph was taken in March 1941 the town council was appealing for compulsory evacuation of local children.

Air Arm killed or missing. HMS *Worcester* had got within 400 yards of the *Gneisenau* and *Prinz Eugen* to launch torpedoes, but the German battleships opened fire and she was crippled after several shells found their mark killing 24 and injuring 45 crew in the process.

The shelling of the coastal towns of 'Hellfire Corner' by the German guns around Calais continued through the ensuing war years. Dr J.W.B. Douglas of the Oxford Extra Mural Unit carried out a study based on interviews with ARP officers and members of local authorities to learn more about the reactions of the people of Dover and Folkestone to shelling on behalf of the Ministry of Home Security.

He noted there were still thousands of children still residing with their families in both towns, although some families had moved away from the areas that were regularly shelled. Many children had been evacuated earlier in the war, but as the weeks and months passed they had been brought back by their parents until by 1944:

The population of both towns is at present about half the pre-war value. After a first heavy evacuation between July and December 1940, there has been gradual return to the areas…There are many children in both towns. This drift back has been more marked in the case of Folkestone than of Dover. It has been estimated that if shelling stopped the population of Folkestone would increase by 1/3rd even if bombing still took place. In Folkestone 3,500 of the population of 19,193 are below school leaving age. Parents have bought their children back because their evacuation (to Merthyr Tydfil) meant almost complete separation from their families. Evacuation of children to country districts in the South East of England would be welcome.

In Dover the population had dropped from 42,000 in 1939 to less than 16,000; fortunately, there was accommodation for 5,000 people in the caves and tunnels in and near the town. Dr Douglas also contrasted the shelter provision for both towns:

In Dover (where there are deep tunnel shelters to accommodate 2/3rds of the present population) during severe shelling many people lived in shelters. For the last 16 months about 2,000 people are accustomed to shelter on nights when – according to rumour – shelling is expected. In Folkestone also similar reactions have been observed. This town has no deep shelters, and surface brick shelters are used by a considerable proportion of the population. At the present day many people, particularly mothers and children, sleep in surface brick shelters when shelling is expected.[4]

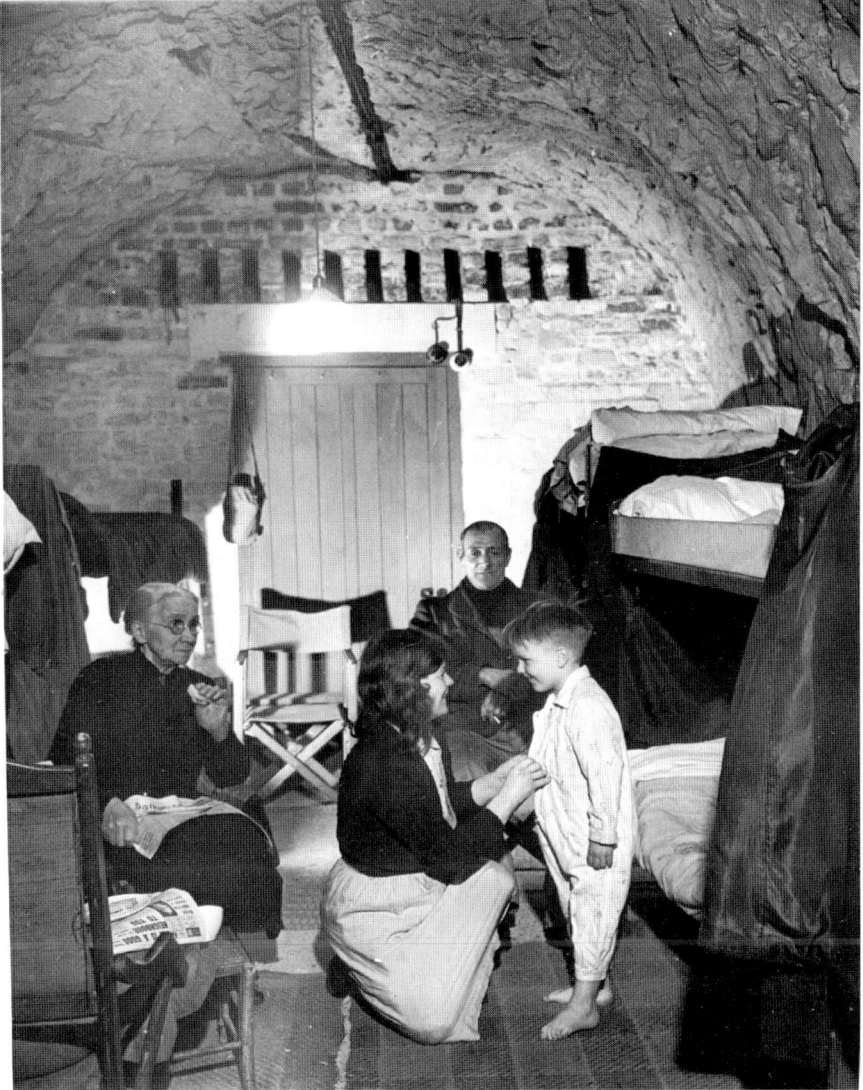

Five-year-old David Day preparing for bed in one of the shelters in the Dover chalk cliffs, April 1944. Throughout the war years thousands sheltered night after night in the natural caves and man-made tunnels on the south coast.

The shelling did not abate as allied forces fought their way across France after the D-Day landings. It was only days after the landings that a bitter reprisal began and Folkestone suffered its heaviest shelling of the war on 13 June 1944 when forty-two shells were sent over during a bombardment that started from shortly after midnight and continued until dawn. As Allied troops closed in around Calais in September 1944 the barrages intensified. One of the worst days during this period was 13 September when a shell exploded outside

Stores (top) and the general ward (below) at the underground Royal Marine Siege Regiment Medical Dressing Station at Townsend Farm, St Margaret's-at-Cliffe, Dover, July 1942.

Priory Station, Dover just after the 1.15pm train from Charing Cross had pulled in. Five passengers were killed by the blast and a further twenty were injured. On the same day Folkestone had a shell warning that lasted eleven hours during which 6 people were killed and more than 30 were injured.

A last gesture of German defiance saw an unprecedented fifty shells fired on Dover on 26 September. The RAF then conducted a heavy bombing raid on the Calais batteries, British and Canadian troops closed in and three days later, on the evening of 30 September the Mayor of Dover received a telegram from 9 Canadian Infantry Regiment:

> *To the Citizens of Dover. Greetings from the Brigade and may you enjoy your pint of beer and stroll on the front in peace from now on. We have all of Jerry's Big Berthas.*

Dover, Folkestone, Ramsgate and Hythe all suffered in the last-ditch shelling, when between 1–26 September 1944 a total of 54 people were killed, 40 of them in Dover.

During the bombardments over the past four years Folkestone had 218 shells fall within the town's boundaries that killed 32 people, seriously injured 64 and slightly injured 102.

> *Front Line Folkestone* (1945) commented: *Damage was not as extensive as that caused by V1s and bombing, the blast effect being limited, but the bombardments caused the greatest nerve tension of all the town's war experiences – you could hear the bombers coming, you had moments if you heard the shell at all; looking back people spoke of shelling leaving people in a state of 'uncertainty' akin to that of V2 attacks.*[5]

Approximately 2,260 shells had landed on Dover and its immediate environs between 1940 and 1944 killing 107 and injuring in excess of 400 civilians. Two thirds of the homes in the town had been damaged by shelling.[6] By September hundreds of workmen had been drafted in for the ongoing repairs. Shortly after the Calais guns fell silent for the last time the *Nota Bene* column in the *Dover Express* concluded:

> *London Press and BBC stressed the trials of people, but Dover did carry on, people worked and amused themselves in very nearly normal ways... The impression is widespread outside Dover that there were shelling warnings sounded because the authorities knew that the enemy were preparing to shell the town and that the alert was sounded in time to enable people to take cover. Of course, this idea is nonsensical. Dover people lived, worked and amused themselves during these four years well knowing that at any moment*

a German battery, hidden away and well camouflaged on the cliffs of France, might open fire and rain shells onto the town as they often did.

On such occasions the subsequent shelling warning was almost redundant. Dover usually got the first of any such shells and passed the warnings on to other coast towns. Often nothing happened in these towns and they did not always appreciate the stoppage of business and traffic that resulted.

Another type of shelling was that which occurred after the guns near Dover had opened fire. For a long time when these guns fired the people did not know whether it was practice or at an enemy convoy. They only found out when the enemy retaliated by shelling the town. After this had occurred several times the chairman of the emergency committee, Major Martin, succeeded in inducing the military to give notice so that the siren might be sounded when they were about to open fire on enemy convoys. This could not be explained at the time for security reasons, but the warning thus given undoubtedly saved many lives. Strangely enough there were grumbles about false alarms if the enemy changed his tactics and did not reply.

In Dover in these past four years we have been 'living dangerously'. Many owe their lives to the merest fraction of a minute which took them away from a spot where the 'first shell' fell. No place was safe but the people who stayed in Dover stuck to their jobs. The tales in the London papers about our living in caves all this time are simply fantastic and insulting absurdities. Though many used the caves to get a good night's sleep, they returned each day to the danger zones for their daily work.[7]

The people of Dover and all those who weathered life in what was not only dubbed 'Hellfire Corner', but also 'Shellfire Corner', through the war years truly embodied their county's motto – Invicta – Unconquered.

Chapter 9

Air Raids

It's mania…And they don't know where to stop. It's limitless. It's the last confusion. They're bombing capitals, smashing up dockyards and factories and mines and fleets.

H.G. Wells

From the standpoint of military strategy docks and harbours large and small were targeted by the Luftwaffe in an attempt to damage Britain's seaborne supply lines. It was also an easier mission for Luftwaffe pilots to fly over the coast and drop their payload than attempt to raid targets further inland. It should not be forgotten either that since the earliest engagements over Britain's coast during the Second World War, as British and German aircraft duelled in the air, the people and properties on the ground below them suffered collateral damage from the sprays of machine-gun fire of each belligerent, not to mention damage inflicted by the fuses and chunks of shrapnel from our own anti-aircraft shells.

So, if you think of just about any coastal town or village along the east and south coast of Britain, although it may have not been a strategic target, it probably had at least one bomb drop on or near it during the Second World War. Indeed many coastal places had endured regular raids, suffered casualties and severe damage before a single bomb fell on London.

When the numerous engagements between British and German aircraft that took place during the first months of the war is taken into consideration, it is surprising it took until 16 March 1940 for James 'Jim' Ibister (27) of Orkney to become the first civilian in the British Isles to die on land as a result of an offensive action by the Luftwaffe when the island was bombed. Jim saw a bomb had hit the house of a neighbour and had just opened the door of his home to rush across to help when a second bomb exploded killing him instantly.

The first fatalities caused by German bombs on English soil during the Second World War occurred on 30 April 1940. A Heinkel He 111H-4 of 1/KG 126, a Luftwaffe coastal unit specialising in mine-laying operations, was off the Norfolk coast intent on sowing two parachute mines when it flew into thick fog. The pilot, Oberleutnant und Flugzeugführer Hermann Vagts (25) flew blindly until when he broke cover over Bawdsey at approximately 11.15pm

Wreckage and wrecked houses after Heinkel He 111H-4 of 1/KG 126 crashed on Victoria Avenue, Clacton-on-Sea on 30 April 1940. Fred and Dorothy Gill became the first people to be killed by the explosion of bombs in England during the Second World War.

and flew near Felixstowe, anti-aircraft batteries opened up and inflicted critical damage on the Heinkel. Witnesses stated the aircraft appeared to circle as if trying to find somewhere to land on open ground when it suddenly came down shortly before midnight in the popular coastal resort of Clacton-on-Sea, Essex. The aircraft crashed on Victoria Avenue and burst into a ball of fire, causing the ammunition and one of the mines it was carrying to explode soon afterwards, devastating the area and killing husband and wife Fred and Dorothy Gill.

After the fall of France the Luftwaffe could launch its bomber attacks from the far closer airfields of France. The smaller fuel tanks of the fighter aircraft had severely limited the fighter support for bombers, but now they were in easy range too and the strategic bombing of airfields in Britain could begin in earnest. Numerous ports and coastal towns all around the coasts of Scotland, England and Wales became targets for enemy bombing raids in June and July 1940.

Dover received its first bombs, a stick of ten, at 5.20am on 6 July 1940, the *Dover Express* would recount:

Few saw the plane high in the sky, apparently attacked by our Air Force, but numbers of people heard the explosions. Fortunately, the bombs [each estimated to be approximately 100lbs in calibre] fell in almost open country, beginning at Coombe Farm, crossing Bunker's Hill and ending near Buckland Rectory, where broken windows represented the only damage caused in this raid.[1]

The outcome would have been a lot worse if the Local Defence Volunteers, who had been on duty through the night near Coombe Farm, had not been homeward bound at first light, but plenty of sightseers came to the site of the bomb craters when they got to hear what had happened.

Plymouth also received its first raid shortly before noon that same bright, sunny day. H.P. Twyford witnessed the event:

With the alert all Civil Defence stations were manned. Soon the sound of aircraft flying very high was heard. Eyes searched the sky for the first glimpse of an enemy raider – the first over Plymouth. High up in the blue dome, making clever use of the sparse cloud cover, the intruder was just a small speck, occasionally catching the sunlight like some silver-winged bird.

The crack of anti-aircraft guns and the puffs of white smoke against the blue sky as the shells burst, helped in the direction finding. Suddenly there was an ominous whistle. It passed high over our heads where I was standing with a warden and 'green like' we both plunged to the protection of the nearest wall. Fortunately, he was a small man, otherwise I might have been a casualty.

The first enemy bomb was falling on Plymouth. With a crumping thud that took my mind back to France in the 1914–18 war, it fell on the Swilly Corporation housing estate. Out of the blue had come the first agent of death and destruction on the city's population. In that blast three houses crumpled like a pack of cards, two more were badly damaged, many others in the area sustained minor damage.

One woman, a man and a boy were Plymouth's first aid raid victims in this overture of Hitler's 'total war.' [Mrs Blanche Ellnor (33), Harry Swinburne (58) died at the scene, Joseph Nicholas (13) was recovered alive but badly injured and was rushed to the Prince of Wales's Hospital (Greenbank) where he died on 8 July.] *The woman was a housewife who had slipped back into the house from the garden shelter to look at the cooking dinner. Six other people were injured, four having to go to hospital.*

Recovering from the dive to shelter as the bomb had passed over us, we saw the column of smoke and dust rising above the devastated houses. 'That's the first taste,' grimly said the warden, as he dusted down his clothes and set his tin hat at a new angle, adding, 'But I am afraid it's only a taste.'[2]

How true he was. Portsmouth was to suffer its first raid in the early evening of 11 July 1940 when bombs fell on the Kingston Cross area of the town killing 18 people and injuring 80. The attacks kept on coming and the damage and casualties rapidly escalated and on 24 August during a daylight raid seventy high explosive bombs were dropped on the city in five minutes killing 125 people and worse was still to come.

The opening stages of the Battle of Britain, a stage known to the Germans as the *Kanalkampf* (the Channel battles) could easily be seen and was watched by many from the cliffs and high ground of the south east coast. The aircraft of *Luftlotten* 2 and 3 conducted more frequent and larger bombing convoys and mine laying along the shipping lanes of the Dover Strait and the Channel. The south-eastern tip of England soon became our front line, falling prey to bombing and the strafing runs of low-flying Bf 109s. Ports, harbours and RAF bases in this area, such as Manston and Rochford (Southend), were soon liberally pitted with bomb craters, as were many other military installations and locations that drew enemy attacks to the degree the stretch of East Kent coast between the North Foreland and Folkestone earned the nick-name of 'Hellfire Corner'. The aerial traffic of friend and foe alike droning in and out over Beachy Head saw it dubbed 'Clapham Junction' by the local residents.

Watching the dog fights in the skies above, a practice known as 'goofing', instead of taking cover was initially a problem for ARP workers trying to keep people safe until casualties began to be incurred. William Ransome, Dover's Deputy Town Clerk was an early 'goofing' casualty in the town:

Heinkel He 111H of 2/KG55 on a mission to bomb Portsmouth was intercepted and shot down by pilots of 145 Squadron, force landed in flames and burnt out on the East Beach, Selsey, Sussex, 11 July 1940.

It was early one morning…there was a raid on and I could hear planes diving as I lay in bed. I could hear the neighbours saying 'Ooh look! There's another,' and things like that, until I could not help getting up, putting on a dressing gown and going out to see for myself. I watched the fun for some time and I was just turning to go in when I felt what I thought was a sandbag fall on my shoulder. I thought my neighbour was having some fun with me, until I put my hand behind me and felt blood. At the time I was by myself, so I called over my neighbour and asked him to come in, because I had been hit. He came in and said, 'By jingo you'll have to go to the doctor; there's a hole in your back.'

In fact, Mr Ransome required surgery, an ambulance was summoned and he was removed to hospital where he woke up in a ward. Resolutely he concluded: 'I don't goof now.'[3]

Churchill watching activity in the Channel from an observation area at Dover Castle during his tour of defences, 28 August 1940. Enemy air attacks were in progress at the time and two German bombers were seen crashing into the sea.

Aerial photograph released by the German press agency to international newspapers in 19 claiming to show a 'British sea town', suggested to be Dover, w an air raid in progress.

Front Line Folkestone evocatively summed up the months when the Battle of Britain was fought in the skies above them:

None who dwelt in this corner of England during those grim days of the autumn of 1940 will ever forget the great battles fought in the skies off and over the coast of Kent and in no part of the coast was the fight more bitter than over Folkestone. Day after day the enemy bombers flew in escorted by large numbers of fighters. Day after day enemy fighters patrolled over Folkestone for the heavily strained RAF could not cope with all the incursions of enemy machines. The plop, plop, plop of cannon fire, the rattle of synchronised machine guns became commonplace to our ears as the fighters twisted and turned, zoomed and whined above our heads, sometimes tiny dots in the heavens sometimes sufficiently low for the marking to be clearly discerned.[4]

Enemy raiders came time and again and air raid sirens would sometimes sound the alarm several times a day. Some people, especially at night, started to ignore it or even slept through not just the alert but even bombs falling. There were numerous terrible bombing tragedies, shelters received direct hits and aircraft dropped their bombs as people were trying to enjoy themselves at dance halls, theatres or cinemas. It happened as part of a planned raid or some dropped their bombs to lighten their load and increase their speed to escape pursuit by British fighter aircraft and the coast often caught these bombs as they were ditched. A prime example occurred on the afternoon of Saturday, 14 September 1940 when a Dornier was being pursued over the south coast by two Spitfires. It ditched its bombs which landed on the Kemp Town area of Brighton. Two of the bombs fell on the Odeon Cinema where parents and children were enjoying a matinee movie: 52 adults, children and two 11-month old babies died and over 100 people were injured as a result.

It should also be remembered that air raids during the Battle of Britain were not limited to the south coast. Along the eastern seaboard many coastal towns, large and small were bombed too. One of the first to suffer fatalities was West Hartlepool on the night of 19–20 June 1940 when four high explosive bombs were dropped on the Musgrave Street and Whitby Street area.[5] There were 2 fatalities and over 60 people were injured as result of this raid. The two dead were Nurse Mrs Lilian Maud Wilkinson (39), who died at the Central Hotel on Musgrave Street[6] and John Punton (54). Mr Punton was an 'Old Contemptible', a veteran of the 2nd Battalion, Durham Light Infantry who fought with the BEF in 1914 and was doing his bit again in the Second World War as a full time ARP Warden.

He had been directing stragglers to get under cover when the bomb came down and he was hit by a shard of bomb casing. Despite being removed to the Cameron Hospital, his injury proved fatal and he died shortly afterwards. Mr Punton has the sad distinction of being the first Civil Defence worker to be killed by enemy action during the war. He was given a funeral with full honours.[7] Considering how densely populated this area was and the scale of the damage caused by the explosions, it was incredible there was not a much larger loss of life.

Hull also received its first bombing raid on the night of 19–20 June 1940 when four HE bombs and around fifty incendiaries were dropped on streets and thoroughfares in the Holderness Road area of East Hull.[8] Hull suffered its first serious daylight attack on 1 July, a lone raider arrived undetected and there had been no siren, before he dropped a stick of bombs aimed at the Shell Mex oil installation at Saltend. The bombs did not achieve a direct hit, but the fragments of bomb casing carried by the explosion pierced one of the petrol storage tanks which contained approximately 2,500 tons of petrol.

The petrol spurted out through the holes and soon caught fire. Thanks to providence of where the bombs fell and the swift actions of the fire crews, the fire was contained and extinguished; the consequences of the tank exploding would have been unthinkable. Two firemen and three Saltend workers were decorated with George Medals for their bravery that night in dealing with the fire and saving over 2,000 tons of petrol in the tank.[9]

The Suffolk fishing port of Lowestoft suffered its first casualties when seventeen bombs were dropped on Clapham Road where the Co-operative Wholesale Society's Store was burnt out, Rant Score, Stanley Street and by the Crown Meadow at 4.30pm on 3 July 1940[10] killing Edith Burnham, George Youngman, Beatrice Baster and her 7-year-old daughter Evelyn[11] with 27 more injured.

The first fatal raids along the Norfolk coast began at 7.30am on the dull, rainy morning of 11 July 1940 when visibility was poor. Nothing was expected to happen and no siren sounded before an enemy aircraft swept in low over Southtown, Great Yarmouth and released seven 50-kilo HE bombs that fell in the areas of the junction of Wolseley Road and Gordon Road. Two houses suffered direct hits. Vera Batley and her 13-month-old son John were killed at their home on Gordon Road, as were Arthur Keable and Harold Richards on Wolseley Road and three more people were injured.[12] Cromer also suffered its first raid later the same day when a lone Dornier 217 dropped a stick of eleven HE bombs that fell across the centre of the town from Hans Place, via Munday's newsagent shop where the blast killed Edward Munday, fatally injured his sister and injured two other family members, then on to the Gangway where a bomb destroyed Joyce's Cafe. The aircraft then wheeled round and machine gunned the streets before it sped back across the sea.[13]

HRH Duke of Kent at an anti-aircraft post, Park Battery, South Shields during a tour of north east defences, August 1940

In Scotland a number of ports and harbours around the coast and Clydebank all suffered their first raids and some Luftwaffe bombers even made it over to the west coast and Wales. Swansea had its first raid at the ungoldly hour of 3.30am on 27 June 1940. Cardiff had its first raids on 3 and 7 July and endured occasional raids by lone aircraft and small groups of bombers for the rest of the year.

The Luftwaffe made a serious attempt to smash the shipbuilding and industrial areas along the banks of the River Tyne in a daylight raid as James Brunskill would record:

On that fateful summer day of 15 August 1940 between 180 and 200 German bombers tried to smash our industrial areas. Lunch hour crowds hurried to shelter as waves of enemy planes droned ominously nearer until their engines sounded like the roar of thunder and only the skill and courage of the RAF pilots and accurate AA fire saved Newcastle and other places from death and destruction.

The attacking force was a mixed formation of Heinkel and Junkers bombers escorted by 36 Messerschmitt 110 fighters flying astern and above them. Into the Luftwaffe formations tore our defiant Spitfire and Hurricane fighters weaving, spiralling and diving, their machine guns spitting death and they speedily converted a desperate and determined attack into what for the enemy was a costly and ghastly failure. Seventy-five German planes were destroyed or crippled within as many minutes, while many more would probably never reach their base. The 'raiders past' sounded and citizens emerged from their underground shelters into the brilliant sunshine. Womenfolk resumed their shopping and men returned to their offices…the life of Newcastle went on as before.[14]

The annals of the Luftwaffe would refer to this day as 'Black Thursday' and would never again send such numbers against the north east but it did not stem their attacks against other targets.

The Birkenhead suburb of Prenton received the first bombs on Merseyside at 12.30am on 9 August followed by another stick of bombs on Wallasey twenty-four hours later. The first bombs fell on Liverpool on the night of 17–18 August. These attacks were intended more to test defences and report back; the Luftwaffe would return with terrible frequency and in force over the months to come. Liverpool city and port was attacked fifty-seven times and 520 had been killed before it suffered its first serious night raid on 28–29 November 1940. In this attack Liverpool was hit by 350 tons of HE bombs, 30 parachute land mines and 3,000 incendiaries that killed a further 300 people.[15]

Wrecked houses on Seed Street, Blackpool after the air raid of 12 September 1940.

Even the 'safe holiday haven' of Blackpool suffered its first air raid with fatal consequences at 11pm on 12 September 1940 when a 500lb bomb, believed to be intended for the North Station, fell on Seed Street killing 8 people.

No matter what was thrown at them the people carried on as best they could and that included in the fields where there was a harvest to be gathered in. This harvest was so essential for the people of Britain when U-boats held such a tight grip around our coast, our imports had been slashed and food was now rationed. Local men, women and children all lent a hand on the land and farmers were also helped by roving volunteer working parties and the mighty workforce of the Women's Land Army. Spare a thought for those farming fields some of whom were killed or badly injured as they went about their work.

Among those working the most dangerous of areas of the coast were threshing machine owner Mr Reginald Blunt and his machine minder William 'Bill' Harris, both of them from Deal. Reginald would recall:

When the Kent War Agricultural Committee asked me to do some threshing with my machine in the Dover coastal area we went over and worked from dawn to dusk for nearly two months and threshed several thousand quarters of corn. It was a hot spot. Almost daily machine gun bullets fell about us and twice the enemy deliberately gunned us. Bullets spattered all around us and we could see sparks fly up as they struck hard ground. On other occasions shells from the French coast and bombs fell near us but we were always at work again at dawn the next day.[16]

Another story tells of when Mr Harris's home in Deal was made uninhabitable after a bomb fell nearby when he was away threshing near Dover. The stoical Mrs Harris, however, claimed she did not send for her husband because: 'I knew he was putting up with a lot more at his job than we were at home.' Reginald Blunt and Bill Harris were both recognised for their work under fire by being awarded George Medals.

Farmer Gilbert Mitchell was also awarded a George Medal and his wife Kathleen and her sister Grace Harrison received British Empire Medals in 1942 for carrying on their work at their Reach Court Farm at St Margaret's Bay near Dover. Their farm was on the nearest point of land in Britain to the continent, their farm buildings were even described as 'the most vulnerable in the country'. They too had carried on through air raids, shelling and even machine gunning by the enemy. They just got used to diving under their tractor or binder for safety. Even when a barrage balloon was shot down in flames and landed on his tractor Mr Mitchell extinguished the fire and just carried on with his work. When other farmers left for safer localities Mr and

Farmer Gilbert Mitchell and his tractor driver Mr C. Rogers keeping an eye on the skies above the fields they were working on the edge of the White Cliffs of Dover, 1940.

Mrs Mitchell and Miss Harrison worked their fields to ensure the crops they were growing were not lost.[17]

British popular history records the Battle of Britain was fought and won in the air by the end of October 1940 but that was not to be the end of the German bombing campaign on London or Britain, in fact London would suffer its biggest air raid on 10–11 May 1941 when 711 tons of high explosive and 2,393 incendiaries rained down on the capital in less than twenty-four hours leaving 1,436 civilians dead.

The airfields and aircraft of the RAF had not been destroyed, Britain had not been brought to submission through the blitz on London so German strategy changed in late 1940 and into 1941 to focus attacks on 'arms towns' where munitions were produced such as Birmingham, Sheffield, Manchester, Coventry, Bristol and Avonmouth. There were also intensified attacks on ports: out of forty night raids on targets other than London, only six were not on ports, indeed some of our ports and other coastal towns would receive the worst attacks they would suffer during the entire war in 1941.

Some of the damage caused by the parachute mine on Potter Lane and the Old Town, Scarborough after the air raid of 10 October 1940.

Despite the barrage that opened up at enemy raiders and deafened the locals because it was just minutes flight from France, by August 1941 Portsmouth had been raided 792 times during which 1,500 bombs rained down on the city. In the raid of 10 January 1941 300 enemy aircraft dropped 25,000 incendiary bombs on Portsmouth starting 2,314 separate fire incidents. Despite the efforts of the fire service, assisted by local military units, there was no effective supply of water to fight the fires. The conflagration rapidly spread through the main

Leaflet issued by the Southampton ARP Committee offering advice on what to do in the event of an air raid.

shopping centres, burning out numerous public buildings, six churches and the Guildhall; 65,000 houses were damaged, 3,000 people were rendered homeless, 171 people lost their lives and 430 were injured.[18]

Their port neighbour Southampton had already taken its hammering on 23 and 30 November and 1 December 1940 which caused fires and extensive damage to the city centre. By 1 December only a single building was left intact between the Civic Centre and Bargate.

In Wales Cardiff was given an unwanted New Year greeting on 2 January 1941 with the first raid that specifically targeted their docks and factories. As ever, residential housing was part of the collateral damage. One story from that night tells of the rescue of a 6-year-old boy who was trapped under the rubble of what had been his home for six hours who was heard to be continually singing God save the King when asked why he replied:

My Father was a collier and he always said that when the men were caught buried underground they would keep singing and singing and they were always got out in time.[19]

Bombers returned to Wales and attacked Swansea inflicting three nights of blitz on the town over 19, 20 and 21 February during which 1,273 high explosive bombs and an estimated 56,000 incendiary bombs were dropped on the town centre, levelling it with bombs and fires. Great swathes of Brynhyfryd, Manselton and Townhill were also destroyed, leaving 230 people dead, 409 injured and rendering 7,000 people homeless.

The following month Clydeside, Britain's biggest ship building area was subjected to its first concentrated attack on 13 and 14 March. The combination of high explosives and fire bombs set large areas of Glasgow and Clydebank ablaze with fires that were recorded as being spotted from the air by British pilots from 100 miles away.[20] Yet again the poor quality of the housing, especially the overcrowded tenements that quickly cracked and collapsed from the bomb blasts, saw 35,000 out of a population of around 60,000 made homeless as a result. Over the two nights of raids 528 people were killed and 617 seriously injured.

The drone of enemy aircraft over Plymouth had become a sickeningly familiar sound by March 1941, and widespread damage had already been inflicted on the city. Their Majesties King George VI and Queen Elizabeth had come personally on a morale boosting visit to tour devastated areas of the city, meeting its people on 20 March 1941; just two hours after they left the bombers were back again:

The attack was started by a circus of 'pathfinders' and the dropping of thousands of incendiary bombs. They were followed by wave after wave of heavy bombers dropping high explosives into the fiery cauldron. In this fearful attack the heart of Plymouth was doomed to destruction. The first major fire was at Messrs Spooners printers at St Andrew's Cross; another was the Royal Hotel. Soon the fires were raging in every direction.

This was easily the most terrifying raid that Plymouth had experienced. The civil defence organisations worked feverishly but it was impossible to cope with the weight of the attack…The dawn revealed the greatest tragedy in Plymouth's history. The scene of devastation was beyond description. Gaunt buildings, piles of smouldering rubble, miles of hoses, the stench and the grime. Hollow-eyed for want of sleep, grimly silent, but still with an unconquerable spirit, the people set about the task of clearing up.

The next night the attack was repeated on identical lines. It seemed that the enemy was determined to complete the destruction…What had not gone down in the previous night was doomed to destruction in this second attack. The havoc was widespread and the second morning revealed a truly stricken Plymouth.[21]

The morning after the raid the people had their worst fears confirmed, the city centre, popular thoroughfares like Bedford Street and Cornwall Street were in ruins, as were churches, stores and shops, even the historic Guildhall

The ruins of Plymouth city centre near Charles Church, 1941.

was reduced to a burnt-out shell and the bustling area around it reduced to what was described as 'a brick filled desert'. The raid of 20–21 March killed 336 civilians and across the city 20,000 properties were destroyed or damaged.

People tried to salvage what they could from the rubble of their former homes, including a significant amount of the precious furniture that had been recovered and stored in two stands of Home Park football ground. There it remained safe and sound until the following month when it was fire-bombed in the next series of raids on the nights of 22, 23, 24 and 29 April. On the night of 22 April, one of the single greatest losses of life from a single bomb occurred when a public shelter in Portland Square in the central area of the city received a direct hit killing 76 people.

Extensive damage to houses on Saltash Road, Plymouth, 1941.

Plymouth suffered again and again, as did Devonport and Stonehouse, as bombers targeted its dockyards and barracks many homes, businesses and places of entertainment were also damaged or destroyed. In this latest round of raids there had been over twenty-three hours of continuous bombardment from 1,140 HE bombs, 17 parachute mines and thousands of incendiaries. The loss of life was appalling with 590 people killed[22] and thousands injured. Nevertheless Union flags on a motley array of poles appeared out of shattered window frames and were planted in piles of rubble each morning and defiantly fluttered in the breeze. The people of Plymouth were not going to give up.

What was less known was the phenomena of 'trekking'. In every badly bombed area many of those who lost their homes went to stay with friends and relatives outside the town, but there were also those who chose not stay in the town at night and left each evening by car, bus, lorry, trade van, bicycles and even walking with their precious goods and bedding in old prams, they made their way out of the city each night to sleep in the surrounding countryside and would return again in the morning. H.P. Twyford saw this

Bomb Disposal squad and the 1,800kg 'Satan' bomb they defused, Frederick Road, Gorleston, Norfolk, 12 June 1941.

nightly procession in Plymouth and wrote: *'It was, indeed a pathetic sight. War was a cursed thing.'*[23]

The Luftwaffe continued to press the east and west coasts. On 7–8 April 1941 bombers attacked Great Yarmouth and Gorleston dropping HE bombs on Southtown Road and a huge shower of an estimated 4,000 incendiaries, many of them the explosive type, across the town from the Market Place, across the Rows and along South Quay to Gorleston starting sixty-five major fire incidents and nearly two hundred smaller fires. Inflicting the most destructive raid of the war on the town, 17 people were killed and 68 injured.[24] The Motor Launch flotilla in the dock was only narrowly saved by crews hosing their decks down and throwing the incendiaries off the boats.

Belfast in Northern Ireland also suffered its first serious raids on 7–8 and 15 April 1941. The latter raid was the most severe as 674 HE bombs, 76 parachute mines and 29,000 incendiary bombs hailed down, inflicting the worst of the damage on the working class terraced streets of North Belfast and along the Antrim, Cavehill, Crumlin and Duncairn Roads. The city streets blazed with fires and reinforcements came from both Eire and across the Irish Sea from Britain, but little could be done to stem the inferno. A death toll of civilians and military personnel killed in the raid exceeded 800, the greatest loss of life incurred in a single raid on the United Kingdom outside London.

Liverpool and Merseyside had suffered raids over 20, 21 and 22 December 1940 and the bombers returned again on 13 and 21 March 1941. German bombing tactics were evolving to not just target a city or town on one night, but to attack it over several nights in quick succession and destroy the repairs that had been effected in the aftermath of the earlier attack in an attempt to inflict maximum damage and break morale. Over 1–7 May 1941 bombers returned to Liverpool and Merseyside almost every night; during these raids it was estimated 2,000 bombs fell on the area and the fire brigades fought over 1,200 fires. Public buildings, churches, department stores, shops, businesses and warehouses were damaged and destroyed and much of the once imposing city centre and its thoroughfares were reduced to rubble and ruins.

At the docks 70 out of the 140 berths were put out of action, roads and railway lines were blocked and all utilities were badly fractured, but Liverpool made repairs, cleared what needed to be cleared from streets, roads and rails and carried on. As a result of these attacks 1,900 people lost their lives, 1,450 were seriously injured and 70,000 people lost their homes. When the last bombs fell on Merseyside on 10 January 1942 air raids on Liverpool, Birkenhead, Bootle and Wallasey had claimed the lives of 3,966 people and seriously injured 3,812.[25] *Front Line 1940–41*, the Ministry of Information's official story of Civil Defence in Britain, stated of Merseyside: *Measured by number and weight of attacks and number of casualties, this must rank as Hitler's Target Number One outside London.*[26]

As Liverpool burned, bombers returned to Belfast with a 'fire bomb blitz' on 4 and 5 May dropping 237 tons of HE bombs, 80 parachute mines and 96,000 incendiaries that caused extensive damage to East Belfast and the city centre where the Great Hall in the City Hall was gutted by fire. Short and Harlands' aircraft factory was so badly damaged full production was not restored until November. Many of the workshops at Harland and Wolff's shipyard were also wrecked, three corvettes were destroyed by fire and a supply ship was sunk. As a result of the raids of April and May on Belfast over 1,000 people lost their lives, half the houses of the city sustained damage and 15,000 were left homeless.[27]

In his excellent booklet to accompany the Northern Ireland War Memorial Home Front Exhibition, John Potter quotes an extract from the diary of a nurse at a hospital in Stranmillis who recorded in her diary on the morning of 5 May, with the smell of the fires from the Belfast blitz still hanging in the air and the grass outside strewn with blackened and charred paper, her eyes were drawn to a sheet from a child's essay book:

On the top of the page were the words 'the end of the world'. It seemed appropriate. It was the end of the world as we knew it….[28]

On 5 and 6 May the Luftwaffe made an unwelcome return to Clydeside in an attack aimed at the shipyards and ships around Port Glasgow, Greenock and Gourock. In this latest attack 1,000 tonnes of explosives were dropped over the area, 217 people were killed and over 10,000 injured, 5,000 people lost their homes and many more suffered damage.

As 1941 progressed the attacks became more sustained and vicious. On 18 March Hull had received its first heavy attack with over 100 HE bombs being dropped on the north and central areas of the town. The bombing caused 700 fires, rendered hundreds of homes uninhabitable, took the lives of over 90 people and seriously injured 70. On the last day of that month, 31 March, the public air raid warning sirens whined at 8.20pm and the raiders returned again soon after. They dropped illumination flares that lit up the city like day and then dropped bombs and parachute mines that fell in almost every area, blowing up roads and water mains, blasting buildings and showering the streets with glass. Towards the end of the raid, about two hours later, landmines fell on the Shell Mex Buildings on Ferensway which housed Hull's Civil Defence Control Centre from which all emergency and Civil Defence services were co-ordinated. Tom Geraghty, Assistant Editor of the *Hull Daily Mail* during the war recounted the incident in his account of the raids in *A North East Coast Town* (1951):

The blast swept the staff in all directions, wounding some, rendering others incapable of action through shock. Ceilings fell, walls caved in, fire broke out. Furniture, filing cabinets, typewriters etc, were piled in indescribable confusion, rendering the evacuation of the falling and blazing structure most difficult. Yet there were some who stayed on to try and fight small fires or give the layout of the building to rescue parties.[29]

As rescue crews arrived at the scene they were confronted by the sight of headquarters' vehicles that had been parked outside strewn over the area like discarded toys after they had been blown sky high, and a concrete section of the roadway stood up vertically in the road like some monolithic tombstone.

Inside, Dr David Diamond (37), the Deputy Medical Officer of Health, had been killed as had RAF pilot Otto Meggitt who was engaged to one of the young lady clerks employed in the control centre and several others were nursing wounds. The casualties in the Ferensway public shelter illustrate the cross section of people that could be wiped out with the explosion of a single bomb: Firewatcher Bramwell Butler (44), Ada Carrington (62), Phyllis Bayton (20) and Lilian Johnson (37), Susan Wood (38) and her children Mavis (7), Geoffrey (11) and Joyce (14), husband and wife Annie and George Jennison (aged 56 and 62 respectively) and widow Emma Howard (80). Sadly,

The Shell Mex building on Ferensway, under which was the Hull Civil Civil Defence Control Centre and a public shelter, after the air raid of 18 March 1941.

the incident was far from unique and can be found repeated again and again all around the coast and across the country.

A search was also made for PC Robert Garton (46) who had been on duty outside the Shell Mex building. Tragically, all that could initially be found of him were pieces of his uniform. Among the official reports however is a description of the discovery of a pile of human flesh recovered on nearby Spring Street.[30] All in all 52 people were killed and 73 were injured in this raid.

Worse was to come when Hull faced its most severe raids on the nights of 7–8 and 8–9 May when 300 HE bombs, parachute land mines and thousands of incendiary bombs rained down on the city. The Guildhall, City Hall, the city centre and surrounding streets were soon a mass of flames and Riverside Quay was gutted from end to end. Over those two nights there were 1,200 casualties, 400 of them lost their lives, in thirty-six cases the injuries they had sustained meant their identities could not be established. Raids continued on Hull into 1942 and 1943, even when they thought they had suffered the last aerial assault the city was machine gunned and bombed in March 1945. All told, in excess of 1,200 people were killed and over 3,000 received treatment for wounds, 86,715 houses were damaged and 152,000 were rendered homeless during the air raids on Hull.

The worst hit cities were often confronted with difficulties feeding those who had been bombed out after rest centres, often based in schools and public buildings, were damaged along with the rest of the city in the raid. This is where mobile canteens run by the WVS and a variety of charitable organisations such as the YMCA and Salvation Army, played such a valuable role providing hot drinks and food when they were needed most. The WVS also provided the staff for the Queen's Messenger 'Flying Food Columns' of mobile canteens for mass feeding. In Hull three big municipal kitchens provided meals to be served and eaten in thirteen British Restaurants (feeding centres), twenty-four cash and carry food offices, forty works canteens, emergency feeding centres and rest centres. Over the eight days after the May raids the Hull Municipal Kitchens were averaging some 25,000 meals a day.[31]

Every bombed city had heroes be they members of the police, ambulance, fire service, Civil Defence or even members of the public helping someone, often a stranger, in their time of need or danger. Many times gallantry went unrecognised, some did receive commendations and awards, but very few could claim the distinction of having been awarded the George Medal twice.

One of that brave few was George Sewell of Hull. Former Merchant seaman, Mr Sewell had worked at the Shell Mex oil installation at Saltend since before the war and was manager of their works fire brigade. George had led his team to attend to the petrol storage tank that had been pierced by shrapnel back on 1 July 1940 when, according to his citation for the George Medal, Sewell had personally: '*clambered on to the tank roof whilst the gas inside was burning, endeavouring to extinguish the flames by playing foam over the tank top and placing sandbags over the roof curb*'.[32]

On the night of 8–9 May the tanks were suffering damage again and an incendiary bomb was spotted landing on one of the petrol storage tanks and, as firebombs are prone to do, it ignited. Mr Sewell led his team in again and as his second citation states:

> *...although enemy aircraft were overhead and bombs continued to fall, Mr. Sewell immediately climbed to the top of the tank and placed bags of sand over the holes, successfully extinguishing the fires. Mr. Sewell then climbed on to another tank and kicked to the ground a burning bomb. Mr. Sewell's gallant action prevented a serious fire and consequent loss of valuable product and installation.*[33]

Tip and Run

As 1941 turned to 1942 the Luftwaffe strategy changed yet again. Where 1941 was marked as the year of horrifically intense and destructive raids by hundreds of bombers on towns and ports, over the remaining years of the war our coastal towns would be subjected to fewer big raids, but there would be tip and run raids by smaller groups of enemy aircraft and the damage and loss of life caused by these raids proved to be the worst suffered in some of our coastal areas.

A prime example is the lone raider that caused the worst loss of life during a single raid in Lowestoft during the conflict. It occurred at 4.27pm on 13 January 1942, as Ford Jenkins recalled:

> *It was snowing at tea-time on this winters day when an enemy Dornier suddenly dived on to the main shopping district and, from only a few hundred feet up, dropped four bombs which in a matter of seconds, created the most complete scene of havoc the port had experienced. The biggest casualty list occurred in Wallers restaurant where many civilians and service folk were at tea. A shrill whistle gave a brief warning of danger, but there was little time to seek safety and only a few members of the staff of the downstairs grocery department were able to save their lives by rushing to the concrete shelter at the rear.*
>
> *Almost a complete block of large shops was devastated, as were several other business premises, while numerous establishments, including the town's biggest cinema, the Odeon on the opposite side of the road, were severely*

blasted. Among others who lost their lives was a girl roof-spotter at a large shop and a girl assistant at another store who died after being rescued from a cellar in which she had lain for twenty-four hours.[34]

In this single tip and run raid 51 civilians and 18 service personnel were killed, 1 person was missing and over 100 were wounded.

King's Lynn also suffered its worst losses from a tip and run at 9.30pm on 12 June 1942 when the last of a stick of four bombs dropped by a lone raider was a direct hit on the Eagle Hotel on Norfolk Street. It was a Friday night, the bar was packed, the bomb wrecked the hotel and buildings collapsed nearby.

Royal Artillery Sergeant Frank Faulkner of Widnes was based locally and was on the scene just minutes after the bomb exploded. He defied police orders and crawled under dangerous debris and through his initiative a number of people were rescued after one and a half hours. He then found a

The ruins of the Eagle Hotel, King's Lynn that received a direct hit on 12 June 1942.

217

The ruins of St Nicholas Church, Great Yarmouth that was burnt out by incendiary bombs during the air raid on 25 June 1942.

woman trapped in a cellar. Working in a confined space heavily polluted by escaping gas, he eased heavy girders off her body and sang to keep up her spirits for six hours. Sergeant Faulkner was awarded a George Medal for his courage, endurance and devotion to duty.[35] A total of 42 civilians and military personnel lost their lives as a result of the raid.[36]

Later that month Luftwaffe bombers returned to inflict another serious raid on Great Yarmouth dropping eight HE bombs and approximately 1,500 incendiaries on the town on 25 June 1942. This horribly destructive raid damaged a number of places that had already suffered in previous raids, including the Free Library and the ancient Toll House. Much damage was caused to homes and shops in the Rows, Lacon's brewery barrel store and workshops were gutted, as was a furniture store containing the furniture of twenty-two houses that had previously been bombed out. Worse still was the medieval parish church of St Nicholas, one of the largest parish churches in the country, was also gutted by fire. Three people lost their lives and 19 were injured.[37]

Many of the hotels and large buildings in Great Yarmouth were being used as billets for the men and women of local military forces. On 11 May 1943 twenty Focke-Wulf 190s sped low across the sea to avoid radar interception and arrived over Great Yarmouth at 8.45am. Despite having the advantage of early morning sea mist cover and the sun low in the sky behind them, one was shot down by F/O Townsend in one of four Mustang fighters from 613 Squadron (Coltishall) who had been on their way to recce shipping off the Dutch coast.

Another raider was brought down by anti-aircraft fire, but the rest flew over the north end of the town machine gunning and dropping HE bombs as they did so. On North Drive a company of thirty ATS girls were marching briskly back to their billet at Sefton House after taking part in physical recreation on the nearby Wellesley Road recreation ground when the raiders screamed towards them, one of them opening up with his machine guns. The girls ran towards the hostel for cover, one of them tripped and fell, this accident undoubtedly saved her life, because just moments later a bomb was dropped on the building.

James Dean was an eye witness and told a *Yarmouth Mercury* reporter:

I heard the roar of the planes and right in front of me a crashing sound. Then there was another and I saw a building burst apart about 500 yards in front of me just as five planes came screaming over my head. The blast lifted me off the motor roller I was driving. The planes were so low I could see the black crosses on them. They seemed to lift themselves up to clear the roof tops. I was on the ground when the bombs fell and when I looked towards the billet I saw the awful wreckage.

Upon later examination bomb fragments were found to have hit the motor roller Mr Dean was driving. He rushed over and assisted with the rescue effort. Soldiers from the 1st Battalion, The Sherwood Foresters manning the AA mounted Bren gun position on the shore-end of the Britannia Pier were also among the first on the scene and were soon working with rescue squads to remove the wreckage to extricate survivors. The young soldiers and the rescuers who worked for hours digging through the rubble had not seen carnage involving so many young women before and the sights they saw haunted them for the rest of their lives. The name of only one that was dug out alive was reported at the time, that of Private Doreen Chappel (22) of Cinderford, Yorkshire who was removed to the general hospital. A total of 26 ATS servicewomen lost their lives as a result of the bomb on Sefton House;

The Hotel Metropole, Bournemouth, scene of the worst loss of life after receiving a direct hit during the town's worst air raid on 23 May 1943.

23 others, mostly mothers and children, were killed and 41 were injured by the bombs that fell on the town in the same raid.

The tip and run raids mentioned were far from unique and were not limited to the east coast either. As ever, being so close to the occupied coast of France, the Luftwaffe raiders kept on coming and seafront properties and hotels suffered badly. Hastings suffered its severest attack on 11 March 1943 when 38 people were killed. Hove also suffered its two most serious raids in March 1943 that left 22 dead. In a raid on Eastbourne on 3 April 1943 there was widespread damage including a public shelter which received a direct hit and 30 people were killed.

On 23 May 1943 twenty Focke-Wulf 190s of II/SKG10 set off to bomb Hastings and twenty-six Fw190s of IV/SKG 10 aimed for Bournemouth to conduct simultaneous raids on the coastal towns.[38] The attack was not unopposed, one aircraft was shot down by an RAF Typhoon pilot and another was damaged by anti-aircraft fire by Royal Artillery Lance Bombardier Norman Lawrence with his triple mounted Lewis guns which he continued to fire from the roof of a shop despite the premises being on fire. His gallantry was recognised with the award of a British Empire Medal.[39]

When the attackers arrived over the coast it was a fine and sunny spring Sunday lunchtime, pubs and hotels were bustling when twenty-five HE bombs were dropped on Hastings and the streets were machine gunned. Widespread damage was inflicted on the seaward part of the town and 25 people were killed, 30 seriously injured and 55 suffered minor injuries.[40] Worse still would befall Bournemouth where bombs were dropped across the town centre causing a death toll of 77 civilians, 46 seriously injured and 150 with minor injuries. Bournemouth also provided billets for numerous military personnel, among them the Metropole Hotel which was being used by trainee RAF aircrew. The hotel suffered a direct hit and 31 service personnel, mostly men of the Royal Air Force, Royal Canadian Air Force and Royal Australian Air Force were killed, 3 were missing and 38 wounded.[41] As rescue parties dug through the wreckage they pulled out both the living and the dead. The wounded were taken away in ambulances while the dead were taken to the Bournemouth Pleasure Gardens which rapidly became on open air mortuary with lines of bodies wrapped in white sheets. It was a sight no one who saw it would ever forget. A number of both the service and civilian wounded who had been hospitalised would also succumb to their wounds over the ensuing days and weeks.

Two days later on 25 May 1943 Brighton suffered another of these lunchtime attacks. The raid lasted just five minutes but that was quite long enough for severe damage to be inflicted on the railway and locomotive works. The London Road viaduct was destroyed, the Black Rock Gas Works was set on fire and 150 houses were made uninhabitable making 500 people homeless. A total of 24 men, women and children were killed and over 100 injured.

Nowhere was beyond the bombers and nothing was sacred. On Sunday, 30 May 1943 churches were busy with large congregations for Rogationtide. A lone Fw190 from SKG10 came into view flying low over Torquay. The aircraft appeared to have been damaged by AA fire and ditched his bombs as he descended over the town, so low, that his tail clipped the cross on the roof of Priory Church and knocked it to the ground. He released a bomb moments later as he went out of control and crashed into houses on Teignmouth Road.

The bomb fell on St Mary's Church blowing it apart. Inside a group of Sunday School children and their teachers caught the full force of the blast, killing 21 of the children.[42]

V Weapons

Even in 1944 and 1945 air raids still took place in Britain but they were far less frequent, however, after the success of the Normandy landings. Hitler still believed he could win the war and began sending a new terror weapon over in the form of pilotless, jet-powered flying bombs, known in Germany as *Vergeltungswaffe* 1 (Vengeance Weapon 1). Fired from launch sites from the region of Dieppe to Calais, launch ramps for the V1s were aimed primarily at London and locations on the south coast of England.

The first V1s were fired at Britain on 13 June 1944. Hitler had ordered that the launch of the first V1s against Britain were to be in concert with a

Margaret Hicks, a member of a mixed Anti-Aircraft battery on the South Coast paints another V1 'kill' on the battery scoreboard, August 1944.

barrage of coastal artillery fire directed to the same area. As a result, unusually, Maidstone was shelled and Folkstone received its heaviest bombardment of the war in a five-hour ordeal from just after midnight until dawn where forty-two shells landed on the town causing damage to over a thousand properties. During all of this the first V1s crossed the Channel and flew over Folkestone.[43]

The arrival of V1s had been expected for some time after the first reports of the weapon had been received by British military intelligence in 1943. The Operation Diver plan (named after the action of the V1 whereby its engine stops and the 850kg of high explosive in its warhead nose causes the V1 to dip and then dive to the ground and explode on impact). For combatting this new menace plans had been drawn up early in 1944. Members of the Royal Observer Corps and Civil Defence had been given special recognition briefing about what to look for to identify one and a code word of 'Diver' if a V1 was spotted. On the night of 13 June the first V1 was spotted as it flew towards the English coast by members of the Royal Observer Corps on duty at Folkestone and Dymchurch and they rapidly relayed 'Diver. Diver. Diver' to their central control centre.

Auxiliary Coast Guard Mr F.C. Marsh BEM who was on watch at the end of Folkestone Harbour had not had quite the same briefing reported at 4.20am: 'Two aircraft with lighted cockpits flying North-West.'[44] At more or less the same time as Mr Marsh's report was received the first V1 landed on English soil at Swanscombe, Kent, followed by a second at Mizbrooks Farm, Cuckfield. Both had landed on fields and no-one was injured; more would soon follow and sadly that would not always be the case. On 15 June the V1s were targetted in force for the first time when 120 were launched at London and more were to follow.

Britain did not stand defenceless against the V1s, Operation Diver swung rapidly into action. Immediately, fighter aircraft were undertaking anti-V1 patrols with radar-guided fighters carrying on at night assisted by searchlight units deployed every 1½ miles along the coast from South Foreland to Seaford in Sussex. There was then a concentrated belt of 192 heavy anti-aircraft guns and 192 light anti-aircraft guns extended along the southern slope of the North Downs backed up by 480 barrage balloons on the higher ground behind the guns, all set up in less than a week after the first attack.[45]

Operation Diver had been superbly executed but it soon became all too apparent the V1s were still getting through. In excess of 100 bombs were landing on London and the south east every day in the first fortnight of V1 attacks, leaving 1,600 dead, 4,500 seriously wounded and 5,000 suffering minor injuries in their wake – a casualty rate as high as the worst weeks of the blitz in September 1940. The difference was the proportion of those killed was far lower. This could well be because the V1s were coming day and night with little or no warning and people on busy streets were being injured by flying glass.[46]

It had also become clear to German military intelligence that the V1s were being thwarted by British defences on the south east coast. The week ending 8 July saw the peak of attacks when Flakregiment 155 (W) launched over 800 V1s, in an attempt to circumvent the Kent defences. In the first of many such missions Heinkels from III/KG3 carrying V1s took off from an airfield in Holland and launched them over the North Sea against London for the first time on 7 July 1944.

A comprehensive examination of the anti-V1 defences saw a revised and co-ordinated plan drawn up and agreed between Fighter Command, Anti-Aircraft and Balloon Commands on 13 July 1944. More, faster aircraft such as the Hawker Tempest Vs, late model Spitfires, Gloster Meteors, Mustang IIIs and Mosquitos capable of the speeds required to intercept the flying bombs were assigned to the south east coast on anti-Diver operations. Acting with

Some of the 3.7-inch QF guns of the anti-V1 barrage on the promenade at St Leonards, Hastings 1944.

No.554 Anti-Aircraft Battery, Royal Artillery demonstrating Searchlight Control Radar near Harwich 1943.

impressive speed GOC Anti-Aircraft Command Sir Frederick Pile organised the redeployment of his heavy anti-aircraft guns from the North Downs to between St Margaret's Bay and Cuckmere Haven by 17 July, with 570 light AA guns sites established in the same area by 19 July. By the 21st the static balloon barrage south east of London increased to 1,000 and by the end of the month crews and equipment had been redeployed to the area from sites all over the country and 1,750 barrage balloons were now maintained against the V1 menace.

The requirement of a 'gun box' at the mouth of the Thames was also initiated to tackle the V1s now being launched from the east and north east. This is when Guy Maunsell's futuristic gun plaform forts truly proved their worth. The redeployment of the AA gunners nearer to the coast meant they had better sight of their V1 targets as they crossed the Channel and thus a far better chance of shooting them down before they made landfall over England. The shells they were firing were also greatly improved with VT proximity fuses to 'detect' their target before exploding, combined with gun-laying radar and searchlight radar, the rate of successful kills of V1s by AA artillery improved from 24 per cent to a remarkable 80 per cent by September.[47]

Crew from 127 Heavy Anti-Aircraft Regiment, Royal Artillery rushing to man their 3.7-inch guns during a morning alert at Southwold, Suffolk, October 1944.

No matter what efforts were taken – and thousands of V1s were indeed brought down in the sea before reaching our coast – just like the bombers, if enough were sent some would always get through. Those living in the flight path of V1s in the south east became familiar with the sound of the V1 as they passed overhead. Its pulse jet engine with a characteristic, gutteral sound, which some described as sounding like an old Ford Model T truck struggling up a hill, were soon dubbed 'Buzz-Bombs' or 'Doodlebugs'. People who lived through that time would recall that as long as the engine was running you didn't have to worry, it was when the engine stopped the nose would dip and the thing would then be heading down. The rule of thumb was if you could count to three after the engine stopped it was not going to land on you.

A regular flight path for the V1s heading for the capital soon became recognised and was nick-named Doodlebug Alley and slap bang in the middle of this flight path was Bexhill-on-Sea, a town that took some pride in describing itself as 'a vital section of the bridgehead on the southern front'. At the height of the attacks no fewer than 480 flying bombs were tracked over Bexhill in one period of twenty-four hours.[48] The coming of the V1 also brought yet another round of evacuations from London and places along the route of the rockets. Some groups of children and parents were evacuated as far away as Newcastle.

Some 9,000 V1s were fired at England but only about 25 per cent of them hit their intended targets. The combined defences brought down over

3,500 V1s destined for London. Mechanical unreliability or guidance errors saw many V1s crash harmlessly into the sea, but there were still many of them that brought death and destruction to the capital, its suburbs, the home and south east counties; some even made it as far up as Durham in the north east and near the Dorset border in the west.[49] As an aside, not all V1s were primed solely with explosives, some also carried propaganda leaflets that would scatter around the area where it exploded. These would show images of groups of people, often children, killed in an air raid accompanied by the message in English 'Do you like that? You do? You may not in a few months' time', or maps and drawings showing London and the south of England in flames.

Rocket powered pilotless weaponry was still in its infancy and with the number of them flying over the area observers in Bexhill saw many strange sights, some terrifying as they feared it might be their turn for it to land on the town. On one remarkable day they tracked a flying bomb from its launch site near Boulogne that was heading straight for the town at low altitude until it was a couple of miles off the coast when it turned westward and passed over Beachy Head. It turned yet again and was last seen heading back to where it came from![50]

The spirit of people on the coast was never broken, damaged houses and premises would have defiant chalked signs hung in front with messages such as 'Still open for business' and 'We are still here!' written on them, but some communities were being pushed to their limits. *Front Line Folkestone* reminisced:

Finally came the flying bombs. Folkestone saw the first of these missiles come across, a yellow light flaring from their tails. For three months the attack was kept up. Some of the flying bombs fell in the town causing widespread damage and some casualties. The racket of many heavy and light anti-aircraft guns attacking the missiles as they came over, coupled with the rattle of the flying bombs and the frequent thunderous explosions as they were destroyed in the air, was a severe test for townspeople but they stood up to it bravely as they had to air raids and shelling.[51]

In late September a poster displayed in the borough of Folkestone reproduced a message that had been sent to the mayor from Home Secretary Herbert Morrison:

Every sympathy with gallant citizens of Folkestone in concluding stages of their ordeal. Hold on! I am assured by the competent military authority that the end for your trial will not be long delayed.[52]

The V1s were curtailed as each launch site was captured, but there were still a few that clung on until December when over sixty were brought down by the AA guns of Harwich and Felixstowe even into the early months of 1945. The last two V1s were launched at England on 29 March 1945. One was brought down by AA gunners at Iwade in Kent at 9.59am and its wreckage was the last fragments of the weapon to land on British soil. The last V1 launched at Britain was destroyed at 12.43pm while still over the sea by AA gunfire from Orford Ness, Suffolk.

Some 775 flying bombs landed in East Sussex; poor old Battle took the brunt of these with some 374 of them landing within its rural district.[53] Kent, however, took the brunt when the fragments of the last V1 fell on the county 1,444 Doodlebugs had dropped on Kent, killing 152 and injuring 1,716.[54]

Hitler was not done either; the first V2 long-range rocket, known in Germany as the *Vergeltungswaffe 2*, launched at Britain landed on Chiswick, London, killing three people on 8 September 1944. Each V2 was 45ft tall, carried nine tons of fuel and one ton of explosive. Difficult to track and so fast they could not be easily be tackled by fighters or held in the sights of AA guns, little could be done to intercept these weapons and all that could really be hoped for was the capture of their launch sites as soon as possible.

The east coast was not going to escape V2s either, rockets aimed at the historic city of Norwich were launched from under the cover of woodland near the hamlet of Rijs, in south west Friesland, Holland. None of these reached Norwich city proper, the nearest coming down on the greens of the Royal Norwich Golf Club in the city suburb of Hellesdon. Some of the V1 and V2 flight lines to London passed over East Anglia and the coastline in Suffolk and Essex suffered several incidents. Fortunately, at least for the residents of the coast, most of the V2s sailed over and landed inland.

The last V2 to fall on Britain landed on a bungalow on Kynaston Road, Orpington, Kent on 27 March 1945, killing householder Ivy Millichamp (34) in her kitchen. In total, over 2,700 people were killed in the V2 attacks and over 6,500 more were injured.

Chapter 10

The Cruel Sea

O hear us when we cry to Thee,
For those in peril on the sea.

William Whiting

The seas around Britain were protected by the presence of the Royal Navy Home Fleet, but the escorts for convoys, armed trawlers for the defence of fishing fleets, day to day patrols and defence of our coastal waters fell to flotillas and groups of submarines, destroyers and light coastal forces in each of the five Naval commands around the country. Clockwise from Scotland they were:

The Operations Room at the Headquarters of Western Approaches, Derby House, Liverpool, 1944.

- Orkney and Shetland Command whose duties included the operation and defence of Scapa Flow
- Rosyth Command (originally known as Coast of Scotland Command) that covered sub commands from Aberdeen to Newcastle
- Nore Command from Humber to Dover
- Portsmouth Command from Newhaven to Portland
- Finally, the biggest of them all, Western Approaches Command (including Plymouth Command).

The Western Approaches was also one of the most important commands because it covered some of Britain's largest shipping ports on the west coast, including Glasgow, Liverpool, Holyhead, Cardiff, Swansea and Milford Haven, as well as the convoy routes across the Atlantic. In late 1940 the original Combined Operations Headquarters at Plymouth was proving increasingly impractical and in February 1941 it was moved to a specially constructed reinforced concrete, bomb-proof bunker under an unassuming office building Derby House on Rumford Street in Liverpool. From this bunker of one hundred rooms, covering 55,000 feet, known officially to its staff of men and women Royal Navy and RAF personnel as 'the fortress' or 'the citadel', the Battle of the Atlantic was planned and controlled.

At its heart was the operations room in the lower basement where fifty Wrens would be on duty twenty-four hours a day updating the position indicators on the huge situation map that showed enemy movements, followed the progress of allied convoys, escort groups and air support. Any issue requiring discussion with the War Cabinet, or even Churchill himself, could be conducted via a telephone hotline. To ensure only the approved senior officers used this telephone it had its own armed guard. It was at Western Approaches the important supply routes from Canada and America to Britain were planned and the strategies developed against German U-boat packs, submarines and fleets by the Western Approaches Tactical Unit (created in 1942). It was a major contribution to victory in the Battle of the Atlantic.

In the day-to-day war on the North Sea and the Channel a new threat of fast, well-armed E-boats emerged too and the fight against these 'in and out' attackers was met by the men of the Royal Navy's Light Coastal Forces. There were three main types of vessel used, as Lieutenant Commander Peter Scott[1] would explain from first-hand experience:

The best known is the Motor Torpedo Boat, which is mainly concerned with attacking enemy shipping in enemy waters. Its hitting power is heavy for its size and in that respect it is parallel with the bomber. The MGB – Motor Gun Boat – is the equivalent of a fighter aircraft. It is mainly concerned with

Royal Navy Motor Torpedo Boats on patrol, 1940.

Motor gun boats MGB 60 with MGB 62 and MGB 65 'the Spitfires of the sea' 1941.

fighting enemy light craft. The ML – Motor Launch – which is slower than the other two, is used for a great many different purposes, such as laying mines or leading in landing parties of a Combined Operations raid, but more often defensive, such as routine patrols and escorting convoys, minesweeping and the invaluable service of Air Sea Rescue.[2]

The first MTB base of the war was formed at Felixstowe and the 1st Flotilla was ready to operate by January 1940 and grew to have over 2,000 craft, based on the east, south and west coast (including Northern Ireland) and a complement of 3,000 officers and 22,000 ratings by 1944. Boats and crews of the light coastal forces not only patrolled the seas for enemy craft and faced the regular danger of attack from U-boats, flak trawlers, and E-boats (a term adopted in 1940 for fast German *Schnellboots* (literally meaning a fast boat), they were attacked from the air and those operating in the 'Narrow Seas' of the Dover Strait and English Channel were subject to shelling from German gun positions on the coast of France. The convoy route off the coast of Norfolk and Suffolk became the infamous 'E-boat Alley' when the menace was at its most intense during the winter of 1941–42.

The Light Coastal Forces also took the fight back and conducted their own sorties and raids on enemy ships and even on ports on the occupied French coast such as St Nazaire and Dieppe in 1942. They too became 'in and out' attackers, who gained the nickname of 'The Beat 'em Up Boys'. Fighting in 900 actions, they sank around 400 enemy vessels and 32 enemy aircraft.

Above all, the shipping lanes around Britain needed not only to be protected from enemy vessels with air and sea patrols and minefields, but the seas, channels and entrances to harbours all needed to be swept clear of mines that had been laid by the enemy. The naval branch entrusted with this dangerous work was the Royal Naval Patrol Service. The Admiralty had foreseen the need to expand their fleet of minesweepers during the summer of 1939 and had started entering into contracts with boat owners to purchase modern steam trawlers for conversion to minesweepers. Among the first were fifty-four trawlers from Hull and thirty-two from Grimsby, quite a purchase that accounted for about a third of the deep-water fleet at the time in the two Humber ports. Assurances were made to the public that the effect on the supply of fish would be counter-balanced by the lifting of the voluntary restrictions on the boats remaining in the ports that would then be working at full capacity.[3]

After the outbreak of war even more minesweepers and crew to man them would be required so the Admiralty made an appeal for volunteers, aged between 18 and 45. Candidates were also expected to have not less than one year's experience in deep sea fishing vessels. Newspaper and magazine features included appeals for 2,000 volunteers for minesweeping, but they could not always afford to be quite so choosy. The Admiralty continued to purchase and requisition trawlers and drifters and – more to try to avoid being out of work rather than through a sudden burst of Nelson-like patriotism – their crews would volunteer to come with them. If found medically fit and more or less in the right age group; boys as young as 15 and men in their fifties and sixties could all be found serving in the RNPS. This did mean many of these men, despite being uniformed and having had some period of training (often of a contracted nature when the need for more men and boats was acute) were often not too keen on strictly observing the rigours of Naval red tape and discipline.

They were, however, extremely brave and very good at what they did. This reputation combined with their hotch-potch of trawlers, drifters, yachts and even paddle steamers in the minesweeping service gained them the nick-name of 'Churchill's Pirates'. In the finest tradition of the men who volunteered to become members of Kitchener's Army becoming rather proud of the *nom de plume* of Fred Karno's Army after one of the great comedians back in 1914, the men of the minesweepers were given another nickname after another great comedian and they became rather proud of being known as 'Harry Tate's Navy'.

Minesweepers returning from a patrol c1940.

The refitted trawlers and drifters were initially equipped with mine sweeping gear for the clearance of moored contact mines.[4] This consisted of a long cable with a serrated edge and a torpedo-like winged float attached to the end. To commence a sweep for mines the float would be lowered over the side by means of a davit operated by crew members. The wireman would be ready at the winch to let out the sweep cable as the float drifted away from the minesweeper, usually around 250 yards, the trawler would then make headway and the sweep would commence. The now extended serrated cable would then sever the cables of the mines as it passed along and the freed mines would float to the surface. The crew not engaged in operating the sweeping equipment were armed with rifles and would then open fire and destroy the mines. [5]

The spikey horns that that stuck out from the surface of a sea mine were its detonators. Each metal mine horn casing would contain a glass tube of acid, so if the horn was contacted and bent by a passing vessel, the glass tube inside would be broken releasing the acid over battery contacts completing the circuit and the mine would explode, potentially with devastating consequences to the vessel that had contacted it. There were, of course, many times that the swept mines would explode when contacted by the sweep cable and a huge plume of water would be sent many feet skyward, or under rifle fire with dramatic and potentially dangerous results. The real aim was to puncture the casing of the mine with the rifle shots and sink it.[6] The minesweepers would then be followed by trawlers that had converted to Danlayers that would lay buoys to mark the passage of the channel that had been swept clear.

Each minesweeper trawler would usually be armed with a 12-pounder gun on the whaleback on the fo'c'stle head and an Oerlikon, Bofors or twin machine guns mounted on a gun platform aft and Lewis or Hotchkiss machine guns mounted on the 'verandah'.[7] Most of this weaponry was of First World War vintage and the crew were also tasked with the removal of the thick coating of grease they had been packed in for decades.

The standard crew of a trawler minesweeper was twenty-three men, consisting of a skipper, second skipper who would act as first lieutenant and would take over command if the skipper was injured or sick. There would be a second hand who would act as petty officer, a signalman (known as Bunts), a telegraphist (Sparks), a gunlayer, a wireman (Torps), a motorman, eight seamen, three stokers, a cook and an assistant steward. Every man would have his designated station and duties when sweeping and every seaman would have his place at one of the guns.[8]

Their work was incredibly dangerous, and by the end of 1940 alone over 100 of the converted trawlers had been lost. Losses continued to be heavy[9] so by 1943 it was rare to find more than a couple of former fishermen among

Officer and crew guiding a paravane float over the side of their minesweeper so it could be lowered into the water and drift away, extending the sweep cable attached to it then the sweep of the area would commence, c1941.

the crew of a minesweeper; instead the men came from all walks of life from bus drivers to butchers, metal workers to market gardeners. One story tells of a minesweeper cook who had been an asphalt mixer before he was called up, apparently his rice puddings reflected his former calling. No matter what their previous calling, after six months at sea they earned the right to wear the silver badge of the Royal Naval Patrol Service.[10]

The silver badge earned by members of the RNPS for six months service at sea. The design shows a shark impaled on a marlin spike against a background of a net and sea mines to represent both minesweepers and anti-submarine vessels.

Every Naval command around the country had its Royal Naval Patrol Service Minesweeping Groups and each and every one of them, quite rightly, was fiercely proud of their achievements. There were large minesweeper bases such as Portsmouth, HMS *Wildfire III* at Queenborough, HMS *Miranda*

Women's Voluntary Service leader Lady Reading gives her blessing to the Vegetables for Minesweepers Scheme that supplied fresh vegetables to crews, Grimsby, Lincolnshire, May 1941.

Some of the Royal Naval Patrol Service 'Sparrows' at HMS Europa *listening to an address from the old pleasure gardens bandstand at Sparrow's Nest, Lowestoft c1941.*

at Great Yarmouth, HMS *Martello* at Lowestoft and HMS *Badger* at Harwich, but Grimsby became the largest base in Britain. The RNPS Central Depot, known as HMS *Europa* however, was housed at the Sparrow's Nest theatre in the Lowestoft municipal pleasure gardens.

The transformation had taken place almost overnight in 1939, the notification of the Royal Navy requisition arrived as Elsie and Doris Waters were performing and the following morning a party of workmen arrived to gut the theatre and, as soon as their task was completed, a naval guard was placed at the entrances of the park and Sparrow's Nest became HMS *Europa*.[11] The wonderful acoustics of the bandstand opposite were also very much appreciated by senior officers when addressing large parades of personnel. During the war years HMS *Europa* was the training and drafting base for over 70,000 RNPS personnel who were very proud to be nick-named 'Sparrows'.

British or German sea mines washed ashore on the British coast could also cause severe damage to beach defences or properties if they exploded, not to mention anyone who may have been in the vicinity. They were dealt with by Royal Navy bomb disposal teams, whereas the Royal Engineers Bomb Disposal teams would be expected to deal with our own anti-personnel mines

A detached sea mine, an occasional and highly unwelcome arrival on the beaches of Britain's coastal areas during the Second World War.

on beaches, as well as devices dropped by the Luftwaffe anywhere in the country unless it fell on or near an airfield, in which case that was dealt with by RAF bomb disposal teams. However, if a German parachute mine was discovered inland by the Naval Land Incident Section it such as if a sea mine was carried inland along a river inland, like the one carried 4 miles up the River Cuckmere to Alfriston in East Sussex in October 1943, then a quandary could present itself over which unit would deal with it.

Great efforts were also made by the squadrons of RAF Coastal Command with their 'kipper patrols' to protect those at sea from enemy action. In fact of the 727 U-boats sunk during the war 192 were sunk by pilots from Coastal Command.[12] There was also the Air Sea Rescue Service whose reconnaissance aircraft and flying boats became a regular sight in skies above our coastline as they sought out aircrew who had ditched in the sea. Then there were the RAF High Speed Launches or 'crash boats' of the RAF Marine Craft Section who could speed to the area where the plane went down or where crew in their inflatable rubber dinghies had been spotted. A similar scheme was also developed by the Royal Navy with larger and slower rescue motor launches aimed at providing emergency assistance for coastal forces craft. Local lifeboats would also join searches and together these rescue organisations saved many lives.

RNLI Lifeboats, no matter who was in danger be they friend or foe, in high seas or dead calm, would launch and attempt rescue even though they now

Some of the officers of Coastal Command making friends with some of the locals in a Scottish fishing village c1941.

faced added dangers of wartime such as attack by enemy boats and aircraft or striking an undetected sea mine.

Nineteen RNLI lifeboats from the east and south coasts, some with their own crews, some with Royal Navy crews, took part in the Dunkirk evacuation and were also used to ferry returned troops from ships to shore. Outstanding service during the evacuation was recognised with the award of Distinguished Service Medals to Howard Primrose Knight, Coxswain of the Ramsgate Lifeboat and Edward Drake Parker, Coxswain of the Margate Lifeboat. Both crews worked in excess of forty hours and together they rescued over 3,000 British and French soldiers.

Time and again lifeboat crews answered the call; there are literally thousands of stories of the rescues they performed during the war. One of the most dramatic was by one of the greatest lifeboatmen of all time, Coxswain Henry Blogg GC and his crew of the Cromer Lifeboat *H F Bailey* on 26–27 October 1941. The call came at 8am on 26 October for a lifeboat to attend a vessel ashore on the notoriously dangerous sandbank of Hammond Knoll, about 22 miles out to sea off Cromer. The crew were summoned and the Cromer Lifeboat launched at 8.15am but the high seas were heavy going and it took until 11.35 for the lifeboat to arrive alongside the stricken vessel, the

British Power Boat Company Type 2 'Whaleback' High Speed Launches of the RAF Maritime Branch off Dover, April 1941.

Dungeness Lifeboat **Charles Cooper Henderson** *landing Uffz. H. Bley, 4/LG2 pilot of Messerschmitt Bf109E-4 after he crashed in the Channel suffering minor head injuries having being attacked by RAF fighters on 7 October 1940.*

The crew of the Cromer lifeboat in front of the No.2 Lifeboat, **Harriot Dixon.**

steamer SS *English Trader* with forty-four men on board. There had been more, but five had already been swept overboard and drowned by the time the lifeboat arrived.

The sea was perilous and the waves so high at times that the only part of the *English Trader* that was visible was the tops of her masts. The first attempt to get alongside and fire a line was beaten back by the storm, a second attempt was made, Coxswain Blogg picks up the story:

> *We were trying to approach about half speed, and when still about 100 yards away a huge wall of water suddenly rose up on our port side, a shout of 'look out' and before I could even give a half turn of the wheel I was lifted out of the boat just as though I had been a bit of cork. We were simply overwhelmed by the sheer weight of water. How the boat righted herself I shall never understand. It must have been the hand of Providence. The boat must have been hardest abaft the fore cockpit. Had she been hit as hard along her whole length there would be no lifeboat crew in Cromer today.*[13]

The captain of the *English Trader* witnessed the incident and would state he saw the keel of the lifeboat come right out of the water. The second coxswain John 'Jack' Davies, and crew members Henry 'Shrimp' Davies, Sidney 'Kelly' Harrison and Signalman Walter 'Primo' Allen were all thrown overboard with Blogg. The second coxswain's son William 'Pimpo' Davies[14] sprang to the wheel and steered the lifeboat to where his father and Coxswain Blogg were floating and they were hauled aboard. Blogg took charge again and went to

241

pick up the other three crew. All were hauled aboard but Walter Allen, the lifeboat's signalman, had been in the freezing water for twenty-five minutes and was unconscious. His crewmates managed to briefly revive him, but he suddenly collapsed and died.

It was now about 3pm and the Cromer lifeboat had been out seven hours, suffered a fatality, the crew were exhausted and the propellors were compromised after being fouled by ropes so Blogg made the decision to make for shore. The Yarmouth and Gorleston lifeboat *Louise Stephens* had already been launched to assist and arrived at the *English Trader* a short while later. The Yarmouth Lifeboat faced the same difficult seas as well as the swinging derricks and floating cargo and suddenly their boat was also swept away. It was now getting dark and the captain of the *English Trader* waved the lifeboat to leave for safety which the coxswain agreed to do.

Meanwhile the Cromer lifeboat arrived at Yarmouth, where a doctor and an ambulance were waiting. Some of the crew were so exhausted they had to be helped out of the boat. The body of Signalman Allen was also taken ashore. The Cromer crew were then taken to the Shipwrecked Sailors' Home where they were given hot baths, warm drinks and dry clothes. At 4.40am the following morning Henry Blogg and his crew put to sea again for a third attempt at the rescue. The ropes were still around the propellors, the weather was still gale force and the Cromer lifeboat had to travel 22 miles against the blast to reach the *English Trader*, which when they arrived had its fore part under water. The Cromer lifeboat managed to get alongside the steamer's lee rail and within half an hour all forty-four survivors were aboard and the *H F Bailey* was making for Great Yarmouth.

For gallantry at the SS *English Trader* rescue Coxswain Henry Blogg was awarded a third clasp for his RNLI Silver Medal and the rest of the crew received bronze medals or clasps to their existing bronze medals. Signalman Allen was awarded a posthumous second clasp for his bronze medal and a pension equivalent to that of a sailor of the Royal Navy who had been killed in action was granted to his widow.[15]

During his fifty-three years of service Henry Blogg became the most decorated lifeboatman in RNLI history and with his crew saved 873 lives. When Henry Blogg's nephew Henry 'Shrimp' Davies was asked in an interview what was his uncle's greatest quality 'Shrimp' answered directly: 'He'd never give in… if he started a job, it had to be done.' In the true spirit of Nelson, he was a Norfolk man.

It was a time of extraordinary gallantry by numerous lifeboat crews. It was also when one of the greatest launches also took place. In a number of coastal communities their lifeboats did not have a lifeboat house at the end of a pier to launch directly into the sea, some had to be hauled out manually, especially if it was low tide. Traditionally, this had been done by both men and women launchers in the rural fishing community of Newbiggin on the Northumberland coast.

It had been a foul night and the north east coast was in the teeth of a gale, the sea was roaring and there were hard squalls of sleet and rain when the call came from the coastguard to the Newbiggin Lifeboat Secretary at 4.30am on Sunday, 4 February 1940 reporting a vessel driving ashore north of Newbiggin Point. The alarm was raised and the men and women launchers faithfully rushed to the lifeboat house and hauled the *Augustus and Laura* into the bitterly cold waters.

The lifeboat struggled to make headway and as it rounded the Point met very high breaking seas; the water kept breaking over her bows washing the crew off their feet and all faced the danger of being swamped out of the lifeboat. Second Coxswain George 'Minty' Taylor wisely decided to put about and it took all his seamanship and physical strength to turn the lifeboat and get it back to shore.[16] Come the dawn they could see the Belgian registered motor vessel *Eminent* was stranded on the East Sands.

The only way they were going to reach the stricken vessel was to launch the lifeboat from the shoreline nearer to it on the other side of Newbiggin Point about a mile away. The call went out to launch again and this time forty-five launchers presented themselves for the task, between twenty and thirty of them were women. They picked up the towing ropes and set off into the howling wind and with sleet and, worst of all, sand driving into their faces they dragged the 32ft long, 4-ton lifeboat off the beach then hauled it along Pant Road and over the undulating moorland to the rocky Whitehole Skears where the lifeboat was launched for a second time.

Finally, the eleven bedraggled crew of the *Eminent* were rescued and returned to shore. The lifeboat then had to be hauled over the golf course and back onto its carriage for return to the lifeboat house. Coxswain Taylor was presented with an RNLI Silver Medal for his leadership in this dramatic rescue and an official thanks on vellum was awarded to the 'Women of Newbiggin' launchers for their gallant efforts and endurance.[17]

Between the outbreak of war in September 1939 and VE Day 1945 RNLI lifeboats launched 3,760 times, a total of 6,376 lives were saved and 204 RNLI gallantry medals were issued. Considering all the dangers the crews of RNLI lifeboats faced, only twelve of them lost their lives while attempting to help others during the war years.

Chapter 11

The Turning of the Tide

*A landing was made this morning on the coast of France by troops of the
Allied Expeditionary Force...*

General Dwight D. Eisenhower, 6 June 1944

As the preparations were made for Operation Overlord, the greatest combined operations assault in military history, the British coast had a key role to play in the training of the troops for the task, the development and testing of the vehicles and equipment that would be required and the distraction of German military intelligence from where the actual assault was going to take place. So let us first begin with the deception.

Operation Fortitude

Operation Fortitude was divided into two main elements in Britain. Fortitude North attempted to persuade the Germans a wholly fictitious British Fourth Army was massing in Scotland in preparation for an invasion of Norway or Denmark. Fortitude South was highly successful in its creation of a phantom force for the invasion of France at the Pas de Calais rather than Normandy. Among them was the impressive First US Army Group under General George Patton. The deception was created by many cunning devices ranging from deliberate 'careless talk', movements of real allied army divisions and extensive radio traffic by the No.5 Wireless Group, Royal Signals to give the impression of massive preparations and troop movements in readiness for the invasion.

To back this up there were guns, tanks, bulldozers, cranes, pontoons and even gliders that appeared to be camouflaged, but could still be spotted from the air as they appeared to be assembling in the Kentish countryside between Westerham and Wye. Lights were occasionally left on and the places appeared to be a hive of military activity day and night. Bridges and road corners were being reinforced to protect them from the passage of the tanks and armour, additional bridges were assembled over the Stour and the Medway,[1] a huge

One of the many film prop Quad, limber and gun sets made to deceive German aerial reconnaissance photographs during Operation Fortitude South before the D-Day landings in 1944.

Some of the dummy landing craft built for Operation Fortitude South in a harbour channel in the south-east of England, 1944.

oil dock and pumping head was built at Dover and fighter aircraft were flying sorties above to protect the forces below. It was all a deception using film props and special effects created and maintained by skilled technicians from the film industry and a range of inflatable tanks and field guns produced in secret by Dunlop.[2]

There were also visiting and movement restrictions imposed from the Wash, around the east coast and down to Lands End which came into effect on 1 April 1944. On 2 April, following a secret reconnaissance around the sectors involved by GHQ, a 'Top Secret' plan was sent to the field commanders and naval officers concerned detailing the construction of buildings and launch sites for fake tank landing craft codenamed 'Wetbobs' and 'Bigbobs'. Made of canvas and erected over a metal frame, at 25 yards the completed LCTs were indistinguishable from the real thing. A total of six sites were created at Folkestone, Dover, Woolverstone, Waldringfield, where the craft were berthed on the River Deben, Lowestoft where the illusion was carried out on Lake Lothing, and at Great Yarmouth where the dummy LCTs were stored, erected and found their launching hard at Pitchers Quay and the railway yard and were berthed on Breydon Water.

From early 1944 intercepted German intelligence reports were claiming thirty-four divisions were in southern England, eleven of which were fictional creations of Fortitude South. Up to D-Day and beyond Hitler and many of his generals were of the opinion the main attack was still to come, led by General Patton on the Pas de Calais and the Normandy landings were the distraction.[3]

Operation Overlord

Four armies – the British Second Army, Canadian First Army and the First and Third United States Armies – needed to be put through specialist training for the Normandy landings. For many the training began in the autumn of 1943. As the orders to evacuate Tyneham, Worbarrow Bay and the South Hams on the south coast were being delivered to property owners, British assault battalions were in the North West of Scotland where they began training in co-operation with armoured divisions and sent for specialist training at the No.1 Combined Training Centre on the remote shores of Loch Fyne, Inveraray, Scotland.

What they were training for or why was not explained, everything had to remain a closely guarded secret but it was clear they were being trained as assault divisions and once they got to grips with the training and heard the briefings they were being given they were left in no doubt it was for 'something

Landing manoeuvres at the newly established US Assault Training Centre at Woolacombe in North Devon, 31 October 1943.

big'. For some, like the men of the 1st Battalion, The Royal Norfolk Regiment in the 3rd Infantry Division, who had returned from India to Britain in 1939 and had spent the war to date on home service, hopes were high they would get to see some action at last. Spare a thought, though, for the men of the 50th Division, some of whom had been serving since the Battle of France, who had been evacuated from Dunkirk in 1940, slogged through the desert campaign and the invasion of Sicily and had only returned to Britain in November 1943. After just two weeks leave they were sent to train as assault divisions for the latest big show and must have been thinking 'here we go again'.

Over the autumn and winter, the British, Canadian and some American assault units such as the Rangers, passed through rigorous and tough training and practised seaborne assaults with landing craft at CTC Inveraray. The majority of American assault troops trained at the US Assault Training Centre that had been established at Woolacombe in North Devon in 1943. This centre, which encompassed Woolacombe and Saunton Sands provided similar training to Inverary on sand and in a setting very similar to that of Omaha beach.

A number of specialist units would also play key roles in the success of Operation Overlord. One of them was the top secret Combined Operations

Sub Lieutenant K.C.J. Robinson at the Hydroplane controls of an 'X-craft' midget submarine, 1944.

Pilotage Parties. (COPP) Created under the instruction of Lord Louis Mountbatten, Chief of Combined Operations, their depot was established at the Hayling Island Sailing Club in 1943. COPP trained men in covert beach reconnaissance techniques and operated in active theatres of war all over the world. In December 1943 and early 1944 COPP teams, usually consisting of five men, two swimmers, two crew and the COPP commander, would travel in a motor gunboat from Gosport to just off the coast of Normandy, changed into what were then bulky wetsuits, transferred to inshore craft which took them to within a quarter of a mile of the beach, swam in to conduct their reconnaissance, take samples if required, then swam back to the inshore craft, back to the gunboat and sped back across the Channel. Others were towed by Royal Navy trawler in X-craft midget submarines from which they would survey the beaches by periscope during the day and the swimmers would leave the subs by night, swim to shore to take samples of beach surface by night. Their work was fraught with danger but essential for planning. COPP teams would also return on D-Day in X-craft submarines to provide navigational markers for the approaching landing craft.

Pipe Major 'Jock' Slattery, 1st Battalion, King's Own Scottish Borderers practising 'Blue Bonnets over the Border' the tune he will play as he leads the men into battle, while his pipers tune their pipes in camp at Denmead, Hampshire, April 1944.

For the final stages of training the south coast of England was ideal because of its similarities to the Normandy coastline. In April 1944 the assault brigades were despatched to the south coast to the concentration areas for their divisions for 'collective training' in combined operations with the Royal Navy and RAF.

The men of the 50th Division would be under canvas on the fringes of the New Forest and their first major rehearsal for the landings to come was Exercise Smash, conducted on Studland Bay, Dorset on 18 April 1944. The history of the 8th Battalion, Durham Light Infantry noted Exercise Smash:

> '…had been primarily designed to test the naval plan for the landing and handling of Beach Groups. The infantry did not go aboard the landing craft but were guided by men of the Beach Groups through dummy minefields on the Dorset coast to an assembly area inland, near to Swanage. There followed a long, strenuous advance when the marching troops of 50th Division were

driven really hard as they had been in North Africa and Sicily. Several mock battles were fought and the exercise was watched by General Montgomery and the senior Naval and Air commanders who seemed pleased with what they saw and the many lessons which had been learned.[4]

In his history of the 50th Division Major Ewart Clay reflected: 'The Studland Bay area gave a fair picture of the problem presented by the assault beaches'[5] but he does not mention how the division witnessed the first use of the DD (Duplex Drive) tanks in a large-scale operation. The DDs had been fitted with flotation screens that were supposed, when deployed, to offer enough buoyancy for the tank to float and would be able to motor through the water by means of a special propeller powered from the tank's engine to the beach.

The problem was older Valentine tanks were used for Exercise Smash instead of the M4 tanks that were being held for use in anger. The larger landing craft for these tanks could not get close to the beach, so the DD Valentines had to be launched from further out than usual. The fatal consequence was four or five of them sank before they reached the beach and their crews were drowned.

The US Army had begun a series of training exercises on Slapton Sands in January 1944 and commanders were keen to rehearse what they had learned on a larger scale and with realistic battle conditions. Exercise Tiger, staged

Children watching US troops practise assault landings at Blackpool Sands, Dorset, April 1944.

US LCVP's landing troops during an invasion exercise at Slapton Sands, April 1944.

between 22–30 April 1944 was first major exercise for the American Force U that was destined to land on Utah Beach. The exercise was for 30,000 troops to practise a landing from nine large LSTs (Landing Ship Troops) from Lyme Bay onto Slapton Sands under live fire from naval guns. It should have been a chance for any problems in logistics or communications or weaknesses in training to be identified. There were issues with command and communications from early on because the various forces were not using the same radio frequencies and there were losses to friendly fire as a result.

Practice assaults began on 27 April and in the early hours of the following morning of 28 April, the 5.S-Boot Flotille under the command of Korvettenkapitän Bernd Klug spotted dark shapes that were in fact eight landing ships of convoy T4 that contained hundreds of men of the 1st Engineer Special Brigade. The E-boats split into pairs, launched torpedoes and opened fire. After a collision the E-boats decided to beat a hasty retreat under the cover of a smoke screen. Two of the LSTs were successfully torpedoed and sunk, others suffered damage. The men aboard were killed by explosions and gunfire, others drowned in the water. Valuable lessons were learned from the exercise, but they should not have come at such a price in life. The exact number of lives lost during Exercise Tiger remains contentious, a figure of 749 US servicemen is recorded on the memorial erected to the incident in Weymouth. All survivors were sworn to secrecy by their superior officers to ensure a lid was kept on the incident, primarily to stop the Germans getting wind of what they had achieved. There were concerns about Operation Overlord being compromised and even cancellation was considered.[6]

Men of 6th Battalion, The Green Howards receiving 48-hour ration packs before embarking onto their landing craft during Exercise Fabius, 5 May 1944.

The rehearsals pushed on with Exercise Fabius, four full-scale exercises for British and Canadian beach units and US troops assaulting Omaha were staged 23 April -7 May:

Fabius 1: US 1st Infantry Division and 29th Infantry Division rehearsed amphibious landings at Slapton Sands in Devon in preparation for their assault on Omaha Beach.

Fabius 2: British 50th Division rehearsed landings on the beaches of Hayling Island in Hampshire for Gold Beach.

Fabius 3: 3rd Canadian Division rehearsed landings at Bracklesham Bay in West Sussex for Juno Beach.

Fabius 4: British 3rd Division rehearsed landings for Sword Beach at Littlehampton. The history of the 1st Battalion, The Royal Norfolk

British troops from assault battalions hit the beach from LCAs during Exercise Fabius, May 1944.

Regiment recalled: *No one was quite sure whether it wasn't to be the real thing. However, Littlehampton beach was the enemy shore and the Downs above Goodwood our objective.*[7]

Fabius 5 and 6: Rehearsals held in the Thames, ports of the east coast and ports in the Southampton and Portsmouth areas for American and British supply units that would be working on Allied beaches.

British troops wading ashore from landing craft and heading up the beach after the initial assualt landings during Exercise Fabius, May 1944.

After the final Fabius exercises it was considered essential for there to be a period of final refit and overhaul of ships and craft before commencement of Operation Overlord. The army also needed a breathing space to complete their preparations such as waterproofing of vehicles and to conduct briefings of exactly what was expected of our assault battalions. Details were not given explicitly, as the history of 1st Battalion, Royal Norfolk Regiment recalled:

> *Briefing was a serious business. Imagine a series of large store tents each with special lighting and flooring and a twenty-foot map. The master plan was unfolded to every man, but security was such that bogus place names were used throughout and even now any reference to any part of the immediate bridgehead is still referred to as 'Hillman', 'Rover' etc. During and after this period of intensive study of air photographs, maps and models, the battalion was 'sealed'. This meant no one was allowed in or out of the perimeter within which we lived; we knew the hour was at hand and that soon we should go through the marshalling camps to our embarkation hards.*[8]

Princess Elizabeth inspecting an honour guard during a Royal visit to 2nd Battalion, Grenadier Guards, 5th Guards Armoured Brigade, Guards Armoured Division at Hove, East Sussex, 17 May 1944.

DUKWs of a 21st Army Group Royal Army Service Corps Beach Group company lined up ready for loading onto LSTs at a south coast port, 1 June 1944.

A visitors' ban was imposed in the coast where the assault divisions were concentrated which extended inland for 10 miles and high barbed wire fences were erected around the camps. Military authorities were determined the invasion was going to remain as secret as possible, but the people of the south coast had an idea something was afoot as the squadrons of allied aircraft flew overhead day after day in May. In early June 1944 ports and harbours filled with all manner of landing craft and tanks, armoured fighting vehicles, lorries and military transports and streamed along coastal roads. Local people could not miss the activity and gave the lads of all the allied forces a wave and a cheer as they went by. If there was a queue of military traffic outside houses people brought out drinks and homemade snacks.

Logistics ran very well, typical of them was the British 50th Division which was bound for Gold Beach. At the beginning of June the 50th Divisional Headquarters moved from the New Forest to on board its headquarter ship at Southampton Docks. Brigade groups of Force G were assembled in separate camps and marshalled into loads ready to board their landing craft. By the evening of 3 June 1944 the entire personnel of 50th Division was afloat, part in the West Solent and part in vessels lying alongside at Southampton.[9] The history of the 8th Battalion, Durham Light infantry recalled:

> *The LCI were moored three or four abreast alongside the quay and with over two hundred men on each ship there was little room to move about. On another quay the carriers and anti-tank guns went aboard LCT.*[10]

US Landing craft engaged in pre-invasion loading at Portland Harbour, 2 June 1944.

USS LST-47 loading her cargo of anti-aircraft half-tracks at Dartmouth, England, 1 June 1944.

Southampton had six LST hards where Canadians loaded for Juno Beach. The majority of Force S bound for Sword Beach left from Southsea Pier, Hampshire. The remainder left from Gosport as did some of the Canadian units bound for Juno Beach.

In Dorset the US 1st Infantry Division 'The Big Red 1' and Rangers of Force O departed from Weymouth and Portland and the US 29th Infantry Division left Plymouth for Omaha Beach. Other units from Force O and Force U departed from Poole followed by the US Coast Guard Rescue Flotilla.

The bulk of Force U bound for Utah Beach embarked from a number of ports in Devon such as Torquay Hard, Brixham and Falmouth. Transports for US XI Amphibious Force departed from Dartmouth. Falmouth hards in Cornwall provided the embarkation point mostly for further elements of the US 29th Infantry Division. Follow-up forces were also embarked from Cardiff, Swansea (Force B) for American troops and British follow-up (Force L), consisting mainly of the 7th Armoured Division and XXX Corps from Harwich, Felixstowe and Tilbury. Some of the prefabricated Mulberry Harbours also departed from Tilbury, others concentrated off Selsey Bill in West Sussex and Dungeness in Kent ready to be towed across to Normandy.[11]

American soldiers of Force O, bound for Omaha Beach boarding their landing craft at Weymouth Quay 4 June 1944.

LCVPs, with full loads of troops, come alongside to transfer men to their landing craft bound for Omaha Beach, Plymouth 3 June 1944.

This gives a good flavour of what happened on the south coast, but make no mistake, other ports and harbours in the area also played valuable roles in the departure of troops, armour and supplies. Such were the preparations for the greatest combined assault in the history of warfare.

D-Day was originally set to take place on 5 June but early on 4 June the weather had taken a bad turn and there was a postponement to 6 June. Some of the units at Southampton were allowed off their landing craft and onto the quay where a very temporary rest camp was organised in a large shed.[12] Other units were not so fortunate and were ordered to remain afloat in their landing craft. At last, at 0730 on 5 June the first vessels of the armada began to move out of the West Solent and crossed the Channel through the night of 5–6 June with minesweepers clearing the way in front of them.

Soldiers often don't make good sailors, and during the crossing the decks of the LCIs were running with so much vomit the leather-soled ammunition

Soldiers on South Parade Pier in Southsea, Portsmouth, some of them wearing the ribbons of decorations and medals from previous campaigns, ready to depart for the Normandy beaches, June 1944.

Sherman tanks of 13th/18th Hussars, 27th Armoured Brigade, embarking LCT-610 at Gosport, 3 June 1944.

111 Commandos of 1st Special Service Brigade aboard LCI (S) at Warsash, Southampton on 3 June 1944.

A Phoenix caisson, part of the Mulberry Harbour that was key to the landing for the supplies for the Normandy campaign, pictured under tow, following its construction by the Portsmouth Dockyard, 17 March 1944.

261

Soldiers wounded on D-Day just off the hospital ship that brought them back home, 7 June 1944.

boots of the soldiers on board had become horribly slippery and the air reeked of bile. Many veterans would reminisce, of course they felt fear in their guts as they approached their landing areas, but would add they were also glad to get off the sick-riddled landing craft and on to the Normandy beaches on D-Day.

So began the beginning of the end of the Nazi occupation of Europe, the fighting would seem at times, that every field, ditch and hedgerow was so hard fought for, but fight on they did. Back on the British coast the success of the D-Day landings and the progress of troops across France, Holland and Belgium over the following months saw the number of our coastal batteries reduced and many of those that did remain were unmanned and simply kept in maintenance. By late 1944 the Home Guard had been stood down, all the batteries were closed, a rolling programme had begun to dismantle them and their guns were sold for scrap metal.

Companies of Royal Engineers, Pioneer Corps and supervised working parties of German prisoners of war had also begun the massive task of removing anti-invasion scaffolding, barbed wire, defensive structures and minefields from our beaches. In some areas, such as Trimingham and Mundesley in Norfolk, cliff falls and movement by tides and storms meant the maps of where the mines had been placed were practically useless and it

BOROUGH   🛡️   **OF DOVER**

This is to record with sincere appreciation the services of

Mrs. K. F. Lenihan

for the Five Years from 3rd September, 1939 to 3rd September, 1944 in the Civil Defence Organization of the Borough of Dover.

Mayor

Chairman of Emergency Committee

She stayed throughout the hell of Hell Fire Corner. A certificate of appreciation presented to Dover air raid warden Mrs Kate Lenihan.

would be the 1970s before such beaches would be certified by the Ministry of Defence as cleared and safe to be opened to the public again. There are still odd mines and groups of mines being discovered along our coast, the last recorded mine clearance of a beach area occurred at Whitsand Bay, Cornwall in 1998.[13]

Defensive structures were also removed from many seafronts and coastal areas but if you look around, you can still spot pillboxes, anti-tank blocks and other fixed defences along our coast today; silent sentinels reminding us of when Britain's coastline became our front line during the Second World War.

Acknowledgements

The author would like to express his personal thanks to: Imperial War Museum, The National Archives, British Library, British Newspaper Archive, National Records of Scotland, Library and Archives Canada, Library of Congress USA, Bundesarchiv-Militärarchiv, Newcastle Local Studies Library, Tyne & Wear Archives, Norfolk Record Office, Norfolk Heritage Centre, Royal Naval Patrol Service Museum, Lowestoft, Hull historian Mike Covell for sharing some of his research from his unpublished manuscript *Hull At War – The Shelters*, Richard Martin at Newbiggin Maritime Centre, Mundesley Maritime Museum, Leo Whisstock, David Oxley, Charlie Cairoli jnr., Austin Ruddy, Andrew Powell-Thomas, Ian Flowers, Fiona Davies, John and Cynthia Read, Ray Cossey, Peter Stibbons, Peter Cox, Colin Tooke, David Hemsley, Ellie Tarratt, Christine and David Parmenter, Henry Wilson and my old friends Bob Collis and James Hayward for sharing their research and sage thoughts with me.

I would also like to mark my sincere appreciation to sadly departed and much missed friends Henry 'Shrimp' Davies, Richard Davies, Eric Reading, Harry Snowling, Noel Cashford MBE, RNVR, Peter Brooks and Alan Childs for their kind help in the past with research for some of the stories now included in this book.

Last but no means least I thank my partner Fiona and my family for all their love and support.

Notes

Chapter 1
 1. Priestley, J.B. *Postscripts* first broadcast on BBC Radio on 5 June 1940
 2. *Dover Express* 13 January 1939
 3. Walmsley, Leo *Fishermen at War* (London 1941)
 4. HO 207/60
 5. *Thanet Advertiser* 19 May 1939
 6. *Gloucestershire Echo* 16 August 1939
 7. *Aberdeen People's Journal* 4 July 1939
 8. *Diss Express* 28 July 1939
 9. *Hastings & St Leonards Observer* 8 July 1939
10. *Hastings & St Leonards Observer* 15 July 1939
11. *Hastings and St Leonards Observer* 10 July 1939
12. Twyford, H.P. *It Came to Our Door* (Plymouth 1946)
13. Peer, Betty, Private correspondence, author's collection

Chapter 2
 1. Twyford, H.P. *It Came to Our Door* (Plymouth 1946)
 2. Ramsey, Winston G. The Blitz *Then and Now* (vol. 1) (London 1987)
 3. Bekker, Cajus *The Luftwaffe War Diaries* (London 1966)
 4. Bekker, Cajus *The Luftwaffe War Diaries* (London 1966)
 5. Bekker, Cajus *The Luftwaffe War Diaries* (London 1966)
 6. *Linlithgowshire Gazette* 20 October 1939
 7. *The Scotsman* 19 October 1939
 8. *Falkirk Herald* 18 October 1939
 9. *Musselburgh News* 20 October 1939
10. Ramsey, Winston G. *The Blitz Then and Now (vol. 1) (London 1987)*
11. Norman, Bill *Luftwaffe Over The North* (Barnsley 1997)
12. *Illustrated* 24 February 1940
13. *Yorkshire Post* on 5 Febuary 1940
14. Twyford, H.P. *It Came to Our Door* (Plymouth 1946)
15. Twyford, H.P. *It Came to Our Door* (Plymouth 1946)

Chapter 3
 1. Crowdy, Terry (ed.) *Donald Dean VC* (Barnsley 2010)
 2. *Portsmouth Evening News* 18 May 1940
 3. *Western Morning News* 17 May 1940
 4. *Worthing Herald* 17 May 1940
 5. *Worthing Gazette* 22 May 1940
 6. *Eastbourne Herald* 18 May 1940
 7. *Hastings & St Leonards Observer* 8 June 1940
 8. *Hastings & St Leonards Observer* 8 June 1940
 9. *Worthing Herald* 7 June 1940
10. *Thanet Advertiser* 11 June 1940
11. Ogley, Bob *Kent at War* (Rochester 1994) pp.37–38

Chapter 4

1. Twyford, H P *It Came to Our Door* (Plymouth 1946)
2. CAB 60/167
3. CAB 63/167
4. CAB 63/167
5. Collier, Basil *The Defence of the United Kingdom* (HMSO London 1957)
6. AIR 20/2087
7. WO 199/2527
8. Geddes' correspondence with Basil Liddell Hart (Feb.1940) Liddell Hart Military Archives 1/311.116
9. *Daily Herald* 24 May 1937
10. *Western Mail* 8 April 1938
11. *Liddell Diary*, 12 September 1939 KV4/185
12. *The Times,* 13 May 1940
13. *Liddell Diary* KV4/185
14. *Liddell Diary* 27 May 1940 KV4/168
15. Macleod, Colonel R & Kelly Denis, *The Unguarded: The Ironside Diaries 1937–1940* (New York 1963)
16. *The Times,* 5 June 1940
17. Charlie Cairoli was never bitter about being interned, he was sent over to the Isle of Man and soon found entertainers and members of the entertainment community he knew and just like many show folk his outlook was stoical and he would reminisce that with all those great chefs interned with him the food was pretty good.
18. *Liddell Diary* 20 June 1940 KV4/186
19. *Liddell Diary* 24 June 1940 KV4/186
20. *Liddell Diary* 24 June 1940 KV4/186
21. Regional Suspect Lists continued to be maintained by Regional Security committees until 1944.
22. CAB 80/14
23. CAB 80/14
24. CAB 80/14
25. CAB 80/14
26. AIR 75/7
27. WO 199/87
28. WO 199/1419
29. WO 199/87
30. WO 199/85
31. WO 166/122
32. *The Times* 20 June 1940
33. *The Times* 8 July 1940
34. *The Times* 6 July 1940
35. *The Times* 8 July 1940
36. WO 193/732
37. WO 193/732
38. WO 199/1446
39. War Cabinet Chiefs of Staff Meeting 26 June 1940 CAB 63/167
40. CAB 63/167
41. Montgomery, Field Marshal Bernard Law The *Memoirs of Field Marshal Montgomery* (London 1958)
42. Addison, Paul & Crang, Jeremy A, *Listening to Britain: Home Intelligence Reports on Britain's Finest Hour – May to September 1940* (London 2011)
43. Levine, Joshua *Forgotten Voices of The Blitz and The Battle of Britain* (London 2006)
44. Collyer, David G. *Deal and District at War* (Stroud 1995)

45. Lewis, Major P.J. and English, Major I.R. English *8th Battalion, The Durham Light Infantry 1939–1945* (Newcastle 1949)
46. Warner, Philip *Auchinleck: The Lonely Soldier* (London 1982)
47. Lewis, Major P J and English, Major I.R. English *8th Battalion, The Durham Light Infantry 1939–1945* (Newcastle 1949)
48. CAB 80/15
49. National Records of Scotland CAB 79/5 Chiefs of Staff Committee, Minutes 1940
50. Shetland and Orkney had been removed from the CinC Home Forces remit and had been under War Office control since 8 August
51. Collier, Basil *The Defence of the United Kingdom* (HMSO London 1957) pp221–3
52. Folkestone, Hythe and District Herald, *Front Line Folkestone* (Folkestone 1945)
53. Lidstone, G.H. (ed.) *On Guard! A History of the 10th (Torbay) Battalion, Devonshire Home Guard* (Torquay 1945)
54. KV2/12
55. KV2/12
56. KV2/1700
57. HC Deb 18 November 1946 vol 430 cc56-7W
58. HC Deb 18 November 1946 vol 430 cc57W
59. Lewis, Major P J and English, Major I.R. English *8th Battalion, The Durham Light Infantry 1939–1945* (Newcastle 1949)
60. Addison, Paul and Crang, Jeremy A. eds. *Listening to Britain* (London 2011)
61. Glover, Michael *Invasion Scare 1940* (London 1990)
62. Hayward, James *Myths and Legends of the Second World War* (Stroud 2003)
63. Banks, Sir Donald *Flame Over Britain* (London 1946)
64. Lidstone, G.H. (ed.) *On Guard! A History of The 10th (Torbay) Battalion, Devonshire Home Guard* (Torquay 1945)

Chapter 5
1. *Liddell Diary* 3 October 1940 KV4/187
2. *Liddell Diary* 8 October 1940 KV4/187
3. *Falkirk Herald* 12 February 1941
4. *Northern Whig* 10 February 1941
5. Mof I Home Intelligence Reports 10 and 12 June 1940 in Addison, Paul and Crang, Jeremy A. *Listening to Britain* (London 2011)
6. Mof I Home Intelligence Report 2 July 1940 in Addison, Paul and Crang, Jeremy A. *Listening to Britain* (London 2011)
7. J B Priestley *Postscript* broadcast on the BBC 14 July 1940
8. *The Times* 10 March 1941
9. Ministry of Information *Beating the Invader* leaflet (May 1941)
10. Ministry of Information *Beating the Invader* leaflet (May 1941)
11. Ministry of Home Security *Front Line 1940–41* (HMSO 1942)
12. *Portsmouth Evening News* 29 July 1941
13. *Portsmouth Evening News* 29 July 1941
14. *Portsmouth Evening News* 24 March 1942

Chapter 6
1. Twyford, H.P. *It Came to Our Door* (Plymouth 1946)
2. Obituary, Guy Anson Maunsell, *The Times* 23 June 1961
3. Turner, Frank R. *The Maunsell Sea Forts* (Privately published)
4. *Thornton Cleveleys Gazette and Herald* 29 December 1945
5. Pawle, Gerald, *The Secret War* (London 1956)
6. HO 196/21
7. ADM 199/848
8. ADM 199/848

9. Records discovered after the war showed the balloons had been the cause of fires, accidents and disruption of power lines see ADM 199/848
10. Churchill, Winson S. *The Second World War* Vol. 2 (London 1949)
11. Clarke, Dudley, *The Birth of the Commandos*, *The Listener* 25 November 1948
12. Durnford-Slater, Brigadier John *Commando* (London 1953)
13. Durnford-Slater, Brigadier John *Commando* (London 1953)
14. *Belfast Telegraph* 19 August 1942
15. *Portsmouth Evening News* 20 August 1942
16. No. 96 Daily Report on Morale, Tuesday, 10 September 1940 (moidigital.ac.uk)
17. Miller, Major General Charles Harvey *Training Area, East Holme near Lulworth* (Southern Command, 16 November 1943) printed letter, author's collection

Chapter 7
1. KV2/1700
2. KV2/15
3. KV2/17
4. KV2/21
5. KV2/1067.
6. KV4/117
7. Hayward, James *Double Agent Snow* (London 2013)
8. KV2/114
9. See *Liddell Diary* 4 October 1940 Liddell declared this was 'obviously an untrue story' KV4/187 and KV2/1700 and KV3/76
10. KV3/76
11. KV3/76
12. Brooks, Peter *Coastal Towns at War* (Cromer 1988)
13. *Daily Herald* 15 August 1940
14. KV4/122
15. KV4/122
16. KV4/122
17. Sadly, although Maurice du Fretay realised his dream to become a combat pilot he did not survive the war. He and his Hurricane were lost at sea while flying air support of Operation Jubilee on 19 August 1942.
18. KV3/76
19. KV3/76
20. KV4/188
21. KV3/76
22. Collyer, David G. *Deal & District at War* (Stroud 1995)
23. *Sunday Telegraph* 14 June 1992
24. Letter from Jack Driscoll to James Hayward (11 June 1992). Private correspondence courtesy of James Hayward
25. War Diary, Black Watch of Canada, February 1942, Library and Archives of Canada
26. Unfortunately, Laycock did not specify where or when the 'one absolutely' splendid' raid conducted by German forces took place but because he was not specific there has also been speculation that the raid he was alluding to was a different one (and one yet to be proved actually took place) conducted on a location somewhere on the south coast of England or the Isle of Wight.
27. Royal United Services Institution. *Journal*, Vol. 92 Issue 568 (1947)

Chapter 8
1. Cook, Raymond A. *Shell-Fire Corner Carries On* (London1943)
2. Illingworth, Frank *Britain Under Shellfire* (London 1942)
3. Folkestone, Hythe and District Herald, *Front Line Folkestone* (Folkestone 1945)
4. Douglas, Dr J.W.B. *An Appreciation of the Reactions of the people of Dover and Folkestone to shelling* (Ministry of Home Security, 1945)
5. Folkestone, Hythe and District Herald, *Front Line Folkestone* (Folkestone 1945)

6. Rootes, Andrew *Front Line County* (London 1980)
7. *Dover Express* 6 October 1944

Chapter 9
1. *Dover Express* 24 June 1949
2. Twyford, H.P. *It Came to Our Door* (Plymouth 1946)
3. Pratt Boorman, H.R. *Hell's Corner 1940* (Maidstone 1942)
4. Folkestone, Hythe and District Herald, *Front Line Folkestone* (Folkestone 1945)
5. Cowley, Charles *Air Raids on the Hartlepools* (West Hartlepool 1945)
6. Commonwealth War Graves Commission *Civilian War Dead Roll of Honour* (London)
7. *Northern Daily Mail* 23 October 1944
8. C TYA/1 Hull History Centre
9. Geraghty, T. *A North East Coast Town* (Hull 1951)
10. Jenkins, Ford *Port War* (Ipswich 1946)
11. Commonwealth War Graves Commission *Civilian War Dead Roll of Honour* (London)
12. Box, Charles C. *Great Yarmouth Front Line Town* (Great Yarmouth 1945)
13. Brooks, Peter *Coastal Towns at War* (Cromer 1988)
14. Brunskill, James *Newcastle Victory Celebrations* (Newcastle 1946)
15. *Liverpool Daily Post and Echo Bombers Over Merseyside* (Liverpool 1943)
16. Pratt Boorman, H R *Hell's Corner 1940* (Maidstone 1942)
17. *Dover Express* 29 May 1942
18. Evening News, *Smitten City* (Portsmouth 1945)
19. Ministry of Information, *Front Line* (HMSO 1942)
20. Ministry of Information, *Front Line* (HMSO 1942)
21. Western Morning News, *Plymouth Blitz: The Story of the Raids* (Plymouth 1947)
22. Twyford, H.P. *It Came to Our Door* (Plymouth 1946)
23. Twyford, H.P. *It Came to Our Door* (Plymouth 1946)
24. Box, Charles C. *Great Yarmouth Front Line Town* (Great Yarmouth 1945)
25. Liverpool Daily Post, *Bombers Over Merseyside* (Liverpool 1943)
26. Ministry of Information, *Front Line* (HMSO 1942)
27. Barton, Dr Brian *The Blitz: Belfast in the War Years* (Belfast 2015)
28. Potter, John *The Belfast Blitz* (Belfast 2011)
29. Geraghty, Tom *A North East Coast Town* (Hull 1951)
30. Hull History Centre C TYA/9 Air Raid Incident File 1
31. Ministry of Information, *Front Line* (HMSO 1942)
32. *London Gazette* 27 September 1940
33. *London Gazette* 4 July 1941
34. Jenkins, Ford *Port War* (Ipswich 1946)
35. *Liverpool Evening Express* 1 March 1943 also see WO 373/67/485
36. HO 192/207
37. Box, Charles C. *Great Yarmouth Front Line Town* (Great Yarmouth 1945)
38. Goss, Chris *Luftwaffe Fighter Bombers over Britain* (Manchester 2003)
39. *London Gazette* 17 August 1943
40. Hastings and St Leonards Observer *Hastings & St Leonards in the Front Line* (Hastings 1945)
41. Goss, Chris *Luftwaffe Fighter Bombers over Britain* (Manchester 2003) also see CWGC Debt of Honour Register
42. Ramsey, Winston G. *The Blitz Then and Now (*vol. 3) (London 1990)
43. Folkestone, Hythe and District Herald, *Front Line Folkestone* (Folkestone 1945)
44. Folkestone, Hythe and District Herald, *Front Line Folkestone* (Folkestone 1945)
45. Rootes, Andrew *Front Line County* (London 1980)
46. Ramsey, Winston G. *The Blitz Then and Now (*vol. 3) (London 1990)
47. Ramsey, Winston G. *The Blitz Then and Now (*vol. 3) (London 1990)
48. Sussex Express and County Herald *The War in East Sussex* (Lewes 1945)

49. Ramsey, Winston G. *The Blitz Then and Now* (vol. 3) (London 1990)
50. Sussex Express and County Herald *The War in East Sussex* (Lewes 1945)
51. Folkestone, Hythe and District Herald, *Front Line Folkestone* (Folkestone 1945)
52. Folkestone, Hythe and District Herald, *Front Line Folkestone* (Folkestone 1945)
53. Sussex Express and County Herald *The War in East Sussex* (Lewes 1945)
54. Ogley, Bob *Kent at War* (Westerham 1994)

Chapter 10
1. After the war Sir Peter Scott became known as one of the BBC TV's leading presenters on ornithology and wetlands.
2. Scott, Peter *Battle of the Narrow Seas* (London 1945)
3. *Daily Record* 26 July 1939
4. The first German acoustic mines were detected in the Thames Estuary in 1940, countermeasure had to be developed quickly and minesweepers were soon equipped with LL cables that generated an electric pulse capable of detonating magnetic mines and a SA (sweep acoustic) device to emit a thump sound wave to detonate acoustic mines.
5. Ministry of Information *His Majesty's Minesweepers* (HMSO 1943)
6. Walmsley, Leo *Fisherman at War* (London 1941)
7. Ministry of Information *His Majesty's Minesweepers* (HMSO 1943)
8. Ministry of Information *His Majesty's Minesweepers* (HMSO 1943)
9. Approximately 15,000 RNPS personnel died during the Second World War.
10. The RNPS badge, approximately the size of an old shilling, consisted of a design showing a shark impaled on a marlin spike against a background of a net and sea mines to represent both the minesweepers and those engaged on the anti-submarine vessels.
11. Jenkins, Ford *Port War* (Ipswich 1946)
12. Bowyer, Chaz *Coastal Command at War* (Shepperton 1979)
13. Royal National Lifeboat Institution *Services by the Life-boats of the Institution and Shore-boats* (London 1947)
14. Tragically William Davies, his wife, their two children and his mother and father in law were all killed in an air raid on Cromer on 22 July 1942
15. Royal National Lifeboat Institution *Services by the Life-boats of the Institution and Shore-boats* (London 1947)
16. William Brown the Coxswain of the Newbiggin Lifeboat was not aboard being bed bound at the time suffering from pneumonia.
17. Royal National Lifeboat Institution *Services by the Life-boats of the Institution and Shore-boats* (London 1947)

Chapter 11
1. Rootes, Andrew *Front Line County* (London 1980)
2. Ogley, Bob *Kent at War* (Westerham 1994)
3. Forty, Simon *D-Day UK* (Swindon 2019)
4. Lewis, Major P.J. and English, Major I.R. English *8th Battalion, The Durham Light Infantry 1939–1945* (Newcastle 1949)
5. Clay, Major Ewart *The Path of the 50th* (Aldershot 1950)
6. Cox, Samuel J. *The Exercise Tiger Debacle* Naval History and Heritage Command H-029-1 (US) (April 2019)
7. Battalion, *The History of 1st Battalion, The Royal Norfolk Regiment* (Norwich 1947)
8. Battalion, *The History of 1st Battalion, The Royal Norfolk Regiment* (Norwich 1947)
9. Clay, Major Ewart *The Path of the 50th* (Aldershot 1950)
10. Lewis, Major P J and English, Major I.R. English *8th Battalion, The Durham Light Infantry 1939–1945* (Newcastle 1949)
11. Forty, Simon *D-Day UK* (Swindon 2019)
12. Lewis, Major P J and English, Major I.R. English *8th Battalion, The Durham Light Infantry 1939–1945* (Newcastle 1949)
13. Evans, Roly *World War II Coastal Minefields in the United Kingdom* Journal of Conventional Weapons Destruction: Vol. 21 : Iss. 1 , Article 9 (2017)

Bibliography

Addison, Paul & Crang, Jeremy A., *Listening to Britain* (London 2011)

Banks, Sir Donald, *Flame Over Britain* (London 1946)

Barclay, Gordon, *If Hitler Comes: Preparing for Invasion Scotland 1940* (Edinburgh, 2013)

Bekker, Cajus, *The Luftwaffe War Diaries* (London 1967)

Bowyer, Chaz *Coastal Command at War* (Shepperton 1979)

Box, Charles C., *Great Yarmouth Front Line Town* (Great Yarmouth 1945)

Briggs, Susan, *Keep Smiling Through – The Home Front 1939–45* (London 1975)

Brooks, Peter, *Coastal Towns at War,* (Norwich, 1988)

Bushby, John R., *Air Defence of Great Britain* (London 1973)

Churchill, Winston S., *The Second World War*, Vol 2 (London 1949)

Clarke, Liam, *Light in the Darkness: A History of Lightships and the People Who Served on Them* (Stroud 2016)

Collyer, David G., *Deal & District at War* (Stroud, 2009)

Cook, Raymond A., *Shell-Fire Corner Carries On* (London1943)

Cowley, Charles, *Air Raids on the Hartlepools* (West Hartlepool 1945)

Crowdy, Terry (ed.), *Donald Dean VC* (Barnsley 2010)

Darwin, Bernard, *War on the Line: The Southern Railway in Wartime* (London, 1946)

Durnford-Slater, Brigadier John, *Commando* (London 1953)

Fleming, Peter, *Invasion 1940* (London 1959)

Folkestone, Hythe and District Herald, *Front Line Folkestone* (Folkestone 1945)

Foynes, J.P., *The Battle of the East Coast (1939–1945): The sea, air and land war from the Humber to the Thames* (Isleworth 1994)

Generalstab des Heeres Abteilung für Kriegskarten un Vermessungswesen (IV.Mil.-Geo.) *Militärgeographische Angaben über England* (Berlin 1940–41)

Geraghty, Tom, *A North East Coast Town* (Hull 1951)

Gilbert, Martin, *Finest Hour: Winston Churchill 1939–1941* (London 1983)

Gillies, Midge, *Waiting For Hitler: Voices from Britain on the Brink of Invasion*, London 2006

Glover, Michael, *Invasion Scare 1940* (1990)

Goodwin, John, *Defending Sussex Beaches 1940–1942* (Midhurst 2010)

Goss, Chris, *Luftwaffe Fighter Bombers over Britain* (Manchester 2003)

Graves, Charles, *The Home Guard of Britain* (London 1943)

Hayward, James, *Burn the Sea: Flame Warfare, Black Propaganda and the Nazi Plan to Invade England* (Stroud 2016)

Hayward, James, *Double Agent Snow* (London 2013)

Hayward, James, *Myths & Legends of the Second World War,* (Stroud 2003)

Humphrey, George, *Eastbourne at War* (Seaford 1998)

Hylton, Stuart, *Kent and Sussex 1940* (Barnsley, 2004)

Illingworth, Frank, *Britain Under Shellfire* (London 1942)

Jeffrey, Andrew, *This Present Emergency* (Edinburgh 1992)

Jeffrey, Andrew, *The Time of Crisis* (Edinburgh 1993)

Jenkins, Ford, *Port War* (Ipswich 1946)

Kemp, Paul, *Liverpool and the Battle of the Atlantic 1939–45,* (Callington 1993)

Lampe, David, *The Last Ditch: Britain's Secret Resistance and the Nazi Invasion Plan* (London 2007)

Legg, Rodney, *Dorset at War: Diary of WW2* (Wincanton 1990)

Levine, Joshua, *Forgotten Voices of The Blitz and The Battle of Britain* (London 2006)

Lewis, Major P.J. and English, Major I.R., English *8th Battalion, The Durham Light Infantry 1939–1945* (Newcastle 1949)

Lidstone, G.H., (ed.) *On Guard! A History of The 10th (Torbay) Battalion, Devonshire Home Guard* (Torquay 1945)

Macleod, Colonel R & Kelly Denis, *The Unguarded: The Ironside Diaries 1937–1940* (New York 1963)

McKinstry, Leo, *Operation Sealion: How Britain Crushed the German War Machine's Dreams of Invasion in 1940,* (London 2015)

Ministry of Information, *Front Line 1940–41* (HMSO 1942)

Ministry of Information, *His Majesty's Minsweepers* (HMSO 1943)

Ministry of Information, *Roof Over Britain: The Official Story of Britain's Anti-Aircraft Defences 1939–1942,* (HMSO 1943)

Ministry of Information, *What Britain has Done 1939–1945* (London 2007)

Montgomery, Field Marshal Bernard Law, *The Memoirs of Field Marshal Montgomery* (London 1958)

Murray, D.L., *Brighton & Hove in Battledress 1939–1945,* (Brighton, 1946)

Norman, Bill, *Luftwaffe Over The North* (Barnsley 1997)

Ogley, Bob, *Kent at War* (Westerham 1994)

Pawle, Gerald, *The Secret War* (London 1956)

Potter, John, *The Belfast Blitz* (Belfast 2011)

Pratt Boorman, H.R., *Hell's Corner 1940* (Maidstone 1942)

Ramsey, Winston G. *The Blitz Then and Now* (vol. 1) (London 1987)

Ramsey, Winston G., *The Blitz Then and Now* (vol. 2) (London 1988)

Ramsey, Winston G., *The Blitz Then and Now* (vol. 3) (London 1990)

Robinson, John, *A Short History of the Women Lifeboat Launchers of Newbiggin by the Sea* (Newbiggin 1987)

Rootes, Andrew, *Front Line County* (London 1980)

Royal National Lifeboat Institution *Services by the Life-boats of the Institution and Shore- boats* (London 1947)

Royle, Trevor, *A Time of Tyrants: Scotland and the Second World War* (Edinburgh 2011)

Scott, Peter, *Battle of the Narrow Seas* (London 1945)

Schenk, Peter, *Invasion of England 1940: The Planning of Operation Sealion (*London 1990)

Storey, Neil R., *Beating the Nazi Invader* (Barnsley 2020)

Storey, Neil R., *Norfolk in the Second World War* (Wellington 2015)

Storey, Neil R., *The Home Front in World War Two* (Stroud 2017)

Stourton, Edward, *Auntie's War: the BBC During the Second World Wa*r, (London 2017)

Sussex Express and County Herald, The War in East Sussex (Lewes 1945)

Taylor, James, *Careless Talk Costs Lives* (London 2010)

Turner, Frank R., *The Maunsell Sea Forts* (Privately published)

Twyford, H.P., *It Came to Our Door* (Plymouth 1946)

Vince, Charles *Storm on the Waters* (London 1948)

Walmsley, Leo, *Fishermen at War* (London 1941)

Warner, Philip, *Auchinleck: The Lonely Soldier* (London 1982)

Wells, H.G., *The War in the Air* (London 1908)

White, John Baker, *The Big Lie* (London 1955)

File references

The majority of file references quoted in the footnotes are from files held at The National Archives. Those that are not from TNA are annotated with their repository.

Newspapers

Aberdeen People's Journal, After the Battle, Belfast Telegraph, Daily Herald, Daily Mail, Daily Record, Diss Express, Dover Express, Eastbourne Herald, Falkirk Herald, Gloucestershire Echo, Hastings and St Leonards Observer, Illustrated, Journal of Conventional Weapons Destruction, Linlithgowshire Gazette, Liverpool Evening Express, Musselburgh News, Northern Whig, Portsmouth Evening News, Royal United Services Institution. Journal, Thanet Advertiser, The Listener, The Scotsman, The Times, Thornton Cleveleys Gazette and Herald, Western Morning News, Worthing Gazette, Yarmouth Mercury, Yorkshire Post

Websites

BBC WW2 People's War website: www.bbc.co.uk/history/ww2peopleswar/

Chain Home (CH) RDF System: ventnorradar.co.uk/CH.htm

www.aircrewremembered.com/ KrackerDatabase

www.cwgc.org

www.lexikon-der-wehrmacht.de

www.assaulttrainingcenterfriends.co.uk

www.moidigital.ac.uk

forum.12oclockhigh.net

www.ww2aircraft.net

https://www.discoverhayling.co.uk/copp-heroes

www.aviation-safety.net

Index